The Gift
in
Sixteenth-Century
France

THE CURTI LECTURES

Sponsored by the University of Wisconsin Foundation and the
Department of History of the University of Wisconsin–Madison

THE MENAHEM STERN JERUSALEM LECTURES

Sponsored by the Historical Society of Israel

The Gift
in
Sixteenth-Century
France

Natalie Zemon Davis

The University of Wisconsin Press

The University of Wisconsin Press
2537 Daniels Street
Madison, Wisconsin 53718

3 Henrietta Street
London WC2E 8LU, England

1 3 5 4 2

Printed in the United States of America

Library of Congress Cataloging-in-Publication Data
Davis, Natalie Zemon, 1928–
The gift in sixteenth-century France / Natalie Zemon Davis.
196 pp.   cm.
Includes bibliographical references and index.
ISBN 0-299-16880-8 (cloth: alk. paper)
ISBN 0-299-16884-0 (paper: alk. paper)
1. Gifts—France—History—16th century.
2. Ceremonial exchange—France—History—16th century.
3. Renaissance—France.   4. France—History—16th century.
5. France—Social life and customs—16th century.   I. Title.
GT3041.F8 D38   2000
394—dc21   00-008913

To the future of my children and grandchildren

Contents

Illustrations

Illustrations

THE GIFT
IN
SIXTEENTH-CENTURY
FRANCE

Introduction

fter Gargantua had defeated Picrochole (in Book One of Rabelais's tale), he called together the vanquished captains and his own men and told them what his father Grandgousier had done after defeating Alpharbal, the pirate king of Canarre. Rather than imprisoning and ransoming him, Grandgousier had sent him back "loaded with gifts" and other signs of friendship. Returned home, the king urged his princes and estates to match this graciousness with their own, whereupon they decided to give Grandgousier all the lands of Canarre to use as he wished. Alpharbal went back to Grandgousier with 9038 ships full of gold, silver, jewels, spices, parrots, pelicans, and porcupines. Grandgousier refused to accept any of it as "excessive," threw the signed offer of the whole kingdom into the fire, and insisted that the good turn he had done the Canarrians was simply what was expected.

What was the result? Instead of the tyrannical extraction of ransom and the imprisonment of the king's children — Rabelais was here referring to the recent actions of Emperor Charles V against King François Ier — the Canarrians voluntarily made themselves perpetual tributaries of Grandgousier, promising to pay him two million pieces of pure gold every year. They even increased the amount as time went on until Gargantua's people thought they would have to make them stop. "Such is the nature of the gratuitous," Gargantua concluded.[1]

In 1925, Marcel Mauss began his great work on *The Gift* with a quotation from the Scandinavian *Edda,* but Rabelais's story might have served him just as well. Exchange and contract in "archaic societies" are carried on in the form of gifts. The gifts are "in theory voluntary, in reality given and returned obligatorily"; "apparently free and gratuitous, [they are] nevertheless constrained and self-interested." Every gift produces a return gift in a chain of events that accomplishes many things all at once: goods are exchanged and redistributed in societies that do not have distinct commercial markets; peace is maintained and sometimes solidarity and friendship; and status is confirmed or competed for, as in the potlatch among Indians of the Northwest coast of North America, where clan chiefs rival each other to see who can give away the most goods.[2] The exchange between Grandgousier and the king of Canarre has some of these features, even the fear of being undone by too many gifts. Mauss would have demurred only at the word "gratuitous," and indeed, Rabelais surely intended some irony when he put that word into the giant's mouth.

Mauss might not have been sure that sixteenth-century France was a likely setting for vital gift economies. On the one hand, certain evolutionary features in his thought led him to see gift exchange as contracting over time. In a "total" gift economy, many functions were compressed into the exchange of presents between groups: markets, credit, contracts, arbitrations, marriage alliance, appeals to the gods, and more. Once markets had developed with money prices and individual contracts, a total gift economy was no longer needed. Further, "the spirit of the gift" in a total gift economy—that which made people feel the obligation to give, the obligation to receive, and the obligation to reciprocate—joined persons and objects in an intimate way. Under the eyes of the gods, donors gave something of their substance with their gifts, a potential danger to the health of any recipient who failed to make a return. Once legal and religious changes brought differentiation into such union, the archaic spirit of the gift was sapped. Mauss saw this shift occurring in the Roman Law, where distinction began to be drawn between persons and things. From this evolutionary perspective, societies go through a stage of total exchange of group services, then through a "very long transitional phase" in which gift exchange is central, and then reach a phase "of purely individual contract, of the market where money circulates, of sale proper, and above all of the notion of price reckoned in coinage weighed and stamped with its value."[3]

On the other hand, Mauss also spoke of gift exchange, with its blend of the voluntary and the obligatory and of persons and things, as a permanent part of social life. He delighted in finding forms of behavior in the France of his day, such as competition through magnificent weddings and banquets, that resembled the potlatch or other gift performances. Despite the segmentation in contemporary society,

a considerable part of our morality and our lives themselves are still permeated with this same atmosphere of the gift, where obligation and liberty intermingle. Fortunately, everything is still not wholly categorized in terms of buying and selling. Things still have sentimental as well as venal value . . . The unreciprocated gift still makes the person who has accepted it inferior, particularly when it has been accepted with no thought of returning it . . . Charity is still wounding for him who has accepted it . . . The invitation must be returned.

Writing in the 1920s as a "non-doctrinaire socialist" and a supporter of syndicalist and cooperative movements, Mauss hoped that the gift ethos and gift practices would expand in Europe.[4]

In the seventy-four years since Mauss's essay appeared, anthropologists have examined gift exchange in many settings, and have reflected on changes in gift economies, the "spirit of the gift," and the nature of reciprocity. In a set of influential essays from the 1960s, Marshall Sahlins went beyond Mauss's simple model of voluntary-obligatory gift-and-return to what he called a "spectrum of reciprocities." At one end is "generalized reciprocity," where gifts and assistance are given freely and unstintingly and the return is not specified. It may come soon, it may never come, but the relation between giver and receiver continues nonetheless. Generalized reciprocity, Sahlins suggested, was practiced especially among close kin. In the middle is "balanced reciprocity," where return comes fairly soon and is comparable in value to the initial gift: marriage gifts and peace-making gifts are an example. At the other end is "negative reciprocity," the effort to get something for nothing and get away with it. This can range from shrewd bartering to outright theft. As one moved from the altruistic to the wholly selfish end of the spectrum, one also moved from the inner circle of close kin to the outer circle of less attached persons.[5]

The actors in these presentations were virtually always described as men, sometimes men exchanging women. Annette Weiner challenged this view definitively in her 1976 book on exchange in the Trobriand Islands, the same location as in the celebrated study by Bronisław Malinowski, which Mauss had used to bolster his arguments. Weiner revealed the world of women's wealth and exchange objects (skirts and banana-leaf bundles) and the shifts in rhythms of exchange throughout the life cycle. Exchange and its associated powers could be understood only over a long time span and not just through short scenes of gift/counter-gift. Rather than Sahlins's spectrum from positive to negative reciprocity, Weiner described exchange and magic as the "two most effective persuasive devices" used by Trobrianders on each other. The latter allowed the magic-doer to control the other (or so it was believed); the former allowed both parties to sustain some autonomy and self-interest while expressing generosity and dependence. Weiner's view resembles Mauss's binary voluntary/obligatory, but she probed the psychology of exchange more deeply and insisted on its dynamic character: exchange is "an ongoing process wherein the donor and the recipient may continually reevaluate the other's and their own current condition."[6]

In regard to change in gift economies, for some anthropologists, such as Claude Lévi-Strauss, the evolutionary view still holds: commercial transactions and the profit motive have replaced the many forms of archaic gift reciprocity and all that is left, besides the irreducible exchange in women, are holiday gifts and those within the bosom of the family.[7] Other anthropologists have been struck, on the contrary, by the extent to which commercial markets and gifts continue to exist side by side and interact. Imperialism and colonial encounters have been a critical part of their story, movements ignored by Mauss in his analysis. In 1982, C. A. Gregory described such a situation in Papua New Guinea: a century of colonial rule from England and Australia turned certain gifts (for example, food) and labor services into commodities, but gift exchange simultaneously flourished and expanded, especially in regard to marriage gifts. Objects, including foreign objects, moved now into the status of commodity, and now into that of gift. More recently, Nicholas Thomas has focused on the objects themselves—given, bartered, and bought—and their changing meanings in various Pacific island societies in the nineteenth and twentieth centuries. The objects are "entangled," in the evocative metaphor of his title, indigenous peoples appropriating European things in their own way, Europeans doing the same with Pacific things. Thomas is critical of the general use of the term "gift economies" to describe the diverse systems of local exchange connected with kinship and alliance: "the older anthropological construct of the gift depended more upon an inversion of the category of the commodity than upon anything which really existed in indigenous Oceanic societies." But the Pacific peoples have themselves also adopted the gift/commodity dichotomy to emphasize the way in which their current prestations and exchanges differ from the " 'money life' of white foreigners." Conscious "gift" practices and ethics have emerged in opposition to markets and wages.[8]

Some anthropologists have now brought gift theory to bear on Europe itself. Things did not turn out the way Marcel Mauss had hoped in the 1920s, but nonetheless, Claude Macherel can claim that "in industrial societies, most exchange seems governed by the market, but entire sectors of social life are ruled by the gift." The two realms can even cross over, gift-givers displaying the calculating initiative of sellers and sellers the elaborate personal courtesy of givers. Under the leadership of the sociologist Alain Caillé, a French team has been rethinking the relation between gift systems and modernity. Meanwhile in England, James Carrier, whose first work was on Papua New Guinea, has followed Mauss's evolutionary scheme in *Gifts and Commodities: Exchange and Western Capitalism since 1700*: "the spread of industrial and commercial capitalism has meant the spread of alienated relations and objects" replacing the (allegedly) more neighborly relations of the pre-industrial period and the more personal relations with things. But Carrier has also insisted on Mauss's other vision, that is, of gift-needs as a continuing part of social life. Modern shopping and holiday celebration, as at Christmas, are ways to retrieve the intimate in social life and the personal in possessions.[9]

Historians' portraits of gift economies, some of them inspired by Mauss or other anthropologists, have been rich in insight into large systems. Already in 1954, Moses Finley's *World of Odysseus* revealed the many spheres in which, during the centuries before the city-state, goods and services moved through gifts and return gifts: for example, war booty was distributed to followers as "gifts," taxes and fines were paid as "gifts," retainers were held by "gifts," and trading was constructed in terms of mutual benefit, for "if there was one thing that was taboo in Homeric exchanges it was gain." Similarly, Georges Duby pictured European societies of the seventh and eighth centuries as a world of both war and gifting. Pillaging goods turned into the orderly collecting of the gift of tribute; war loot was distributed to followers and to the church, an important form of sacrifice; peasants brought required offerings to their lords under the name of *eulogiae* or presents; metals and spices crossed the Alps from France to Rome as royal gifts; magnates rivaled each other in gift presentation at the royal court; gifts for the dead were buried in graves, and when this practice gradually stopped, "treasure hoarding . . . was simply transferred to Christian sanctuaries where consecrated valuables were deposited." Duby concludes, "Society as a whole was shot through with an infinitely varied network for circulating the wealth and services, inspired by . . . 'necessary generosity.' "[10]

On the whole, these early works saw gift exchange as gradually but inevitably giving way before market practices and values. For Duby, the initial impact of the urban money economy was to intensify and produce new forms of giving, but "after 1180 the profit motive steadily undermined the spirit of largesse." Elaborating on this, Lester Little examined the paradoxical accommodation of the Franciscans and Dominicans, with their celebration of poverty, to the commercial life of thirteenth-century cities. The friars encouraged merchants to turn their gains into generous gifts to the poor, to hospitals, and religious movements. Thus "even with th[e] maturation of Christian Europe's profit-oriented commercial economy, gift-economy behavior . . . did not altogether vanish . . . [But it] was complementary to commerce; it no longer opposed [it]."[11]

Other scholars put the watershed later. Karl Polanyi's *Great Transformation*, a pioneering book when it appeared in 1944 in its representation of pre-modern European economy, placed the shift from a system of reciprocity and gift redistribution, local markets, and barter to the all-encompassing self-regulating market only at the end of the eighteenth century. Gareth Stedman Jones has talked of "The Deformation of the Gift"—here in relations between the rich and poor in London—in the 1860s.[12] Whatever the date, the direction of change is always the same.

More recently, as with a new generation of anthropologists, historians have been redrawing this picture in important ways. Rather than a gift system eventually being superseded by a market system, gift elements persist with new connections and consequences. With regard to ancient Greece, Gabriel Herman has shown that ritualized gift exchange of an individual man with a foreigner—the *xenia* or "guest-friendship" of Homeric times—did not fade away when the city-state set up communal standards for dealing with foreigners. Instead, "dense webs of guest-friendship still stretched beyond the bounds [of the polis]," linking elites and influencing the mentality of territorial rulers. Examining many kinds of exchange in the archaic and classical polis, Sitta von Reden finds gift sensibilities holding their own as commercial transactions expanded, with frequent crossover between gifting and commercial activities. In their thoughts about persons, money, and political status, the Greeks made distinctions very different from those assumed by evolutionary economics.[13]

For the medieval period, Barbara Rosenwein's examination of the "social meanings" of the property of the great Benedictine house of Cluny showed both donation and purchase playing roles in the acquisition of land in the tenth and early eleventh centuries. Saint Peter, the patron of the monastery, was present as owner in both cases. Rosenwein comments, "The gift-exchange 'system' and the commercial economic 'system' therefore are two conceptions, or ideal types, of exchange behavior. They can function together, and economic activity of every sort is produced by their mix in greater, lesser, or equal degrees."[14]

Important studies of European state-building and patronage in the sixteenth and seventeenth centuries—by Linda Levy Peck, Alain Guéry, and Sharon Kettering among others to be cited in this book—have provided gift theory a context beyond the economic. Gifts and power were present but a minor motif in Mauss's study of exchange, where he assumed that the elaboration of formal law would cut back on the need for gifts. Early modern royal state-building did not put aside medieval gift transactions but rather used them, perhaps increased them, until "corruption" seemed an ordinary part of centralizing government.[15]

Finally, as with Marshall Sahlins's spectrum of reciprocity in "kinship-tribal" societies, attempts have been made to widen the choices in regard to gift bestowal and return in the historical past, rendering them more nuanced than Mauss's pairs of voluntary-and-obligatory, gratuituous-and-interested. I myself have essayed this for printed books: as I will suggest again later, the new printing industry with its multiplied commercial networks also inspired diverse strategies of book dedication, some with return as a distant expectation. In Italy, as we learn from art historian Alexander Nagel, the gifts passed between Michelangelo and Vittoria Colonna were not just the exchanges of patronage, but the efforts of friends to restore gratuitous and non-calculating values both in art and in religious doctrine.[16]

The gift landscape thus has many more paths through it, and its boundaries are more open than when Marcel Mauss tried to map it seventy-four years ago. I venture into that territory with several goals. I am asking what were the status, meanings, and uses of gifts in France of the sixteenth century, when Rabelais's giants could extract more by gift obligation than by force; when editions of Cicero's *Offices* and Seneca's *Benefits*—those great Roman guidebooks on gifts—were pouring off the printing presses; when the Catholics and Calvin were quarreling about what humans can give to God; when the king was trying both to enhance his prestige and fill his treasury; when patronage systems were becoming more complex; when parents were scheming about the best way to pass on the patrimony; when regional markets were thickening, even in the countryside, and the fairs of Lyon were circulating products and credit across Europe; and when Jacques Cartier was loading his ships with knives and beads to give to the so-called "savages" on the other side of the world.

I will also be asking about gifts and gift circuits in many different settings, from the king's bounty to the beggar's alms, and of diverse forms: objects and services, favors and blessings. Who presented what to whom, when and why, and what did it mean? Such a spread allows us to see where gift practices varied according to status or gender or wealth and whether gift rhythms resembled each other in different milieus. It gives us a chance to look for a range in expectations for return: When were they tight? When loose? Were there paths for gift flow so long that they might never lead back to a donor?

Additional justification for so wide an inquiry comes from observers in sixteenth-century France. However different might appear, say, the passage of an office to a client, of a book of hours to a noble niece, and of pins to a serving girl, they were still linked together by the categories and words used to describe them and by the virtues and values they were thought to express in the giver and arouse in the recipient. The same "spirit" flowed through them, which I will explore in the next chapter: gratitude engendering obligation. Nicholas Thomas may be right that The Gift was in part invented through the encounter of Europeans with Pacific peoples, but it was also inherited from a long tradition of moral commentary.

This book is not so much about The Gift as it is an ethnography of gifts in sixteenth-century France and a cultural and social study of what I call a "gift register" or a "gift mode." Though there are big shifts in systems of gift and exchange over time, there is no universal pattern of evolutionary stages, where a total gift economy dwindles to occasional presents. Rather, gift exchange persists as an essential relational mode, a repertoire of behavior, a register with its own rules, language, etiquette, and gestures. The gift mode may expand or shrink somewhat in a given period, but it never loses significance. Its sixteenth-century features will emerge in the pages ahead: among the most important are techniques and manners for softening relations among people of the same status and of different status and for preventing their closure.

The gift mode exists along with two other relational modes: the mode of sales—of market buying-and-selling—and the mode of coercion, that is, theft, punitive seizure, and forced payment (as in taxes to which one has not assented). The gift mode may sometimes be in competition with the sales mode or the coercive mode; they may also cluster around each other, be in close interaction, or overlap. I will be asking about overlaps and rivalry, and in doing so, will not just be following a late-twentieth-century concern. Sixteenth-century people were evaluating gifts all the time, their own gifts and those of others, deciding what was at stake, and judging whether it was a good gift or a bad gift or even a gift at all.

The bad gift will also have an important role in this study. Often gift exchange is examined only at its best, say, as a source for peaceableness or confirmation of status. We will be looking at such ordering qualities of gifts especially in chapters

2 and 3. But gift systems always have the potentiality for trouble brewing within them. They are not simply benign; reciprocity is not assured. Gift practices can explode into unbridled and violent rivalry (the *destruction* of goods at the Kwakiutl potlatch went beyond the ordinary rules of competition at that event[17]) or collapse under excessive domination by the donor. We will hear much about sixteenth-century gift-trouble, not only about "bribes," but also about bitter quarrels, humiliation, and unresolved conflict around the nature of reciprocity.

Some gift rhythms and quarrels would look the same well before and well after the sixteenth century in France. But the century of Rabelais, Marguerite de Navarre, and Montaigne also had special consequences for gift practices. There were expansive opportunities, such as those arising from the printing press, and undermining pressures. I will argue that an over-determined culture of obligation, stemming from family life, state development, and religious custom, placed a heavy burden on the gift register. Some people tried to rethink the nature of reciprocity, but could they persuade their fellow Christians, and would God listen?

I

The Spirit of Gifts

hat conviction or prescription kept gifts moving in sixteenth-century France? What in principle impelled a recipient to make a return on a gift?

Sixteenth-century people built this disposition from two age-old core beliefs, neither one as corporeal as the Maori *hau* of Marcel Mauss. The first belief linked human gifts to divine ones: everything we have is a gift of God, and what comes in as a gift has some claim to go out as a gift. Scripture spoke most frequently of spiritual gifts, such as the wisdom, justice, and righteousness of Isaiah 11, the "measure of faith" of Romans 12, and the supreme grace of Christ's redemption. But the whole world, which the Lord created and governed, could be construed as his gift, as could his promise to multiply human numbers "as the stars of the heaven." How were men and women to respond to these blessings? By gratitude toward the donor, by magnifying his name, and also by more gifts. "Freely ye have received, freely give," said Christ to his disciples.[1]

These biblical motifs were recast over and over again in the sixteenth century. In a moral treatise of 1536, the Poitou lawyer Jean Bouchet listed God's benefits, from the universe to a good spouse, and said we must express our thanks to him in heart, mouth, and deed. Some years later Pierre Coustau commented in his emblem book that "the good we receive from God we must return to him: we must do all we can to help the poor to whom, if we give a benefit, God receives it as if done for him." A popular proverb put the matter in terms of simple self-interest: "Who gives, God gives to him."[2]

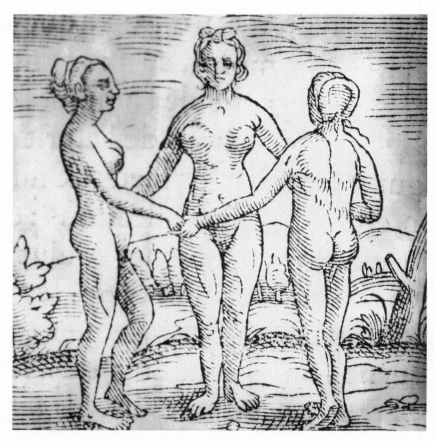

Figure 1. The Three Graces, from Giovanni Pierio Valeriano and Caelius Augustinus Curio, *Commentaires Hieroglyphiques . . .* , 1576

Along with this generative linking of divine and human gifts, a second core belief justified gift exchange in this-worldly terms. Humans were held together by reciprocity, as Aristotle had pointed out long before, and reciprocity was created by gifts and benefits, as it was also by production and trade. "To promote the requital of services," the Philosopher said, "[the Greeks] give a prominent place to the temple of the Graces, for this is characteristic of grace: we should serve in return one who has shown grace to us, and another time take the initiative in showing it."[3]

The Three Graces turn out to be a favorite way for learned people to image gift reciprocity in the sixteenth century (fig. 1). Their guide was Seneca, who insisted on the "naturalness" of gratitude — even fierce elephants were made gentle and dutiful to their feeders — and who thought the three circling sisters illustrated well the mutual advantages of gifts. In his much-quoted phrase, "One of them bestoweth the good turne, the other receiveth it, and the third requiteth it." Why did they dance "in a roundell hand in hand"?

It is in this respect, that a good turne passing orderly from hand to hand doth neverthelesse returne to the giver: and the grace of the whole is marred if it be anywhere broken off: but it is most beautifull if it continue together and keep [its] course.[4]

For French people who had never heard of the philosophers, there were many popular sayings by which they could reassure each other in like fashion of what gifts accomplish:

> One favor begets another.
> [Gratia gratiam parit.]
>
> A thing well given is never lost.
> [Chose bien donnée n'est iamais perduë.]

Or remind each other of the costs of ignoring reciprocity:

> Who nothing gives and always takes
> His friend's love forsakes.
> [Qui tousiours prent et rien ne donne
> L'amour de l'amy abandonne.][5]

These two core beliefs—one evoking the Lord and a vertical cycling of gifts, the other evoking social need and a horizontal movement of benefits among humans—were thought to complement each other in the sixteenth century. Each was also strengthened by compatible values in regard to property and contract. To make gifts, things must be individual or "private" enough to be given away—within a convent, where all things were held in common, the brothers or sisters could make few individual presents to each other—but not so "private" that owners could not imagine separating themselves from them. Sixteenth-century property law still had this mixed quality: generations of descendants had an interest in family property, even while parents could make some bequests of their own choice; real estate was often held by a form of dependent feudal or manorial tenure (and thus multiple persons had rights in it), even while it changed hands briskly on the land market. The movement toward a concept of full private property, as something which "signifieth the highest right that a man hath or can have to any thing, which is in no way depending upon any other man's courtesie" (to quote an English text of 1607) was slow in France.[6]

The image of the Three Graces rested on the assumption that gratitude was as necessary to make society go round as the formal agreements of written contract and the pressures of coercion. Rural notaries took contracts of land sale, rent, marriage, and testament deep into the countryside, and their parchments and papers might fill the coffers of peasant families where no one could read or sign a name. But formal contract was not viewed in the same way as in our own day. For jurists, the contract did not have volition or free individual choice at its heart, as it would in the eighteenth century, but was marked by concerns about the common good. A Poitiers lawyer celebrated contracts as "compensating for the inequality of things among men . . . since [through them], each can attract to himself from the other, mutually and reciprocally, the thing he needs." The learned jurist Charles Du Moulin thought it quite fitting to put "Thou shalt love thy neighbor as thyself" on the title page of his *Summaire du livre analytique des contractz* (Analytical book of contracts).[7]

In short, gift reciprocity and formal contract shared some of the same moral terrain in the sixteenth century. The spread of contract did not necessarily sap conviction about the importance of gratitude.

These core beliefs justified gifts of many kinds and purposes, but interestingly enough, the diversity of gifts was not matched by a diversity of general terms for gifts. The ancient *don* and the medieval *présent* were the most frequently employed, the first more formal than the second and the two sometimes uttered in the same breath, as in 1539, when Emperor Charles V was visiting Orléans and the city councillors "luy firent don et présent d'ung très beau buffet," "made gift and present to him of a very handsome sideboard."[8] The Greco-Roman word *xenium,* a gift to make a friend of a stranger, had no French counterpart; the French *cadeau* still meant only a decorated capital letter in the sixteenth century.[9]

In addition to "don" and "présent," one other word covered a large number of gift situations and objects: *aumône* or alms. Where the recipients were "poor" or in circumstances evoking "pity," things were said to be given "en aumône," "pour aumône," or "par aumône" (as alms, for alms). The accounts of Queen Anne de Bretagne record seven livres to a studious Franciscan friar as "donnée et aumosnée"; those of Charles IX mention twenty-five livres for a painter with an injured hand, "Luy a faict don en faveur de pitie et aulmosne"; those of the young Henri de Navarre list eighteen livres "données en aumône" to the poor of Périgueux.[10]

Apart from these large classifications, there were words that identified things as gifts on special occasions. For example, *legs* was the legacy made in one's will; *offrande,* the offering to God and the church made during religious service or after prayer; *les étrennes,* one's New Year's gifts; *sa bienvenue,* a welcoming feast given by oneself to colleagues at the time of one's arrival at or advancement in a new position or post. There were also gift terms particular to a region or time of year or an event. But whatever the extent of this vocabulary in sixteenth-century France, we are not dealing with a word supply like that for Inuit snows, for example, where every change in consistency brings another noun. Rather, objects and actions moved into the status of a gift whether or not they had a distinctive label attached to them. Setting, phrases, and gestures allowed giver and recipient to understand that a gift relation had been established. The spirit of gifts was carried not by names alone, but by whole situations.

Figure 2. Allegory of Charity, with almsgiving scenes

Beyond these core beliefs, sixteenth-century France had received from the past and was in the process of redefining four powerful prescriptions for human exchange: Christian charity, noble liberality, the favors of friendship, and neighborly generosity. Each offered ideals for giving and receiving in different social milieus.

Whether talked about by *Shepherd's Calendar,* ethical treatise, or confessors' *summa,* Christian charity always began with love of God, which then led to love of others. Charity could be expressed toward friends, kin, and neighbors, but it was described most characteristically in terms of compassion and mercy for those in need and affliction, whether they were close to one or not (fig. 2). The services performed could be spiritual, such as giving advice and teaching the ignorant, or they could be material, as in alms and the Seven Acts of Mercy (giving food to the starving, drink to the thirsty, clothes to the naked, lodging to the homeless, visiting the sick, ransoming prisoners, and burying the dead).[11]

Both volition and obligation were expected to inspire the charitable gift. The Acts of Mercy were God's commands: to refuse to give to someone in danger of death was the mortal sin of avarice. What robbed charity of its virtue was performing it without the love of God and only "for the praise of the world." "Don't blow your own horn," warned Georgette de Montenay in her 1571 emblem book, which showed a donor as busy with his trumpet as with handing money to a beggar (fig. 3).

NE TIBIIS CANATVR

Quoy qu' en tout temps l'aumofne foit vtile
Aux fouffreteux, point ne faut de trompette
A l'annoncer, comme dit l'Euangile.
La Charité de cœur vraye & parfaicte
Ne veut tefmoins de fon œuure bien faicte.
Car il fuffit que Dieu bien apperçoit,
Que l'indigent de ton bien a difette.
Le publiant fon falaire reçoit.

Ceft

Figure 3. "Don't blow your own horn," from Georgette de Montenay, *Emblemes, ou devises chrestiennes,* 1571

16

When Jean Bouchet said alms must be given "without constraint," he meant "with joy . . . to God's honor," not that one had no obligations toward one's fellows.[12]

As for the return on charity, the donor was supposed to expect it from God alone: the Lord would be "pleased" by acts of mercy made in the right spirit and, by the Catholic view, they would contribute to one's salvation. A Breton gentleman spelled this out reassuringly in his "Moral Advice" to his son, and added some material rewards as well:

> Be charitable and merciful toward the poor and share your goods liberally with them, at least your superfluous goods. Your mother and I . . . have always taken care to do this, and God has blessed our work and household and multiplied our goods, as he will do yours if you imitate us or do better . . . And don't just give a piece of bread at the door as you would a dog, but seek out the people who are poor and sick and old . . . Give clothes to at least a dozen needy people every year . . . Doing this you'll prepare the path to heaven and you won't be poorer at the end of the year.[13]

As for the recipients of alms, the donor was enjoined to make sure they were genuinely needy and not false beggars. If there were not enough gifts to go around, he or she should follow the ancient rule of preferring poor neighbors over indigent strangers. But nothing was said about extracting promises from recipients for future service. "I seek not my own" is Charity's motto in an important sixteenth-century picture of a woman with infants pressed to her body.[14]

The human return on the charitable gift was to come only through the grateful sentiments of the recipient. The recipient was to remember the gifts, praise the benefactor—though without flattery—and perform "services." The return might flow back to the donor, but if one did not know who the donor was, it would have to go elsewhere. Moreover, the return would probably be asymmetrical: an indigent recipient of benefits would have nothing but voice and body with which to express gratitude, and that would have to suffice. A common proverb summed up the situation wherever there was a great imbalance in power between giver and receiver:

> To father, to master, to God omnipotent
> No one can return the equivalent.
> [A pere, à maistre, à Dieu tout puissant,
> Nul ne peut rendre l'equivalent.] [15]

Along with the Christian construction of the charitable gift existed the secular and ethical value of liberality. An amalgam of medieval ideals of feudal hospitality and largesse with classical notions of benefits and generosity, liberality was especially recommended to educated noblemen and princes and princesses. It was also a virtue to be sought by the head of any great household in the sixteenth century and, in slightly reduced form, by the women in such families as well.

As a style associated with the medieval past, sixteenth-century readers could hear about it in the reprintings of the old fairy tale of *Mélusine*. The guests at the

fortnight-long wedding festivities of Mélusine and Raimondin were constantly "as-
tounded" and "marvelling" at the abundance of food, at the wines served in gold
and silver cups, at the splendor of their lodgings, at the gifts and jewels ("moult
grans dons et joyaux") that Mélusine gave each of them. This medieval tradition
was followed at sixteenth-century royal weddings and other great festivities when
a herald would appear crying "largesse, largesse," and then, naming all the titles
and lands of the bridegroom or champion, throw gold and silver into the crowd
of spectators.[16]

For most occasions the sixteenth-century prescriptive literature found this largesse too indiscriminate. Jean Bouchet provides a characteristic definition of liberality. He drew from classical texts—Aristotle's *Ethics,* Cicero's *Offices,* and Seneca's
Benefits—and also from his own experience as attorney for the dukes of La Trémoille and longtime recipient of their benefactions. Liberality grew out of benign
sentiments toward one's fellows, which prompted "gifts and rewards," "pleasures
and benefits," but it must never lead to prodigality. One had to live within one's
means. Frequent and excessive banquets and hunting parties were dissipation, as
bad in their way as the isolating vice of avarice. Better to concentrate one's hospitality on the great affairs of life, such as weddings and the taking on of new office,
where magnificence was in order. Better yet to go beyond "private matters" and
extend one's benevolence to relatives, friends, and people in one's service, to pupils
at school, merchants in difficulty, and the like. Gifts for "public and common
things"—for churches, monasteries, hospitals, fortifications, and other buildings—
were also much recommended, another occasion for rightful magnificence.[17]

Bouchet thought his late patron, Louis II de La Trémoille, a splendid example
of liberality, devoting his revenue and income to royal service and public profit.
Bouchet did mention in passing that some of Louis's servants wished he had also
pressed the king for gifts of royal office for them.[18]

Volition and obligation in liberal bestowal were conceived of as conjoined
rather than in conflict, just as they were in charitable bestowal. To be truly liberal,
said Bouchet quoting Seneca, one must give because one wants to, with a cheerful
face and with no regrets. At the same time, with Cicero he viewed generosity as "a
moral obligation to do most for the man by whom we are best treated." Sorting
out one's obligations was an essential step in liberality, even more so than in the
compassionate gifts of charity. "The tunic is nearer than the cloak," Erasmus reminded readers of his *Adagia,* "the knee closer than the calf"; "we must establish
order among those we love."[19]

The return on the liberal gift was talked about now one way and now another.
On the one hand, return was to be generated (as with the charitable gift) only by
the gratitude of the recipient. The liberal man, said Bouchet, must keep himself
from reminding the recipient about all the good he has done for him, "for the
law of benefits is that he who gives a pleasure must soon forget it and he who receives it must always remember it." On the other hand, the advantages of liberality
to the donor were described with frankness. Gifts and benefits brought "friends,"

and there was no wiser course, said Bouchet, expanding on the common proverb that "Friends are worth more than money." Writing several decades later, the Forez judge Jean Papon agreed: through liberality, "you will acquire friends, who will stay with you and help you in your needs . . . friends, who are a most assured treasure, returned to you with a profit greater than any usury."[20]

Unlike the charitable gift, the model situation for the liberal gift was not an anonymous one. Donor knew recipient and was enjoined to know him or her so as to be sure that the gift would be helpful not harmful.[21] Recipient knew donor and, indeed, was permitted to ask for a gift. The request was not to be in the low style of a street beggar, nor was it to be in the style of the medieval "boon," whose granting could be asked without saying ahead of time what one wanted ("Sire, grant me a boon . . ."). Rather one was to specify the gift, using the polite formulas of past service, present need and worth, and future gratitude, which one had learned from Erasmus's *De Conscribendis Epistolis* and other letter-writing manuals.

Though we can see the potentiality for conflict between the charitable ideal and the liberal ideal of a gift relationship, especially in regard to the size of the circle of recipients and the return on the gift, sixteenth-century observers often coupled the two. Writing in 1574, the chancellery officer Pierre de L'Estoile mingled them in every sentence as he described the late Marguerite de France, Duchess of Savoie. When French gentlemen passed through her lands and asked to borrow money, she simply gave it to them, saying, "My friends, it's not me you must thank, but God who has made use of me . . . I am the daughter of kings so great . . . that they have taught me not to lend, but to give liberally to whoever implores my aid." "In short," concluded L'Estoile, "she was a true Christian."[22] A decade later, the Protestant soldier François de La Noue was urging both traits on his fellow nobles "as accommodating well with each other." To be sure,

the most worthy must go first, the precepts of the Gospel to be preferred to those drawn from the teaching of the philosophers. The former direct our charity downward to the very poorest; the latter extend our liberality outward to friends and to those who merit it. Still, they are more alike than different, for both actions are benefits that must proceed from cordial affection.[23]

The word "friend" has emerged several times in our review of Renaissance discourse on gifts, especially on liberal gifts. This is partly because "friend" had so expandable a reference in the sixteenth century, only slightly contracted from its medieval range. It was used intimately between husband and wife, who signed their letters to each other in affectionate friendship: "your faithful husband and assured friend" ("vostre fidele mary et amy asseuré"), "your most affectionate husband and sure friend" ("vostre plus affectioné mary et certain amy"), "your eternal wife and best friend forever" ("vostre famme perpetuelle et meilleur amye a Jamais"), "your wife and perfect friend" ("vostre femme et parfaictte amy"). The word stretched to relatives, who were among the "parents et amis" who gave advice at an orphan's marriage contract and other times of need. It was used for a mere acquaintance, a near stranger, who had suddenly turned threatening and needed to be pacified: "Mon amy, je ne vous demande rien," "My friend, I'm not asking you for anything," was the standard phrase to try to deflect a fight.[24]

"Friends" could also be located at different levels of the social ladder, a few rungs up or down from each other, though the intiative in using the word always came from above. In Rabelais's tale, Prince Pantagruel called Panurge "mon amy" at once because he looked a man of rich and noble lineage, even in his tatters; Panurge stayed with him as servitor and companion, invited by the prince to form "a new pair in friendship." Of course, a prince would not be "friends" with his cook, and great men were counseled not to let their familiarity extend too far downward. Nonetheless, there existed large networks through which gifts moved, generating at least temporarily the language of friendship.[25]

Along with this loose definition of friendship in the sixteenth century, there was a tighter one, with implications for the spirit of gifts. Whether talked about in the learned fashion of Aristotle's *Ethics* and Cicero's *De Amicitia* or in the widespread language of proverbs and spiritual kinship, this deeper friendship applied only to a small circle. "Christian charity extends to the whole world; intimate friendship should be restricted to a few," wrote Erasmus, who placed the ancient saying "A friend is another self" second in line in his *Adages*. Male artisans and traders, in making bequests and setting up executors in their wills, spoke more simply of "[mon] bon amy," "my good friend," "[mon] especial amy," "my special friend," or "[my] good neighbor and friend." (Women of the same milieus used terms of kinship or service about women to whom they made bequests and almost never added "my good friend," but then close friendships between women received less literary celebration than did those of men.) True friendship was born of love and sympathy, not of utility, but it was sustained by mutual services, benefits, and obligations: "one friend watches out for another." Gifts were part of this rhythm, nourishing *amitié* and acting as its sign; for Jean Bouchet, gifts were the fifth law of friendship.[26]

In the favors of close friendship, we have a prescription for gift reciprocity that was strict, yet unaccountable. Givers and recipients, recipients and givers always remained the same; there was no uncertainty about that. But what went back and forth was not to be weighed and measured as in the liberal gift, and, preferably, things should be given before they were asked for.[27]

Our fourth prescriptive tradition — neighborly generosity — represented for the peasant, artisanal, and burgher household what liberality represented for the great and wealthy household. Though theorized less than liberality, it surely covered many more everyday events. According to Jean Bouchet, neighborliness was a form of "familiar affection" among people of "a street, a parish, a town, a burg, a village, a community." [28] Holy Scripture enjoined Christians and Jews not to turn a neighbor away empty-handed, while common proverbs, if not quite asking that one love one's neighbor as oneself, argued for the practical advantages of a "familiar affection" among people on the same street or in the same parish:

Who has a good neighbor has a good morning.
[Qui a bon voysin, il a bon matin.]

He has good in his house who is loved by his neighbors.
[Bien a en sa maison, qui de ses voysins est aymé.]

Who watches his neighbor's house burn must fear for his own.
[Qui la maison de son voisin voit ardre doit avoir paour de la sienne.] [29]

Other popular sayings defined the right kind of neighbors primarily in terms of exchange. "It's not good to have a neighbor too poor or too rich," said the writer Bonaventure Desperiers in summing up "the common language." "If he's too poor, he'll be asking you for things all the time without being able to help you with anything. And if he's too rich, he'll keep you in subjection and in your place and you won't dare borrow anything." In any case, at a time of geographical mobility when children might be far away, neighbors might be the best you could count on: A good neighbor is worth more than a distant relative ("Il vault mieux un bon voysin qu'un parent esloigné") [30]

Charity, liberality, friendly affection, and neighborliness constitute the ideal categories by which many gift relations were evaluated in the sixteenth century and the feelings and virtues that were supposed to be expressed through them. They do not cover all cases: specifically, the sacrificial offering and the gift of awesome reverence (as in the much-pictured three kings presenting their gifts to the infant Jesus) require additional justification, to which we will return later on. For all the complexity in the core beliefs about God's gifts and requisite human reciprocity and in the four prescriptive traditions, nonetheless there was a common thread that joined many different actions under the single register or mode of "gift." We can see this grouping in the disposition of sixteenth-century ethical treatises, where various categories of donation became branches of a single tree of virtue. We can see it in religious tracts, where failures in regard to different kinds of gifts were usually attributed to the single vice of avarice. And we can see it in sixteenth-century account books, where the verb *donner* was used for honorable pensions, customary gifts, family presents, and modest alms and where, in a newer, more ordered mode, diverse gifts were sometimes all subsumed under the single heading of "dons, prix, et bienfaits." [31]

The notion of a gift mode also appears in an innovative fifteenth-century work that had much impact among the learned in the sixteenth century: Lorenzo Valla's *De Falso Credita et Ementita Constantini Donatione* (The falsely believed and forged Donation of Constantine), which had an edition in French already in the 1520s. Valla made several arguments, including linguistic ones, to show that the newly Christian emperor Constantine the Great had never donated his western lands and temporal power to Pope Sylvester back in the fourth century. [32] Part of his reasoning concerned the nature of gifts: the emperor would never have made such a gift, the Senate and Roman people would never have allowed such a gift, and, if such a gift had been offered, the pope would not have accepted it. Along the way, Valla considered alternate donations: the succession to the western lands by Constantine's sons; rewards to Constantine's kindred, friends, and noble soldiers; biblical animal sacrifice; the reward offered to and refused by the prophet Elisha after he had cured Naaman the Syrian of leprosy (2 Kings 5). All of these actions Valla placed within the discursive realm of gift.

Sixteenth-century people were also attentive to the borders of that realm, to the signs that might distinguish a gift from a sale and a gift obligation from a coerced payment. The teachings on the spririt of gifts suggest that this might not always be so easy to do. Volition and obligation were both expected to be present. Human return was to be generated only by the gratitude of the recipient, but gift theories always assured donors that return would come. Gifts were to express sentiments of affection, compassion, and/or gratefulness, but they were simultaneously sources of support, interest, and advancement. The actual practices of gift exchange brought many other feelings and functions into play, but even before turning to them we may suspect that the Three Graces sometimes stayed in concert and sometimes missed a step.

2

Gift Practices and Public Times

ift bestowal was informed by ideal expectations, but was shaped even more by the repeated practices and rhythms of actual exchange. Let us here follow some of the major patterns in gift-giving in sixteenth-century France. What objects and services moved as gifts, and when, and from whom to whom? What ties were established by gifts and what positions affirmed? In this first search we will concentrate on gifts that, on the whole, created amity rather than enmity and coexisted relatively easily with modes of market and formal contract.

Some gift-systems revolved around the year's calendar, each season with its own sequence. New Year's, in the midst of the festivities of the Twelve Days of Christmas, was the most important public gift day of the year. Here two different gift traditions coincided, one going back to the Romans, the other to the Druids (or so sixteenth-century scholars believed).

The *étrennes,* the Roman *strenae,* were gifts of good omen. They had persisted for centuries despite the protests of the early Church that "special days" were in vain. (Religious concern was all the stronger because until 1564, the new year was dated numerically in France from Easter, not from the pagan 1 January.) At the very least, "the Great give Étrennes to the small," as one seventeenth-century commentator noted.[1] The accounts of a queen or a Norman country gentleman or a Breton canon all show small amounts of money bestowed on musicians and players, servants and chambermaids, choirboys, and the children of friends "for their étrennes for the first day of the year." New Year's could also bring grander gifts, as when King Henri III created knights in his new Order of the Holy Spirit on 1 January and presented each of them with a thousand gold crowns. And it could bring more intimate gifts, as when a Paris chancellory officer gave his wife and daughter a purse, gloves, and rings, even while asking himself whether étrennes were not a silly and erroneous custom.[2]

New Year's gifts also moved upward, though perhaps with less frequency. Around 1540, the Duchess of La Trémoille told her daughter, a nun, to provide a richly decorated corporal cloth as étrennes for her uncle, the Bishop of Dol: "this could give him the occasion to do some good for you."[3] Meanwhile authors and writers used 1 January as a privileged day to dedicate their publications to important persons and to friends and presented individual poems or a whole book to readers as "étrennes." Clément Marot sent forty-one "estreines" to ladies of the royal court on 1 January 1541; Charles Fontaine's *Estreines, à certains seigneurs, et dames de Lyon* of 1546 brought New Year's wishes in verse to more than seventy-five people, from judges and their wives to printers and goldsmiths, while in 1608 the curate of the church of S. André-des-Arts in Paris presented New Year's poems to his parishioners, or at least to those who had been sufficiently generous in their weekly offerings.[4]

The étrennes thus moved up and down categories of rank and age, mixing good omens with an acknowledgment of past service and a hope for its continuation or for new benefits in the future.

The other New Year's gift moved across categories of age, but stayed within the same social milieu, reinforcing the notion of group reciprocity. In many parts of France outside Provence, young people of the lower orders would go out in groups on New Year's Eve or Day to ask for "l'aguilanneuf," to make the "quête [collection] de l'aguilanneuf." In the time of the Druids, so learned treatises taught, the search had been for the sacred mistletoe; now, in the sixteenth century, young unmarried men—sometimes with young women, more often on their own—took bagpipes and other instruments, sang songs at the houses of neighbors and village families, and asked for presents of food or coins. "Aguilanneuf de coeur joyeux," their song might begin: "Aguilanneuf with joyous heart, all together we demand"; "chase avarice from your heart . . . don't refuse to start the year off in happiness." The customary gifts were chicken, ham, sausage and other meat. "We'll sing your praise." And if the neighborly generosity was not forthcoming, there was the threat of a curse from the young and bad luck and bad reputation for the year ahead.[5]

The *quête* (collection) was a fundamental form of gift-seeking and gift-receiving in artisanal and peasant milieus in the sixteenth century, and the New Year's round set a model for it. Participants remembered the message long after the bagpipes had stopped and the sausage had been eaten. The elders had been reminded of their responsibility to the community; the young, in their gratitude, would use the collective voice of their Misrule Abbeys to support generous householders rather than cause them trouble. The hint of violence lay behind this gifting, the trick behind the treat.

Though 1 January was also the Feast of the Circumcision, following fast after the Nativity of Jesus and only a few days before Epiphany (celebrating the adoration of Jesus by the three kings), étrennes and the gifts of aguilanneuf drew little on Christian themes and charity.[6] In the diocese of Angers in the late sixteenth century, the Church got the young people to promise that money from their aguilanneuf would be used to purchase a candle for Our Lady or for the parish patron-saint, but this may have been unusual. At Epiphany, the young people sometimes costumed themselves as the three kings and the star of Bethlehem and brought gifts to their neighbors, but the purely Christian reference was overshadowed by banqueting, dancing, guessing games, and forfeits. On into the seventeenth century there were Catholic complaints about the pagan or Saturnalian features of celebration and reciprocity during the Twelve Days of Christmas.[7]

The period on the calendar when public gifts were most associated with Christian themes and charitable gifts was Lent and Easter. Presents went first and foremost from lay people to the clergy and parish institutions. The Lenten preacher might be rewarded, as at Lyon, with whatever men and women could collect at Sunday service and from confraternity donations. Everywhere each person who confessed and received communion—an annual affair for many Catholics—made an offering to the priest or to the parish. Indeed, this Easter money might itself have been a gift to the penitent, received from a master or a patron so that one could "faire ses pasques," "do one's Easter duty."[8] In Norman villages, the contributions from the parishioners for the parish treasury were at their height on Good Friday and Easter Sunday, surpassing the offerings at Christmas and other feast days and many times what they were on ordinary Sundays.[9]

Meanwhile there was a secondary flow of alms to the poor, especially in the cities. Public distributions of alms were made at other times of the year, of course: at selected holy days by religious houses and every week by the new municipal welfare institutions. But the season of Christ's sacrifice and resurrection called for some distinctive expression of human charity: thus king and bishops followed Christ's example and washed the feet of the poor on Maundy Thursday.[10] In Lyon, the rectors of the Aumône-Générale gave their annual alms to prisoners at Easter "in honor of the Easter feast," and the annual Procession of the Poor took place during the Easter fair at Lyon and during Lent at Paris.[11]

Apart from the lay-to-clergy, rich-to-poor flow of charity, there was a third movement in Easter gifts, that of eggs, a food that could be eaten now that Lent was over and a sign of spring fertility. Easter eggs had been used for competitive games in medieval France, as in rolling contests and hand fights, and eventually they were given as presents, colored and decorated, to persons of different ages. In the sixteenth century began the organized collecting of eggs by youth groups (students, choirboys, law clerks, and young villagers), who went from door to door with songs linking Christ's resurrection to neighborly generosity.[12] As with the aguilanneuf, young as against old was the boundary across which gifts moved.

Pentecost, when the sevenfold gifts of the Holy Spirit were remembered, inspired diverse festivities (including, in some places, water pilgrimages and dancing), but it also included some of the charitable gifts of Easter. The offerings to the parish treasury jumped above the usual Sunday figure, while in Maine and the Chartrain, there was a special distribution of grain and money to the poor known as "la charité de la blee."[13] By the time the Christmas feasts had rolled around again, there had been a harvest feast for the laborers in the rural parishes, and even the dead had had their due. In Brittany on 2 November, the Jour des Trépassés (the Day of the Dead or the English All Souls) when the souls of ancestors were likely to visit, food was left out for them in the house so they would be content and give help, not trouble, to the living in the year ahead. There was no youth collecting—indeed, the young men and women might have spent the night in the cemetery dancing—but at least one Norman gentleman thought it appropriate to give coins to the "petits garsons," the "boys," of his parish on the way out of church on All Saints, the day before.[14]

This picture of calendrical gifts reports only the high points of the year and ignores regional variations, which could give great prominence to a special saint's day. Then members of an urban or rural confraternity treated each other with a common banquet in honor of their patron, made sure that they were all at peace with each other, prayed for the souls of their predecessors, and sometimes distributed food and clothing to poor people outside the confraternity membership. At Lyon, for example, the annual banquet of the Confraternity of the Trinity was a big affair, drawing upon its approximately three thousand male members in the early decades of the sixteenth century. On Trinity Sunday, along with their feasting, the brothers distributed a one-pound loaf of bread to any "poor people" coming by their church. When they discovered in 1519 that artisans and "other non-needy persons" were arriving for these alms with their wives, children, and servants, they converted the loaves to a week of dinners for the poor sick people at the Rhône Bridge Hospital.[15]

Whatever the contrasts from place to place, these holiday gifts acknowledged the main lines in social organization—rich and poor, clergy and laity, young and old, living and dead—and were all marked in a similar way by time. Because they were annual, they projected a gift relationship that could be repeated, that *should* be repeated, whether the participants saw each other often or rarely. They suggested a time limit during which the grateful gift requital, whether direct or indirect, should be enacted. Further, the gifts took on meaning from the day on which they were presented. If God's gifts initiated the occasion, then human gifts should bear with them an extra freight of gratitude. If it were a day of omens or ghostly visits, then the gifts should carry some of the day's magic.

Also stretched along a time frame were the multiple gifts that accompanied the life cycle of the individual and the family. Here the rhythms of giving, taking, and giving were much more complex than with the calendrical presents, both in the short run and in the long run.

A child is born in a Normandy village: the peasant wives rush over to the mother with cider, honey, and nutmeg, the last contributed by the local seigneur, Gilles de Gouberville. (When his sister delivers her baby, however, Gouberville sends white wine and oranges.) At the baptismal ceremony soon afterward, the new parents offer a feast to the godparents and the kin, but most of the gift flow seems to move the other way: godfathers' accounts show them paying for the candles at the baptism and making gifts of money to the midwife, to the wet nurse (used only in well-off families at this period), and to the new mother herself. The newborn, meanwhile, receives not presents from the godparents, but promises—spiritual ones, as enjoined in the baptismal liturgy, and practical ones that could be drawn upon, for instance, at the child's apprenticeship or marriage. Another banquet follows some weeks later, important in families of noble and commoner alike: the *relevailles,* after the new mother has returned to church for a blessing and her mass of "purification." Then the house is crammed with guests to join in thanks that the child has lived that long and that the mother has survived.[16]

In the birth cycle, food, money, and other presents came outward from the parents to express their gratitude for their good fortune (kings made the birth of a dauphin the occasion for new pardons and privileges for their subjects), but they especially went inward to the parents, in gratitude for their having supplied a new member for their family and community. (In contrast, a peasant couple who had not produced a child after a few years might have a charivari turned against them and have to give the young revellers money to make them stop their rough music and go away.) Further, the gifts gave expression to the spiritual kinship established between the new parents and the godparents.

Marriage was the life-cycle event where gift exchange was the most symmetrical. Often we look back at the early modern wedding as a one-way transfer, with the dowry coming from the bride's family and kin (and for the serving girl partly from her own wages) to the groom for the course of the marriage. And the dowry was immensely important, in poor families (where its payment might be stretched over years) as in rich, its amount in money, land, rents, and/or equipment often known beyond the marriage contract and discussed among relatives and neighbors. Depending on the inheritance customs of her region and social group, and whether or not she had brothers, the dowry might be the last claim a daughter could make on the patrimony of her family. The dowry then became part of the property of the new household, administered by the husband while he lived.

But there was much other movement of goods as well, including (as Christiane

Klapisch-Zuber and Jane Fair Bestor have pointed out for Italy)[17] counter-gifts from the husband. These provided both concrete and symbolic support for the mutual donation of the bride and groom to each other in the course of the marriage liturgy.

The presents began with the courtship. A peasant in the Île-de-France took a small sum with him on his first visit to the parents of the servant girl he wished to wed; if they accepted it as a "denier à dieu," "God's penny," then their accord would be fixed.[18] Gaspard de Saillans, a financial officer from Valence, started off his efforts to win a second wife by sending her mother two hundred écus (golden crowns) along with herbal rue as protection against the plague. He begged the mother to show his letter with its compliments to her daughter Louise and said how pleased he would be by a bouquet of flowers cut by Louise's hand. The bouquet, "marvelously arranged," enflamed his love all the more, and soon he was writing her father, "As for the dowry of marriage, I will be content with whatever it pleases you to give me [in fact, he received an ample four thousand livres] and you'll find me ready to pass over [to your daughter] whatever part of my goods you advise." At the engagement party Louise allowed him to untie her blue taffeta garter, which he then wore around his neck. Subsequently he gave her a scarlet mantle and money for golden fancies and bracelets, and offered to buy her wedding clothes.[19]

After he was married, Saillans published a description of all these hopes and gifts, but less visible arrangements than his had some of the same features. The breach-of-promise complaint of a young Lyon washerwoman against a printer's journeyman hinged on the silver ring and serge cloth he had given her "promising marriage." (He claimed it was only for bleaching his shirts.) Among the high Breton nobility, when a young baron found himself exchanging promises with Dame Claude du Chastel, his father said he would take it seriously only if she accepted the family jewels as a gift, which she finally did.[20]

At the *fiançailles,* engagement ceremonies, the gifts emerge again, exchanged between the families along with wine, flowers, and kisses.[21] Nor did the marriage contract concern only the dowry. The dresses, bed, and other furniture given to the bride by her family were often spelled out, and in many parts of France the future husband promised to give his wife in the course of their marriage clothing and jewelry "according to her estate." Here the amount was not fixed, and a Breton gentleman warned his sons against wives with expensive tastes, for whom they would have to eat up their dowry money in laces and diamonds.[22] The contract then went on to the husband's ultimate return gift, that is, what he would leave his wife in addition to her dowry (*augmentation de dot*) if he should predecease her. Usually the increase was a third of the dowry's value.

During the marriage ceremony itself the groom gave his bride a ring and the *trezain,* thirteen coins or tokens, which some have seen as a vestige of the old Frankish bride price. The wedding banquet was at least as often held at the house of the groom's family as at the bride's. In Normandy, the bride's family sometimes gave the groom a "don mobile," separate from the dowry, to help him defray all these wedding costs and the first expenses of the marriage.[23]

The marriage was also an occasion for the presentation of gifts other than those between bride and groom and their families. Relatives and associates of the bride contributed to her dowry: her godmother, her master or mistress (if she was in employ), her uncles and brothers. The parents of the groom might also give him an advance on, or sometimes his total share in, his inheritance—and not only in great families, but in peasant families, as in the Maconnais, where a groom received as his "dot" in 1575 a calf, eighty livres, and three measures of local cloth. Patrons and sometimes friends sent gifts as well, though not as extensively as we do today. Henri III bestowed a necklace of a hundred pearls on the daughter of a favorite; the queen of Navarre, Jeanne d'Albret, gave her tailor two hundred livres "in favor of his marriage"; and the Sire de Gouberville presented game for the wedding of a local captain's daughter and paid for the minstrels at the wedding of a tenant's daughter. Meanwhile on the Île-de-France four plowmen were promising their comrade four pewter pots for his marriage—they would carry them in procession to the church and to the feast—and he was promising them, as his men of honor, foods and wine, gloves, and bouquets.[24]

These multiple gifts reinforced the perception of marriage as an alliance with varied possiblities for the future. There was to be an alliance between the new couple and the community and between the two sets of kin. There was to be an alliance between the new couple and parents on either side, who might look to them one day for help when they were old or widowed. There was to be an alliance between the husband and the wife, who, if their marriage prospered, might one day redraw the customary or expected gifts at the marriage's end to favor more fully a "dear and much beloved" spouse. Gifts added festivity and courtesy to the formalities of contract. Gifts could soften the legal subjection of wife to husband, that is, the husband's responsibility to govern and correct his wife and the wife's duty to obey her husband. That hierarchical order could be tempered by affectionate companionship and common causes, but also by the leaven of mutual gratitude.

Marriage was a group affair, but some rites of passage focused more strictly on the individual. On one's saint's day, which was what Catholics celebrated rather than birthdays, one gave presents to others rather than receiving them. For Saint Gilles's day, Gilles de Gouberville bought pins and distributed them to women at his dinner table and to girls in the parish. For Saint Catherine's day, Catherine Satin of a Brittany seigneurial family sent her godmother hippocras cordial.[25] The giver was acting out of reverence for the saint, thankfulness for having lived another year, and hope for protection for the year ahead. To receive presents at such a time might tempt one's fate.

In a like vein, a journeyman arriving in a new town or rising to the status of a master, offered his own *bienvenue*, his "welcome banquet," to his peers and to those in his corporation. A young lawyer sworn as a barrister in Normandy and a cleric summoned to a new canonry in Brittany did the same, the latter making gifts to the choirboys as well.[26] It was well for the newcomer to try disarm jealousy and initiate the process of exchange and obligation with those whom he would see frequently.

With death, the rhythm shifted once again. The gifts flowed mostly outward from the dead person and from the family from which he or she had been subtracted. Neighbor women, alerted by the death knell or ritual laments, came over to offer their services in laying out the body. The flyleaf of a sixteenth-century Bible lists more than a hundred people who crowded into the dead man's house and offered *pain bénit* (blessed bread) to the company and to the heirs.[27] But the food for the wake and the feast after the burial were presented by the bereaved family.

Gifts to the poor were made in many forms, in the Catholic case with the hope and/or stipulation that the recipients pray to God for the soul of the deceased. For example, twelve or thirteen poor people were dressed in black or white clothes and given torches for the funeral, all of which they could keep afterward; a distribution of money or food was made around the door of the dead person's house right after the burial; alms were specified for individuals whom the executors of the will would eventually track down; funds were left for dowries for poor girls or for dinners at the poor hospital, served at the anniversary of the death; and money was given to a civic welfare organization, to be used as the rectors saw fit. Clerics and clerical institutions also received gifts, most consistently when the testator was a priest. Lay people's gifts could range from the dead person's shroud, removed from the corpse by relatives and left next to the grave for the priest in an Auvergne village, to the many golden crowns bequeathed by a merchant to five religious houses in Lyon and to two religious houses back in his native Foiano in Tuscany.[28]

Death was, of course, mainly the occasion for passing on one's property and goods to one's children. Inheritance operated under such carefully defined customary laws, with children having the right to sue if denied their "legitimate share," that readers may wonder whether parental volition had anything to do with the movement of patrimony. Indeed, in Normandy, the equal divisibility of patrimonial lands among sons was so firmly established that a 1578 commentary on the *Coutumier* declared, "No one can make a testament about his inheritance property." Daughters' dowries could come to no more than one-third of the patrimony; if there were no sons, inheritance was strictly equal among daughters; any gifts that parents had made in their lifetime exceeding these limits were to be undone after their death. All that was left for a Norman will was a slice of the movables.[29]

Elsewhere in France, however, under other Coutumes, parents enjoyed or seized more scope, dividing their property among children even though the Custom prescribed the eldest, or insisting on a single heir even though the Custom called for division. The possibility of disinheriting a child also enhanced the image of parents passing on patrimony as a gift, rather than simply channeling their progeny's due. Then in the course of the sixteenth century, some Coutumes were reformed in a Roman-law direction to give parents a freer hand. Lawyer Claude de Rubys, commenting in 1579 on the recently revised Customs of Burgundy, was especially pleased that the traditional "yoke" of the ancient customs of that province, by which parents could not advantage one child above another in inheritance, had been lifted. Now parents could enjoy "one of the greatest liberties of humankind," that is, "to dispose freely of their goods in testament," and "recognize at their death those of their children or other heirs who best deserve it." Had not Abraham and Jacob advantaged one son above another? Seneca had said that we must teach those who receive "a pleasure" from us to be ready to render pleasure in return; our children would learn that lesson from parental freedom to make a testament as they pleased.[30]

The will also included legacies to other relatives and friends. Especially revealing are those in which an item of personal property, rather than being passed on with the bulk of one's goods to one's "universal heir," was selected out for a special recipient. Feather beds, bed frames, linen sheets, and blankets moved this way, including the bed upon which one had been lying in ill health. Men chose books, swords, artisanal tools, hats, capes and mantles for their friends and *compères* (fellow godparents), apprentices, and servants. Much more often it was the women who turned their belongings into signifying gifts, and not just rosaries, rings, jewelry, and cloaks, but intimate items of apparel. Dresses, skirts, shirts, headclothes, and collars were sorted out, described in detail ("my coral rosary with the silver ornaments," "my black dress, half-lined with fur," "my new violet skirt," "my black wool skirt that I wear every day," "my gray skirt and new blouse," "my dress of scarlet velvet and good underskirt," "my linen garments used on my person"), and assigned to sisters, daughters, cousins, goddaughters, neighbors, and servants. Even a man might be bequeathed a woman's garment, a serge dress to be restitched as a cloak.[31]

These gifts introduce a highly individual element into an event where much property was passing according to the concerns of family strategy or prescription. One's clothes continued one's person. As a Lyonnais peasant explained, he was donating his tunic to the Corpus Christi confraternity in his village "in order to be a participant in [their] prayers and services."[32] That the women were specialists in this kind of gift may be related to the fact that they had large amounts of real property to dispose of less often than men, but this cannot be the whole story, for the pattern is found among women of wealth and of modest means alike. Women came into marriage with gifts of clothing; they received clothing and ornaments from their husbands; they then turned them into gifts once again as a memento of a relation of intimacy or neighborhood patronage or gossip networks. Perhaps they hoped their gift would pave the way for a continuing relation of the recipient with their children.

One other form of gift also left some scope to the individual, even while closely connecting her or him to life-cycle events. Sometimes people did not want to wait till their death to pass on inheritance property, that is, the real estate, houses, perpetual annuities, and the like that they had acquired either from their own ancestors or by their own efforts. Perhaps they wanted to advantage a child before their death or make a gift to someone who was not an heir at all. They turned to an old Roman conveyance known as a "donation between living persons" (*donatio inter vivos* in Latin, *donation entre vifs* in French). The donor explained in a notarized contract that "entirely by her free will, good pleasure and without constraint, desiring to recompense the services that she has received from a certain person in the past (and sometimes it is added) and hopes to receive in the future," she gives some property—it might be a house or vineyard, it might be all her goods—irrevocably to the donatee for himself and his heirs.[33]

The recipient might be grateful for such a gift, but that pleasure might not be shared by everyone. Were there heirs or creditors being cheated? The possible objections to an inter vivos donation are suggested in a text-book sample for beginning notaries, drawn up in the gross language of Mardi Gras parody:

Master John Gayballs the attorney, desiring to recompense Helen, present stretched out on her bottom on the floor, accepting for herself and for those who will have rights from her in the future, gives her half of the fat syphilis which by the sweat of his pendulum and long labor he has honestly acquired from the hole of Sibille of Rouen, with the charge that the said donatee will pass on to all good comrades the fruits and profits that come to her from the said donation. He will deliver the gift on the top floor of the Black Room Hotel this coming carnival at 3 A.M. Since Master John holds all his goods in joint community with his wife, Dame Alice the Grumbler, he promises to obtain proof in good form that she ratifies the present act.[34]

It was out of concern for the Dame Alices that a royal edict of 1539 insisted that donations between living persons could not be secret and had to be recorded in a notarized document.

There are many such acts in sixteenth-century France. Some of them were surely efforts to get around the constraints of customary law in regard to inheritance, as suggested by the Normandy example. But inter vivos donations were used for other reasons—such as paying off debts, or supporting a son during his university studies, or providing a priest's concubine with a house, or giving up one's inheritance claims because one was entering a convent—and many of them either reward persons who have done some charitable service for the donor and/or make provision for the donor's old age. In Lyon a young notable gives a royal notary, "his special friend" and godsib, a house that he has inherited from his late father; the notary had helped him during his "captivity in prison." A widowed gentlewoman from central France gives a good burgher of Paris half her dower and other monies in recognition of all that he has done during her eight years in Paris prisons at the instigation of her children; he provided her with clothing and food and paid her debts. A farmer's daughter in the Île-de-France gives all her goods and all she hopes to win in a suit against her father to a guard at the Paris mint; he had befriended her and taken her into his house after her husband had been murdered, leaving her pregnant, and her father had browbeaten her into a wrongful donation of her goods to him. A surgeon of Saint Chamond in the Forez gives a chapel dedicated to the saints Cosme, Damian, and Catherine to a local priest and schoolteacher "to reward him for teaching his children." Back in Lyon a young shoemaker gives a little house inherited from his father to the man who had taught him his trade; the master had cared for him when he was ill and now he can no longer work to return the services.[35]

A last example from a Lyonnais village shows how the donation entre vifs served in the maneuvers of an elderly couple to get one of their children to take care of them. A certain Jeannette Venette finds she has fallen into "poverty and old age, is unable to work and earn her living," and that her husband is even more feeble. She goes to one of her daughters, well married to a rural notary. The young couple point out that times are dear and they have children of their own. Promised a vineyard adjacent to their land, they finally agree to do all that is necessary "for God" and so their mother does not have to go out to beg. And their duty is spelled out in the contract: to provide food, fire, bedding, and clothing sufficient to their parents' estate, see that they have their final sacraments and a funeral worth ten livres, and pay their confraternity. Jeannette's son was also present at the act, as evidence that other heirs approved their mother's gift.[36]

Is this a gift? readers may be asking. Isn't it just a contractual payment? By the criteria of the sixteenth century, it was a gift, one of the variety of gift practices that flourished. Its validity before a French court would not be impaired by its contractual dress or explicitly stated return obligations; it would fail on the donor's side only if it were proved that the donation had not been voluntary or had not been made (to quote a 1565 court case for non-delivery of a donation) with "liberality, without constraint or force."[37] Patrimonial property in principle was never to be sold, but to pass through inheritance or inter vivos donation. The donation had to be accepted by the recipient with "humble thanks."[38] In many cases the services rendered—care for the sick and the old, helping prisoners—were thought to be like the traditional Acts of Mercy. It would have been unseemly, even insulting, to reward them by an ordinary payment. They were services that could not be sold.

Life-cycle gifts, whether linking groups or linking individuals, seem to have a more systemic structure than those around the year's calendar; that is, they seem to be responding more finely to credits and debits in life history than when the gift is set in motion by a holy day. But here too the accounting was not especially strict outside of the inter vivos donation. Birth, marriage, and death were shaped by an intricate choreography of gifts. Some were measured, some not. Some came all at once, while a bequest or a dowry might stretch over years. The gift/counter-gift model and even the circling gift cannot by themselves represent the shifting relations of families in a community. We might better imagine moving fields of gift action, generating intense connection now among certain groups, now among others.

3

Gift Practices and Social Meanings

usy though the gift networks were with holiday gifts, many presents changed hands irrespective of the rhythm of season and rite of passage. They were part of the complicated history of obligations and expectations between persons and households of roughly the same status, including those of kin, and between superiors and inferiors. The stakes were in part social and economic, but other messages were being carried as well. As before, volition and obligation were often in play together, and gift modes clustered around or entwined with contractual modes.

Among villagers of the same status, it was primarily food that passed from house to house—fruit or vegetables from the women's gardens, cakes, honey, extra fish from the catch, or a rabbit—to express appreciation for help at the harvest, for remedies and soups brought over during an illness, for the loan of a harness, or simply as a sign of courtesy and communality. Every Sunday right after mass there was a symbolic enactment of such exchange in the distribution of "pain bénit," "blessed bread," to all the parishioners. The records for a small-town parish in Brittany show each family supplying the bread or wheat in turn around the year in whatever amount they wanted to give or could afford. One Poitiers observer thought the ceremony resembled the Agape or love feasts of the early Christian Church: "still today," he said, "the villagers, especially in Poitou, popularly call our blessed bread 'la charité.' " [1] In a noisier way, the aguilanneuf collection at New Year's reinforced the same pattern.

The importance of this exhange helps us understand why food was so central in village conflict, as when a villager withheld it from a neighbor in need or was accused of witchcraft for having given another poisoned bread and cheese. It also ✓ helps us see why famine and drought were so devastating: the chain of food-giving was undermined since virtually everyone in the village was hit at once.

Meanwhile at his manorhouse in Normandy, Gilles de Gouberville was either sending to or receiving from other seigneurs and relatives wine, boar, venison, kid, hare, partridges, wood pigeons, salt cod, white herring, artichokes, apples, clocks, stones for quarrying, hunting dogs, and larks, to give only a partial list. Over in Poitou, Anne de Laval and Claude de Foix, sisters-in-law married into the ducal house of La Trémoille, were exchanging fruits and peas and the books that one of them had received from Paris. Farther south in Gascony and Béarn, the wife of a high-ranking judge was receiving from her sister four pairs of gloves and "thousands of affectionate greetings." [2]

The tables and beds in these high-ranking households were open for visits from kin and neighbors without any notice at all. Such liberality not only confirmed local ties, but established reputation and rank. Here is how the Baron de La Moussaye described his years in Brittany with his late wife Claude.

We lived with such happiness and blessing from God that we were the admiration of all our neighbors, and principally because we made handsome and large acquisitions, rebuilt [our chateaux], constructed mills and roads at La Moussaye, bought rings and jewels in great number and at high price, accumulated furniture in our houses, and beyond that lent money to those who needed it and held abundant open house, where anyone who did us the honor to come was very well received and honorably treated. [3]

City neighbors also used food as a primary gift, wine being a frequent present. (Game and fruit could be purchased in urban markets, but to offer them as gifts one would prefer to say they had come from one's farm or estate.) Especially they had each other to meals. Artisans paid each other's share of the bill ("l'escot," as they called it) at inns and taverns. This could solidify companionship but also occasion a fight, as in Paris in 1544, when some journeymen butchers offered to treat the men they had just defeated in a tennis match, and the losers answered "they didn't want to be beholden to the winners" and began to throw the plates. Artisans also gathered around each other's tables, as did the families of merchants and lawyers and groups of canons and priests. Sometimes the guests sent part of the dinner over ahead of time, while Guillaume Bouchet of Poitiers lauded "the honest custom in several towns of France" for relatives, friends, and neighbors to bring a dish to a dinner—a sixteenth-century "pot-luck"—going one day to one person's house and another day to another's. [4]

The popularity and frequency of such dinner parties is suggested by a 1563 royal edict on Banquets, where "superfluity" was found "increasing every day in all estates." No dinner—not even for a wedding or other festivity—was to have more than three services (or courses, as we would say) of six dishes each, and only one kind of meat would be allowed at the main course. Everyone was threatened with fines for violation: the host, the cooks, and the guests, who were required to denounce their host to a judge the next day.[5] No spate of denunciations followed this decree, not even from guests who had indigestion or hangovers or felt jealous.

For the humanist Erasmus the banquet was a setting not for superfluity, but for generosity and discussion. His "godly feast" was a setting for conversing about Christian charity; when the guests leave, the host gives them little books, Christian and classical; clocks, so they may treasure their time; a lamp to read by; and reed pens. His letters provide us with further evidence about gift relations among friends, whether they lived near to each other or far away. Dedicating a book from Basel to Pieter Gillis in Antwerp in 1515, he contrasted their connection with other male friendships:

Friends of the commonplace and homespun sort, my open-hearted Pieter, have their idea of relationship, like their whole lives, attached to material things; and if ever they have to face a separation, they favor a frequent exchange of rings, knives, caps and other tokens of the kind, for fear that their affection may cool when intercourse is interrupted . . . But you and I, whose idea of friendship rests wholly in a meeting of minds and the enjoyment of studies in common, might well greet one another from time to time with presents for the mind and keepsakes of a literary description . . . Our aim would be that any loss due to separation in the actual enjoyment of our friendship should be made good, not without interest, by tokens of this literary kind. And so I send a present—no common present, for you are no common friend, but many jewels in one small book.[6]

So Erasmus sent him his new collection of metaphors.

In fact, Erasmus's circle sometimes resorted to gifts of a more corporeal kind: for instance, Andrea Ammonio sent Erasmus a white horse, telling him, "Rest assured I shall never expect anything in return." But books were the present most readily circulated among learned friends, sometimes with formal dedications, sometimes with a letter, which might well be published afterward. The letters were infused with the courteous language of benefits and gratitude, but also contained mutual teasing, barbed comments about enemies, praise for other scholars, and requests for favors: for assistance in preparing a new edition or selling an old one, in finding out why the pension from an existing patron was late, and in acquiring a benefice from a new one.[7]

Especially important, the dedications also addressed the contents of the book. In 1527 Charles de Bouelles dedicated his Latin collection *Proverbium Vulgarium* (Popular proverbs) to a jurist friend in Paris; his epistle talked of Erasmus's *Adagia* and other proverbs. For the poet and mathematican Jacques Peletier, *L'Aritmetique* (1552) was a testimonial to his years of intimacy with Théodore de Bèze, now an emigré to Calvin's Geneva. Each of its "proems" to Bèze raised an important issue about mathematics, music, and the French language, making known to readers the educational program that he, Bèze, and their circle had talked about in Paris late into the night.[8] The gift provided a frame of civility and friendly exchange for the discussion of subjects that might be new or controversial.

Erasmus's books went not only to scholarly friends, but also to powerful figures in church, kingdom, and duchy. Not "of the homespun sort," they sent back to the Prince of Letters golden clocks, silver cups, ruby rings, and ducats, both the token and the substance of patronage. Gifts from the patron could also initiate the relationship, as in 1516, when the bishop of Rochester asked Erasmus what he should send to the Hebraist Johann Reuchlin, and Erasmus suggested a ring or a garment. The next year offers arrived for Erasmus without preliminary presents: the bishop of Bayeux invited him to come and live with him, "that I might be refreshed by your extraordinary gifts," promising to start off with an "honorarium" of two hundred ducats. A few months later, Guillaume Budé passed on François Ier's offer of a benefice worth more than a thousand francs if Erasmus could be induced to move to France and join a royal "nursery-bed of scholars."[9]

These examples introduce us to the variety of exchanges between persons at different levels of a hierarchy of status, wealth, and/or power. In a sense, the whole patronage system was carried on under the rhetoric of gifts (as Sharon Kettering has demonstrated for the seventeenth century), even while the accounts of great households arranged their lists of "pensions" and "dons" in a very businesslike manner. When Brother René Martin sought a vacant hermitage in Anjou from François de La Trémoille, he wrote the viscount "in humble supplication," promising to be "held and obliged" to pray for La Trémoille, his wife, and whole noble lineage for the rest of his days. When a Breton nobleman wanted a vacant position as "pancionnaire" with the Duke d'Étampes, governor of Brittany, he mentioned past favor from the duke, asked his advice about taking a military post offered him by someone else, then turned to his "humble supplication," which, if granted, "would increase my means to do you service, having no greater happiness in this life than remaining near you and in your good grace."[10]

This language of gift, service, and gratitude was used in relations where the client may well have had or expected to have more than one patron or to change patrons. In this regard, it had advantages over the more exclusive and, by sixteenth-century standards, more intimate language of feudal homage. The element of mutual interest was softened without being obliterated. Grants and promises were made without kneeling and kissing, which were increasingly coming under criticism in the homage ceremony of the sixteenth century. (In 1530, when Montaigne's father, Pierre Eyquem, did homage for the seigneury of Montaigne, he was kissed on the cheek rather than on the mouth as in the medieval ceremony.) As a client one could become grateful to the patron without becoming the other's "man."[11]

Sustaining the patronage relationship as a gift mode were smaller presents passed on as each side saw fit. Here the language widens, as Kristen Neuschel has shown so well, into a courteous and reciprocal acknowledgement of honor and noble status. A Picard nobleman sends special hunting birds with a gracious letter to the Duke de Montmorency, who heads one of the major clientage systems of France. Claude du Chastel sends the Duke d'Étampes a falcon and a tercel, having heard that he desired them and "finding happiness above all things in doing [the duke] agreeable service." He explains he has been ill and thus was unable to come serve the king in person at the duke's side. Then the gifts move downward in the other direction. The Cardinal de Bourbon sends a Picard nobleman a gift of fruit, thanking him for helping him to stop disorder in the province during the religious disturbance of 1562. And Jeanne d'Albret and later Henri de Navarre buy gold and silver engraved rings, belts, hats, sweets, and other small objects for the young noblewomen and men in their suite, quite apart from their regular pensions.[12]

Gilles de Gouberville's presents to important nobles or governing figures in the Cotentin region of Normandy illustrate the gift process outside of a strict system of clientage. Sire Gilles lived primarily from the rents and produce sales from his estates and, during some years, from his income as a local officer in the royal court supervising streams and forests. He was dependent on major figures not for pensions, but for more general favor and support. Gift courtesy also established him as part of their noble world of honor. Two persons of high status emerge in Gouberville's accounts as recipients of gifts beyond his web of kin, seigneurial neighbors, and officerial cronies: the Duchess of Saint-Paul, whose chateau was at Bricquebec about two hours away by horse from his manor of Le Mesnil au Val; and the Sire de Hurtebye, governor of the royal chateau in the administrative, legal, and commercial center of Valognes an hour away. In each case, the relation was more formal and less symmetrical than Gouberville's exchange with his kinfolk, the timing of the gifts more artfully aimed at maintaining a tie without always being associated with a specific request or favor.

With the duchess, Gouberville's association began in January 1554, when he went to her chateau, dined there, and discussed a suit involving one of his tenants. The next day, he sent over a kid to Madame, the first of many kids from his flocks, capons from his barnyard, and leverets from his men's hunting expeditions which flowed to her chateau over the seven years till her death in 1560. Madame de Saint-Paul sent a gift only once in return—some venison in 1560—and she did not visit his manorhouse. Rather her chateau was open to him, both when she returned to Bricquebec from elsewhere and he rode over to do her "reverence," and other times as well, when he could laugh with her about the tricks her pages did to the girls at the Feast of Innocents, mingle with the various officers and ladies from the best families of the Cotentin, and dance. Marriage seems to have been on his mind more than once in these visits: his own perhaps with some local noblewoman and the remarriage of his high servitor Cantepye, though neither of these worked out.[13]

Gouberville sent the Sire de Hurtebye some of the same gifts, but the issues at stake were different and the relation more unstable. Gouberville first met Hurtebye when the latter was tutor of the young Counts de Tende, who resided frequently at the royal chateau of Valognes. From 1553 to 1555, when both young men died, Gouberville went up now and and again to the chateau "to do them reverence" and also sent them pigeons, partridges, and fish. They invited him to dine and to hunt with them (not his favorite activity, though he was happy to lend them his dogs). Meanwhile Gouberville was getting to know Hurtebye, seeing him in the course of his tasks as forest officer, doing errands for him, and dining with him at the chateau. In October 1554, for instance, after an investigation of the acorn crop in one of the king's woods, Gouberville invited all the officers, of which Hurtebye was the most prominent, for a specially catered supper at his manor, where they then spent the night. The next day Hurtebye sent Gouberville four pigs.[14]

After the death of the young counts, the Sire de Hurtebye became the governor of the territory of Valognes. Gouberville's gift relation with him continued for a time along with his judicial tie, Gouberville sending a boar to Hurtebye and dining with him at the chateau. Then in December 1555, before the governor's very eyes, Gouberville had an acrimonious public quarrel on a forest matter with a man of higher status than himself, the Viconte de Valognes. (According to Gouberville, the viconte, citing his many services to the king, asked that he be given fifteen oak trees from the royal forest to use for beams for his new house. Gouberville refused, saying it was against the ordinances.) Abruptly Gouberville's visits to Valognes were cut back: "I scarcely stopped [in Valognes], for the viconte was there."[15]

A year passed, and in mid-January 1557, perhaps as a late New Year's gift, Gilles had his high servant Cantepye take a kid to the governor. The very next morning, Hurtebye was at Goubverville's manor requesting that he come immediately as a forest officer and question two men who had seized a cartload of wood from his servants. Gouberville refused on a conflict of interest: one of the men was a nephew of the viconte, with whom he still had "a quarrel." Someone else should do it. Hurtebye left impatient and displeased. For yet another year, there were no gifts or visits, and the few connections between Gouberville and Hurtebye were strictly in the course of payment or officerial duty.[16]

On 1 January 1558, things changed again as Gouberville sent Hurtebye a bittern, a gift clearly outside the usual game or farm meat. His relations with Valognes officers were also beginning to revive, as the king's advocate was negotiating marriage with Gouberville's cousin. The next years saw a return to the earlier rhythms that combined gifts and duties. Hares, kids, capons, and once even a fawn passed from Gouberville's manor to Hurtebye's chateau, and not only at New Year's, but other times—say, to accompany a regular payment owed from his collecting on the royal domain. In return, there was the occasional present of wine, but more often the chance to dine with and visit the Sire de Hurtebye at the chateau.[17]

In sum, gifts helped initiate those relationships, establishing through their asymmetry the distance between simple seigneur and duchess and between minor officer and governor, while affirming at the same time—through the presence of game and the delivery by servants—that they were all honorable noblemen and noblewomen. Presumably these identities were confirmed as well by appropriate compliments, but in rural Cotentin they were more often exchanged orally than in writing. Gifts and associated courtesies facilitated communication and mutual help. Entwined with the performance of judicial duties for the crown, a gift relation could reinforce officerial solidarity and the sense that royal service need not be in tension with noble loyalties (though this tension was by no means eliminated, as we will see later).

The absence of gifts did not necessarily signify a feud — Gouberville was feuding with the Viconte de Valognes, not with Hurtebye — but it represented distance, a cool zone where correct behavior and prescribed payment could operate, but not favor and communication. Once the gift flow resumed between Gouberville and the governor, the talk resumed.

The gift pattern of the rural nobility clearly had its own shape and customs, as we recognize when we compare it to the objects and letters that passed among Erasmus, his friends, and their patrons. Gouberville's mastery of the rural pattern is nicely revealed in 1560 and 1561, when he set himself up for long stretches at Russy, several hours away in the Bessin, where he had become co-heir to the property of an uncle. Over the weeks as he straightened out the accounts and supervised the farming, he reproduced exactly the kind of gift network he had at Le Mesnil au Val: an exchange of game birds, fish, ham, and pudding with his nearby kin, and woodcocks sent to the viscount and royal judge at Bayeux, where he had increased legal business.[18]

Knowing one pattern did not automatically bring understanding of another, even if the general spirit of gratitude and obligation were expected to prevail in all gift registers. In the winter of 1556, Gouberville went to the royal court, then being held at Blois, in a vain quest for a higher office in Forests and Streams. He had no idea of how to maneuver and seemed most at his ease when watching a comedy, chatting in the royal kitchen with a young squire, and drinking with the queen's wine steward. He did get his request in, but the master of requests never even took Gouberville's papers out of his pouch.[19]

Gouberville's *Journal* also provides a rare glimpse of how gifts moved between peasant and seigneur. From his tenants and leasers, the Sire de Gouberville received occasional presents suitable to their station — fish, fruits, capons, goslings, and rabbits — which were not simply annual rents in kind. Sometimes they were gifts reinforcing or lacing around contractual payments. Often they were gifts acknowledging Gouberville's status as seigneur and certain services he provided them that could be recognized in no other way. A resident landlord deeply enmeshed in the running of his fields, apple orchards, flocks, and beehives; a not inattentive collector of what was due him; an employer paying to five men opening up a field less for a week of digging than he paid for some black taffeta for himself, and to five mowers less for four days of harvest work than he paid for a velvet bonnet for his uncle; a prosecutor of tenants who stole his pigs or his bee hives—Gouberville was also an arbitrator of peasant quarrels, an advisor on and even negotiator for their marriages, their supporter in court cases against others, protector of their interests against the royal tax collector, and sender of cider, honey, beer, and goat's milk (but, of course, never claret, kid, or pigeons) to sick villagers.[20]

Consider Martin Birette, who owed Gouberville rents in grain and barley for his land and payment for leasing a mill. In May 1550, a month after the lease on the mill has been extended, Birette comes by the manorhouse with a couple of goslings, and then stays for Sunday dinner. At the Feast of Kings in 1552, 1553, and 1554, Birette has his grandson bring Gouberville a Twelfth Night cake for the festivities. In January 1555, he accompanies Gouberville to Cherbourg where Sire Gilles purchases a new millstone; Gouberville buys him some beer for his trouble. Two weeks later, the seigneur finds the miller at the manorhouse, his foot badly injured by the millstone. Gouberville sends for and pays a barber to care for him, and then after Birette's death and burial, has a dinner for the family at the manorhouse tables. A few months later, one of Martin's sons stops by the manor with some chickens and a spice cake, and another son is given a year's lease on another of Gouberville's mills.[21]

For most peasants on Gouberville's manors, gifts to the seigneur were infrequent, a respectful action to be taken on special occasions or when one needed a favor. In the spring of 1552, when Gouberville was ill for a month, several tenants stopped by with apples, chickens, and rabbits, their presents duly recorded by the seigneur in his journal along with the kid and the oranges sent to him by his own relatives. Early in the month of December a good farm wife appears with twelve blackbirds and several villagers bring herring; while a lad carries over two chickens for his mother on 31 December. Another villager brings butter as he comes by not long after the Feast of Kings, another two goslings on a summer's day. Tenant Jacques Burnel leaves off two woodcocks at the same time he pays Michaelmas rent. Sometimes the favors for which the gifts prepared the way can be traced in Gouberville's record, though he himself made the connection no more explicit in his journal than he did for his gifts of game to Governor Hurtebye. So Joret Gaillard brings pigeons the day before he has to appear in front of the church court in Valognes, and the next day Gouberville goes with him and speaks to the curé on his behalf.[22]

Gouberville's gifts to his tenants were also less frequent and than those to his kinfolk and fellow seigneurs and officers, but they went beyond New Year's étrennes, Saint Gilles's day pins, and the birth, marriage, and death gifts already mentioned. Considerable money, shirts, and a letter of recommendation are provided for one village lad as he departs for his apprenticeship in Paris; a few pennies are left for tenants in prison. Coming upon a peddler one day, Gouberville suddenly buys eighteen deniers' worth of laces and pins and distributes them to four different villagers.[23]

But Gouberville's major gift return to his peasants was the hospitality of his manor. Favored tenants might be invited to dine along with a priest or two after Sunday or holiday mass, and any villager who was visiting the house at mealtimes could find a place at a table and put down a pallet for the night. There were no special preparations—no dispatching the household staff to Cherbourg for fish or to the woods to hunt for fine game, as one did for important guests. But that table could be counted on the way cider was for the sick or honey for the woman about to deliver. When Gouberville finally made peace with tenant Nicolas Quentin after months of prosecution for his alleged rebelliousness and petty thefts, the seigneur immediately had the peasant to dinner.[24]

These peasant-seigneur gifts had a different style to them from the noble exchange among seigneurs and the courteous or festive exchange among villagers. The food, objects, or small amounts of money given sustained social distance and distinct identities: the seigneur sent artichokes and venison pâté to his cousins, honey and beer to his tenants. A peasant would not dare present game to the seigneur. Not only would it be presumptuous, but also it would be illegal for a mere commoner to hunt deer and large forest animals except in the service of a nobleman.[25] (If a peasant had a deer through "poaching," he would conceal it from his landlord, especially if the latter was an officer in the royal forests.) When the same object could move as a gift in either social direction—such as the woodcock, on one occasion given by a tenant to Gouberville and another given by Gouberville together with partridges and ring doves to the young counts of Tende—the presentation was different. The villager carried his own gift, or sent it by a family member like Birette's grandson; the seigneur sent it by a household servant. Though we have no record of the language, postures, and gestures used in peasant-seigneur exchange, we can assume that these too varied from what was said and done among villagers and among seigneurs.

Gift exchange did not prevent conflict between seigneur and peasant any more than it did between nobles. Gouberville had disputes with his tenants and his servants both. New Year's money and Saint Gilles's day pins did not stop the servant Guionne Curdon from leaving the manor without saying goodbye and taking with her silver rings in place of the back wages she was owed. Still, her brother returned her to the manor and two months later she was given a new pair of shoes.[26] Gifts opened channels of communication here across boundaries of status and literacy. They gave expression to the highly strained but genuine reciprocity between unequals in the social and economic order.

4

Gifts and Sales

ifts sustained relations where regular payments or pensions were part of the picture, and sometimes, as we have seen, they literally accompanied a payment. This timing returns us to the border between gifts, sales, wages, and other formally contractual payments. Did the gift side of the border get pushed back when markets expanded, as some of the early anthropological and historical theory of gifts suggested?

The Brittany lawyer Noël du Fail was certainly wondering about this in 1547 when he published his *Propos rustiques*. In these rural tales, an old and well-off peasant reminisces about his youth.

> Then there was never a feast day when someone in the village didn't invite all the rest to dinner to eat his hen, gosling, and ham. But nowadays . . . the hens and goslings are scarcely fat enough when they are carried off to be sold for money to pay Monsieur the Lawyer . . . to mistreat his neighbor.[1]

Yet du Fail's peasant is bewailing present times even while he and his cronies sit peacefully under an oak tree during a village feast, watching the young men play at archery and other games. Neighborliness is still a reality, and the farmer is reminding his listeners of the difference between two modes of exchange and their continued presence in the village. A similar juxtaposition is made by the next old-timer, who compares the balanced banquets of his youth with those today, when variety is sought through pepper, saffron, ginger, cinnamon, mace, cloves, and other spices "transferred from Towns to our Villages," and originating, as his listeners would

well know, in overseas trade. Healthier though the speaker insists the earlier banquets were, he concedes that people today would find them them tasteless and
lacking splendor.[2]

What is interesting about the sixteenth century is this sensitivity to the relation
between gift and sale, this concern about the border between them. Rather than
imagining a zero-sum game between gifts and commercial markets, or even a historical tug of war, we might better conceive of enduring interactions between gift-
systems and sale-systems. Certain of these interactions may have curtailed gifts,
others freed them to go in new directions. Especially important in the sixteenth
century was the possibility of moving back and forth between the gift mode and
the sale mode, while always remembering the distinction between them.

The gift mode was sustained in these interactions not only by general beliefs
about gratitude, reciprocity, and property, but also by the conviction that it was
unseemly and even somewhat unethical to deliver certain services only for a fixed
payment or price. We have already seen that the Acts of Mercy and the paternalistic
interventions of Gouberville for his tenants were to be recognized solely by a donation or a gift. Services in the liberal arts and liberal professions were not so strictly
categorized in the sixteenth century, but they carried with them strong claims to
be acknowledged by gifts as well as remunerated by payments.

"Knowledge is a gift of God, and cannot be sold" was the medieval aphorism,
itself going back to a Greek ideal. In the village, much lore was inherited or collective and passed on by the storyteller or priest, whose recompense was gifts of food
and a place of honor near the hearth. In the castle, the poet Marie de France spoke
of the obligations of and returns from knowledge.

> To whom God has given science
> And the eloquence of good speech
> Must not be silent or conceal it
> But willingly show it.
> When a great good is heard by many
> Then it begins to seed
> And when it is praised by many
> Then it bursts into flower.[3]

In the medieval monastery, copying manuscripts was considered a meritorious and godly act (rubrication was compared to the blood of martyrs), and lending a manuscript an act of mercy. In the university, where the store of learning
was enlarged by new manuscripts, disputations, and commentaries, the medieval
canon law prohibited fee-taking by professors and the sale of scribal productions.
Fortunately for the teachers and the university copyists, many of whom had no
benefices to support themselves, the biblical text that "the laborer is worthy of his
hire" (Luke 10:7) was finally used to justify some payments. By the late medieval
period, university stationers were renting out manuscripts for copying and busy lay
scriveners were paid salaries for their work by authors and would-be owners. Still,

the careful regulation of rates for the rental and sale of manuscripts was in part a recognition that knowledge was a gift of the Holy Spirit and should not be too dearly sold. In the early fifteenth century, a few decades before the invention of movable type, the theologian Jean Gerson was reminding princes that they must collect books not just for themselves but for the use of those around them.[4]

Sixteenth-century authors, book producers and book possessors thus inherited not only patterns of gift-giving, but also a belief that property in a book was as much collective as private and that God himself had some special rights in that object. In this view, the book was at its best when given, should not be sold beyond a just price, and must never be hoarded.

With the development of the printing industry, these ideas were afloat in one of the most commercially organized businesses of sixteenth-century Europe. They survived in modified form. Book production and sale seemed less "mercenary" than other trades: "You practice the most honorable commerce possible in this world," said a Lyon notary in a printed letter to an important merchant-publisher in Paris.[5] Property in the printed book was still diffuse: the publisher or printer often acquired the royal *privilège,* or exclusive right to publish the book for a specified number of years, but sometimes the author or editor did. The author was closely identified with his or her book in its dedication, but had no formal copyright, and many sixteenth-century printed books had no known author, but only a translator or editor.

The mixture of gift claims and sale claims, of the language of property and the language of benefit, is vividly shown in a suit argued before the Parlement of Paris in 1586. An edition of Seneca's *Opera* had appeared in Rome in 1585, with annotations by the late French emigré Marc Antoine Muret and with no privilège from the French king. Now a Parisian publisher wanted to reprint it with an exclusive six-year privilège for himself, and two competing publishers objected. The lawyer for the latter maintained that each person is the lord or seigneur of what he or she makes. "The author of a book is wholly its master, and as such can dispose of it freely, even keeping it always in his own private hands . . . or granting it common liberty . . . holding nothing back . . . or reserving some right of patronage over it, as in saying that no one but him can print it for a certain time." The Seneca/Muret edition had been given to the public freely and should remain free. The privilège-seeking publisher was "ungrateful" toward God and humankind:

It is ingratitude to contravene the law of benefit, to ravish this book from the breast of the public, to which it belongs by the munificence of those who produced it, and to arrogate it to oneself privately.[6]

He was also ungrateful to the author, who wanted to acquire immortal life by the book, for if "honest emulation" among printers was limited, the number of copies of the book would be reduced and its cost would go up for the studious reader. The privilège-seeker was violating "in his private favor" both "the public liberty of the

Printing Industry" and the spirit of gift and gratitude. The competing publishers won their case.[7]

As physical objects, sixteenth-century printed books operated under the sign both of sale and of gift. The publisher's address was on the title page for potential buyers; the dedication of author, editor, or translator was on the inside, inserting the book into a gift relation. In his request for a royal privilège, always printed in the book, the publisher stressed his efforts and expenses in finding and preparing a correct and useful text, efforts that deserved recompense; in his dedication or preface, the same publisher might present himself as a giver of books. So in 1559 the wealthy Lyon merchant-publisher Guillaume Rouillé dedicates Lodovico Domenichi's *Ragionamento* on military matters back to its author: "Accept this book with the same good heart in which you sent it. You presented it to me in a beautiful script and with pictures made by hand. I return it to you printed in beautiful characters and with engraved illustrations. Think of me," the merchant publisher says to his author, dissolving the commercial relationship into another kind of reciprocity, "as your friend and brother." When the French translation comes out two years later, Rouillé dedicates it to Catherine de Médicis, still presenting himself as a performer of services. He has published the work to celebrate the glory and splendor of her ancestors, mentioned within, and he hopes the queen will receive the book graciously as she has others he has addressed to her.[8]

Over its material lifetime, the same book might pass through a sale, then become a gift, pass on as a bequest to heirs, who might then hold on to it (especially if it were a folio Bible or a book of hours) or sell it. These different trajectories are recorded in the flyleafs, where owners, donors, and/or prices are listed over generations. Sometimes printed books were just given away, an unlikely gesture with earlier costly manuscripts. In 1560, in a Lyon swarming with heretics, the Jesuit Antonio Possevino had Catholic catechisms published at his expense and distributed them in the streets. In 1574, Protestants published satirical attacks on Catherine de Médicis, King Charles IX, and his council and, in the words of one observer, "had them strewn about as far as the wine cellars of Avignon, where the chambermaids and valets going to draw wine for their masters often found them at their feet. So great was the fervor of those who escaped the [St. Bartholomew's Day] Massacre to make known the innocence of the slain, the cruelty and perfidy of the killers, and the injustice of the councillors."[9]

Sometimes a printed book stayed for a very long time or permanently in a great collection: the royal library, to which from 1536 all printers were legally required to donate a copy of each newly published book, and the large private libraries that emerged by the end of the century. The latter were built up by gifts enticed from friends and by astute purchases. Gabriel Naudé used both techniques in acquiring an enormous collection for Cardinal Mazarin and counseled readers to do the same in his 1627 *Advis pour dresser une bibliothèque* (Advice on establishing a library). Symbols of status and power though these collections were, they were not (in Naudé's words, echoing Scripture) "to remain hidden under a bush." "Rather they were to be consecrated to the usage of the public and so far as practicable, be accessible to the least of men."[10]

A related duality is found in the teaching profession. In 1536, in a new ordinance for the Paris Faculty of Theology, the Parlement of Paris was still using the traditional gift formulation: "the knowledge acquired by the doctors in the Faculty is a gratuitous gift for the edification of the Church and ought not to be hidden away."[11] The regent doctors were not to go unrewarded for that edification: they had stipends from the faculty, payments for endowed lectures, and income from benefices and from administrative posts at colleges. They also received fees from their students, which were paid them for directing students' studies and presiding over the academic disputations that were the heart of the long doctoral training in theology.

In addition the students gave the regent doctors frequent customary gifts: sugar and other sweets after candidates pronounced their solemn lectures; fruit and wine to the chancellor on many occasions; and banquets after disputations and the granting of the license and the doctorate. A "biretta" went to every professor who attended the candidate's final disputation before the doctorate. Once it may have been an actual bonnet, such as that conferred the same day on the candidate himself; by the sixteenth century a "biretta" was a gift of one-half golden crown.[12]

The medical faculties of Paris and Montpellier had similar practices, though gloves—the sign of the unsullied hands of the physician—were part of the exchange. Students paid fees to the doctors assessing their examinations and disputations, which covered techniques of consultation as well as questions of medicine and pathology from Hippocrates on. They also provided their examiners with white wine, cakes, and fruit before and during their performance, a feast for everyone at major sessions, and a banquet after the awarding of the doctorate. In return for his bonnet and gloves, the new doctor at Montpellier sent gloves embroidered in gold to each regent doctor present and sweets and a candle to every doctor in town. In Paris, the sugar confections after the licentiate were often shaped into a likeness of the dean of the faculty.[13]

These gifts were costly, often more so than the fees, and had considerable symbolic importance. They should not be collapsed, as some have done, into "disguised payments." In part they sustained the old idea that knowledge came as a divine gift and should be reciprocated by gifts and gratitude. In part they gave expression to the corporate solidarity and prestige of the theologians and the physicians, shown as well through their elaborate ceremonies and distinctive garb. At the licentiate ceremony, the candidate was constructed as a bridegroom wedding his science and his faculty; after the panegyrics, he had the license to speak jocularly and even a bit sharply about his teachers. At the banquet table successful candidates and their doctor professors were joined by the students who had witnessed the day's events. Gift occasions, rather than the payment of their fees, marked the move of young men from one status to another.[14]

Further, gifts were used by the students to compete with each other, in regard to the amount of food, wine, sweets, and guests. This competitive spirit was in part stimulated by the faculties, or at least by the Faculty of Theology, where every cohort of licentiates was ranked, from first place on down. The faculties tried to set limits on banquet fare: neither too spare nor too sumptuous, said a Theology ruling of 1524. In 1536 the Parlement of Paris put a cap on the amounts that could be spent and the number of guests that could be invited, and said that theology students from the mendicant orders (about 30 percent of the graduates) had no obligation to put on banquets at all. It is doubtful that such regulations had much effect except for the mendicant friars. At Montpellier, efforts were made at mid-century to limit the amounts spent on candies, but new graduates continued to use their banquets to help win a good appointment for their first post as doctors of medicine.[15]

The practice of healing provides a third example of the relation between gifts and sales in connection with the privileged realm of knowledge. Long-term changes were taking place in both the "liberal" art of medicine, where doctors centered on diagnosis and prescription, and the "mechanical" art of surgery, with its hands-on setting of bones, applications of leeches, and treatment of wounds. The physicians were continuing their unending efforts to set standards for the medical profession, trying to see to it that all practitioners were licensed, including the midwives, and to exclude "charlatans" and "empirics." The surgeons, or at least an elite among them, were trying to upgrade their education and prestige and expand their activities into the women's world of midwifery.

One of the targets of the professionalizing doctors of medicine was an age-old practice called "the promise to cure." In advance of any treatment, the healer made a pact with the sick person to cure him or her for a specified payment. No cure, no payment. Studied in depth by Gianna Pomata from the medical court records of Bologna, the "promise to cure" was known in France. As the 1612 statutes of Bordeaux put it:

Physicians are forbidden to make pacts and conventions with their sick patients, under a promise to cure them, in which the physicians specify a certain salary or donation that they can extort as they wish from the sick, who hope for cure and health.[16]

Such pacts, when made at all in France, seem to have been initiated, as they were in Italy, by barber-surgeons and popular healers rather than by maverick physicians. So Gilles de Gouberville tells the story of finding his friend Guillaume being treated by a barber for a cancer he has had on his face for nine years. Gouberville remonstrated with the barber that, according to what physicians and surgeons had written on the matter, such a cure was impossible and his enterprise was sheer folly. The barber answered "he would ask nothing if [Guillaume] were not cured." [17]

Insofar as doctors of medicine were reimbursed by salaries — or what some of them preferred to call "honoraria," as befitting their liberal art — they were usually paid a sum by the month or year when the physician was employed by the city or a hospital or a great household, and by the visit when he was summoned by an individual sick person, without any regard to whether the patient was actually being cured. Beyond that, as one Italian text put it in 1527, a physican accepted "the gifts that his patients, out of courtesy or kindness, wish[ed] to present him." Those too poor to pay would be visited out of charity, "with no hope for recompense except from God." ("He took no money from the poor," Jeanne du Laurens said of her physician father, Louis du Laurens, in Arles. "When they really needed it, he even furnished them money.") As for the promise-to-cure contract, the doctors denounced it as both "mercenary" and "presumptuous": healers should not make magical promises.[18]

Such collective self-perceptions readied physicians to be recipients, indeed collectors of gifts, even while they received fees. François Rabelais—himself, of course, a doctor of medicine—suggested that the gift mode was preferred at least for public display: in *Le Tiers Livre,* after Panurge has consulted Dr. Rondibilis about his fear of being cuckolded, he announces he will send some tripe to the physician's house, grandly proclaiming, "You will always be our friend." Meanwhile he quietly slips four crowns into the doctor's hand. Rondibilis acts indignant: "Ha, Monsieur, nothing was needed. Still many thanks. From nasty people I take nothing, from good people I never refuse. I'm always at your service." [19]

Bonaventure Desperiers told a similar story about medical relations in a little town in Gascony. Passing through Saint-Antonin, a Toulouse law student was persuaded by the local apothecary to present himself as a medical doctor since the old physician had just died. Tutored at every turn by the apothecary, the impostor physician was so successful a healer that "people sent him a thousand presents, like game and flasks of wine, and the women made him [special Gascon dishes]." At the same time, he and the apothecary, who filled the prescriptions, became "as stuffed with golden crowns as a cock ready to go into the oven." [20]

Unlike these examples, Gilles de Gouberville's relations with his physician Raoul Dager of Valognes over many years seem never to have involved the payment of a fee. Master Raoul studied Gouberville's urine (carried to him by servants), visited him often in bed at the manorhouse, sometimes examining his high servants and tenants as well, and prescribed remedies. Gouberville paid small amounts to Dager's servant and larger amounts to the barber who occasionally accompanied Dager. He paid for Dager's horse when it was rented, had him to dinner and sometimes as an overnight guest, and made sure he had company back to Valognes. Gouberville offered payment each time, and each time the physician "did not want to take money." Eventually Gouberville would send him a fat pig or a substantial piece of venison. In contrast, with two physicians from Bayeux whom Gouberville summoned only once or twice, a fee did change hands, and then considerably more than Gouberville gave to barbers.[21]

Game was not the only gift that went to doctors of medicine. From Toulouse and his Gascon estate, Judge Jean de Coras wrote lovingly to his wife Jacquette, who was suffering from illness in Montpellier and being treated by eminent physicians from the Faculty of Medicine.

I'd like to know what you think I could locate here, not available in Montpellier, to present to your physicians in recognition of the good and continual services that they do for you every day, more important to me than if they were to bring me back from the dead . . . I've been thinking of some knife holders and nicely ornamented scissors for them and their wives, but perhaps those are things one can find in [Montpellier].

In addition, Jacquette should let her doctors know that he was attending to their case before the Parlement of Toulouse "not only because I hold their excellent virtues in high regard, but also to recognize the obligations that attach me to them through the praiseworthy services they provide you, which I can never forget." [22] Patients hoped to keep the good services coming by the added reminder of gifts; physicians appreciated the link of gratitude.

As for barbers, surgeons, midwives, and other healers, gifts played a similar role in their relations with the sick. Indeed, those healers who used the promise-to-cure pact might answer that they were less mercenary than the physicians, and virtually all healers had fees lower than those of doctors of medicine. Among surgeons, there was evidently a customary schedule for gifts: a linen bedsheet for a hernia, a tablecloth for the stone, and two napkins or headcloths for cataracts.[23] Gifts passed also from pregnant women and new mothers to their midwives along with payments. For Louise Bourgeois, who had served both poor and rich in Paris before becoming *sage-femme* to Queen Marie de Médicis, the relation between mother and midwife must involve more than money payment: the midwife was not a mere "woman of the wine-harvest, hired, paid, and then changed every year."

Ungrateful women do not recognize the good offices that they receive during their deliveries when they are closer to death than to life . . . Where there is a service that concerns life, neither gold nor silver can recompense it. Here there is an obligation to love, according to God first and nature.

Gratitude and love were shown by loyalty to the midwife from one birth to the next, and by gifts. Catherine de Médicis had given her midwives a velvet collar and a golden chain. Marie de Médicis gave Louise Bourgeois a velvet hood and money gifts now and again; Henri IV provided her with annual pension of three hundred écus and promised a five hundred écu payment when she delivered a son and three hundred écus when she delivered a daughter.[24]

Meanwhile a woman like Catherine Genas, mother of the chancellor of the medical faculty at Montpellier, but long a practicing healer in her own right, must have been recompensed only by gifts brought to her estate. As a woman of high status, her treatments had to be given "in charity." Creator of remedies, salves, and bandages for the poor and the sick, Genas had invented an ointment for maladies of the nipples whose use had spread to surrounding provinces. Her son Laurent Joubert dedicated a surgical book to her so that future generations could know of her skill and her qualities.[25]

In each of these examples of compensation for the purveyance of knowledge—through publishing, university teaching, and healing—the gift mode and the sales

mode persisted together in the sixteenth century. In publishing there was a double ✓✓
expansion: of the world in which sales operated and of the ways in which gifts
could signify and be used and directed. In teaching, gifts helped define and sustain
corporate identity, which in the case of theology was soon to be under attack from
Protestants. In healing, they gave expression to the dependencies and hopes in the
relationship between sick person and physician or other healer, even while the instability of gifts as the major remuneration for doctors of medicine was apparent.
The sixteenth-century reformulation of the medieval saying might be: "The gifts
of God can be sold and given, it depends on the circumstances."

In more everyday forms of economic life, where the products and services were
less closely connected with the privileged realm of knowledge, payments and some
presents still went side by side at every step of the social ladder. The king's officers
received "wages" (*gages* or *gaiges* as they were called in the royal accounts) and were
also granted annual pensions of a fixed amount. To start with, the pensions were a
present—"to reward him for his services in battle on land and sea," as one request
went, "and oblige him more and more to do you humble service all his life"—but
then they were accounted in a salary-like way along with the gages.[26]

Royal officers were also given gifts of garments, money, and property apart
from any schedule. The language of the record keepers and treasurers in thousands
of such "dons" shows how fluid the boundary was between the two forms of recompense. In 1543, a vice-admiral of the Levant fleet is given as "don" in "reward
for his services" a property and seigneury near Marseille, recently fallen to François
Ier as an estate belonging to a foreign resident. The next year, the king gives two
soupmakers in the royal kitchens 225 livres each "beyond their wages and [previ-
ous] gifts . . . in favor of their good and agreeable services." In 1569, Charles IX
provides the Duc d'Anjou with forty thousand livres to distribute as "gifts" to those
gentlemen who had done most to win the battle near Montredon "in consideration
of the good performance of their duty" and "to give them the means to make up
their losses in horses, weapons, and baggage, and equip themselves to serve in the
future." Meanwhile, Charles has given the queen-mother's chambermaid a gift of
sixty-two livres "in favor of the services that she has done [for Catherine de Mé-
dicis] for such a long time." A gift in 1575 to a gentleman in the suite of Henri III
is much more ample: 5,250 livres "in consideration for services around his person"
and to contribute toward the expenses he had incurred in accompanying the king
to Poland.[27]

In short, these are "dons" because they are irregular and out of the ordinary,
and because they express the king's appreciation for services and bind the officer
in his or her duty by gratitude. A similar mixture of wages, pensions, and gifts was
dispensed in other great or royal households, such as that of Jeanne d'Albret.[28]

Like practices are found in employment in the trades and household. In several parts of France, artisans' journeymen and other hired laborers and servants accepted a "denier à dieu," "God's penny," from a future master or mistress as a sign of agreement to a job. "[My wife] Gillette hired Paulette, daughter of Guyon Le Palle, to serve here," writes the Vitré merchant draper Jean de Gennes in his accounts in 1519. "She must pay Paulette 40 sous per year, and two shirts and a headcloth. [Gillette] gave her the *denier à dieu* in the presence of Paulette's mother." "Jean Gillebert came to live here and asked to earn 100 sous for each year," Gennes records in 1523. "I offered him 80 sous and gave him the *denier à dieu,* which he took."[29]

God's penny was not literally a penny—Gennes once gave a double, a coin worth twice the denier/penny—but it had significance for a shared definition of employment. Evidently offered and accepted even when a notarized document was used for hiring, the denier à dieu (also known as *arrhes* in French, *arrha* in ancient Latin, arles and arles penny in England) was earnest money, a pledge or confirmation of an agreement. As a transaction, it participated both in the contract mode and the gift mode, an agreement with precise details but which had an affective side and summoned God as a witness.

In notarized hiring and apprenticeship contracts, phrases are sometimes included that also express sentiments and hopes beyond the required agreement of work time and payment. In Lyon, a journeyman hires himself for six months to a master buttonmaker and promises "to serve him as a good journeyman spinner and not leave him"; the master promises to pay him seven livres in two installments, and to feed and lodge him "as a good master is held to do and accustomed to do to a journeyman spinner." A farmer's son is apprenticed to a Lyon taffeta maker, who commits himself to instruct the lad in taffeta making and "in good conduct as best he can." Male apprentices in Lyon sometimes promise to give not only a fee to the master, but a hood or pins to the master's wife.[30]

Such phrases evoke the gratitude-and-obligation processes of the gift mode. Further, the master and mistress always had the possibility of stretching the food and clothing promised the servant or journeyman into something extra—a plump capon here, a well-stitched hosen there—a kind of gift. Jean de Gennes surely did this with Jean Houllier, for four years a favorite among those who worked for him preparing and selling cloth. Contracted to pay him sixty sous, a pair of shoes, and two shirts each year, Gennes gave him extra cloth and money for his garments, a beret, a doublet, and a pouch, and passed on a worn coat to make over into a jacket. For Glenerte Gandiche, a female servant in the Gennes household, Gillette saved the major gifts till she had worked for four years and was about to marry. To Glenerte's annual two shirts and two headscarves were added stockings, shoes, sheets for the marriage bed, and a bale of hemp.[31]

Beyond the individual workshop or household, what we call "tips" and gratuities were universal. All messengers were given a sou or two by recipients of their parcels or loads—whether manor servants bringing game, fish, and fruits from one gentleman or lady to another in Normandy, shop servants delivering satin to a purchaser in Nantes, or a family servant bearing a letter from a sister to a brother. All chambermaids and men-servants at inns, hotels, or other way-stations received small amounts of money from those who had dined or spent the night there. These money tips had a special name: "wine" for the boys and men ("le vin des garçons," "le vin des serviteurs") and "pins" ("les épeigles") for the girls and women. In Brittany in the spring of 1555, the cleric Claude de La Landelle stays the night at Nivillac on his way to taking possession of a new benefice and leaves four sous for "les espigles à la chambriere et le vin du garsson." In Nantes for the meeting of the Estates of Brittany a few months later, he gives four sous to the chambermaid for "les espeigles," noting that she also washed his shirt. Back in Nivillac the next year, he leaves four sous "pour le vin et espigles" for the servants—a youth and an old woman—at the cleric's house where he stayed, adding four sous more for "la belle cuysiniere," "the beautiful cook."[32]

Tips were also given to journeymen by customers along with payments to their masters for goods or services. La Landelle gives a sou to the locksmith's journeymen "for their wine" while he pays their master ten sous for a lock and two keys, and six pennies to the stocking maker's journeymen for "le vin aux garssons," as he pays their master sixty sous for the new stockings.[33] And wine is either paid for or provided directly to male workers beyond their wages and food at sites where they are temporarily employed: wine at Mesnil Le Val for Gouberville's mowers; wine for the carpenters repairing a church for La Landelle; wine for the workers who finish an oven on a judge's estate near Rennes, enough for them "to enjoy themselves, as is the custom"; a whole feast provided by the vestry for the carpenters who finish a new bell tower at the parish church of the village of Izé.[34]

These forms of recompense gave a double authority to the employer, the one defined by the rules of sales contract, the other by the reciprocal and open-ended spirit of the gift; and gave a double self-image to the hired person, the one defined by measured work and the other by a relation of personal service. Gifts did not conceal sales from the participants. Rather sixteenth-century people drew on both self-definitions in their daily dealings with each other, moving, if need be, from one register to the other, as they collaborated, exchanged, and quarreled.

For example, the printer's journeymen of Lyon and Paris argued with their masters about wages and their meals in both registers. In their sale mode, they accused their masters of "trying to put them, their wives and children in the poorhouse," of greedily "acquiring every day great and honorable wealth at the price of their sweat and marvelous toil." In their gift mode, they said they labored not out of coercion, but "as free men working voluntarily at an excellent and noble calling . . . Given the quality of the parties involved, there should be mutual and reciprocal love between us." When their masters proposed to replace meals with wages, the journeymen said no: they wanted to eat at the master's table, with wine of the same quality as the master's and a good capon now and then. The master printers denounced their workmen as gluttons, that is, Golfarins (the journeymen immediately adopted this as the name of their clandestine company, the Company of the Golfarins), but then sustained the meals sufficiently so that collaboration was possible all during the dangerous decades of production of heretical books.[35]

Small commercial transactions were sometimes accompanied by symbolic actions at their start (Gouberville gave one sou denier à dieu and a teston as arrhes in pledge for his purchase of a millstone) and at their finish (La Landelle spent four sous for the "vin du marché," the wine marking the sale, after he had purchased a horse).[36]

But perhaps the most interesting example of the proximity of and yet distinction between gifts and sales is in connection with loans. In his 1547 text on *Contracts,* the important jurist Charles Du Moulin criticized the Catholic system of prohibiting usury in principle, but then allowing it to be taken by a complicated system of special contracts and exceptions. Moderate interest should be allowed in all business loans, he said; simple repayment without too much time pressure in loans to those of modest means; and straight alms to the indigent. What Du Moulin found perfectly acceptable, however, was the burger of the town of Siena

who often lent his money to poor rural folk in order to help them without any profit or interest, except that some of them, in returning the amount, gave him a little voluntary gift according to their capacity, and others if they could not return the amount at term would likewise give him a little present and be allowed a delay without any formal pact or extortion.

After his death, this man had been declared a "mental usurer" by the Church because he had hoped for the voluntary presents, and his heirs ordered to make amends as the bishop of Siena required. Du Moulin thought this unjust and wicked, but more important so did the poor peasants who testified on his behalf. Never had they found a more charitable man to help them. They were grateful to him and feared that such treatment would discourage other good persons from making loans on the same basis.[37]

The burger of Siena and his peasants can not have been alone in their borrowing-and-lending style. To be sure, those making business loans or providing substantial sums of money to important personages resorted to one of the allowable contracts for interest (*lucrum cessans, damnum emergens*); or to repayment in another currency at a rate of exchange certain to allow interest; or to rent charges on fictionally mortgaged property. But many loans were small and made to meet an immediate need among people who knew each other: innkeepers, hotelkeepers, butchers, physicians, textile workers, adult serving women, and many others. Doctor Pierre Tolet of Lyon lent rather substantial sums to two of his patients "in great need and necessity" along with treating them for their ills. Butcherwoman Benoiste Penet of Lyon made small loans to butchers, a woman hotelkeeper, and her relatives as well as borrowing herself from a merchant-butcher. Over in Vitré, draper Jean de Gennes made repeated loans to his relatives and in-laws, including lending his priest-brother the twenty livres needed for gilding a silver pyx. In another part of Brittany, cleric Claude de La Landelle was lending small sums to the archdeacon's groom; to fellow priests; to the choirmaster; to a scribe "in great

Figure 4. Hélisenne de Crenne presenting her translation of Virgil to François Ier, ca. 1542

need"; and to the woman who washed his shirts, "without hope," he said of her in his accounts, "of its being returned." He himself borrowed a few crowns here and there, including from his favorite male servant.[38] These examples, coming from surviving IOUs, account books, and wills, suggest the range in petty indebtedness in the sixteenth century, much of it lost to our eyes or unrecorded.

Sometimes these loans were secured by pawns: Jean de Gennes' brother put up silver cups; a Lyon woman, a red petticoat for a loan from a woman hotelkeeper; a Lyon artisan, two sheets and a woman's black dress for a loan from a foundryman's widow; Claude de La Landelle's borrowing rector, a golden ring which turned out to have a false stone. Often the loans were simply made on trust alone, and here is where the gifts come in. Two weeks after he had borrowed from his favorite servant, Claude de La Landelle took the man out to dinner "for love of him." Gilles de Gouberville's tenants stopped by the manor with a woodcock or chicken when they were two months late paying the rent, and that was the end of it.[39] In all likelihood, loans made to friends, associates, kin, and neighbors were rewarded by "voluntary little presents."

Figure 5. Jacques du Fouilloux presenting his book on hunting to the king, 1562

The sale mode and gift mode coexisted and interacted in sixteenth-century France, distinguished from each other by the roles in which they cast donor and recipient or buyer and seller and by certain features of the transaction. Each had its own etiquette, language, and body posture for presentation. Gift presentation, as rendered in illustration if not always acted out in practice, had one of the parties lower than

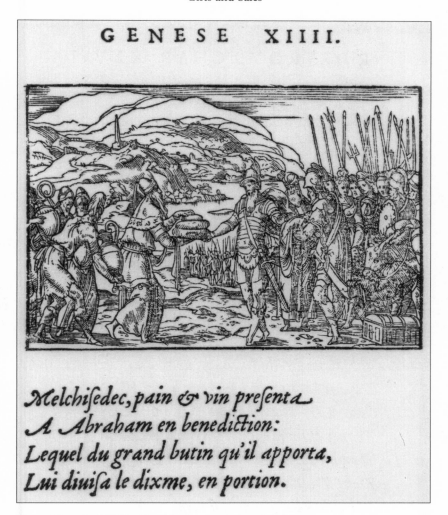

GENESE XIIII.

Melchiſedec, pain & vin preſenta
A Abraham en benediction:
Lequel du grand butin qu'il apporta,
Lui diuiſa le dixme, en portion.

Figure 6. The priest Melchizedek offering bread and wine to Abraham, 1553

the other, bowing or bending in a graceful or rounded position. Often it was the donor who was lower (figs. 4, 5, 6, 7), not merely the author on his or her knees presenting a book to the king, but also the slightly bowed priest Melchizedek offering bread and wine in blessing to an erect Abraham, returned victorious against the Sodomites (Genesis 14:14–20) and the kneeling Abigail deflecting the anger of David by her gifts (1 Samuel 25:14–29). Sometimes it was the recipient who was lower (fig. 8; also see figs. 2 and 3, pp. 15–16), accepting a gift from the king or from a parent or taking alms from a charitable Christian. A 1587 book presentation pictured a seated Duc de Nivernais with his hat on, while Christofle de Savigny, the

Dauid fafché & de faim,& de voye,
  Voyant l'ennuy de l'exercite fien,
  Gens vers Nabal(riche Pasteur)enuoye:
  Requerant ayde,& fecours de fon Bien.
Le fol refufe,& ne leur tranfmet rien,
  Dont Dauid iure anichiller fa race:
  Abigaïl y ha pourueu fi bien,
  Que fon Prefent l'Ire embrafee efface.

N 3

Figure 7. Abigail offering gifts to David to assuage his wrath, 1564

Figure 8. Christofle de Savigny presenting his book on the liberal arts to the Duc de Nivernais, 1587

author, strode forward hat in hand with his knees slightly bent.[40] In both images, difference in social status was maintained where needed, but posture either sweetened the claim to obligation being placed on a powerful recipient or strengthened the promise of gratitude on the part of a weaker recipient. Interestingly enough, a 1536 emblem for the saying "The gifts of enemies are no gifts" (fig. 9) pictures Ajax and Hector handing each other a sword and a belt with rigid upright posture and stern faces.[41]

Ἐχθρῶν ἄδωρα δῶρα. In dana hostium.

Bellorum cœpisse ferunt monumenta uicißim
   Scutiferum Aiacem Hectoráq; Iliacum,
Balthea Priamides, rigidum Telamonius ensem
   Instrumenta suæ cœpit uterq; necis.
Ensis enim Aiacem confecit, at Hectora functum
   Traxere Aemoniis cingula nexa rotis.
Sic titulo obsequij quæ mittunt hostibus hostes
   Munera, uenturi præscia fata ferunt.

Figure 9. "The gifts of enemies are no gifts": the bad exchange between Ajax and Hector, 1536

60

Figure 10. The farm owner paying his harvester, book of hours, 1522

Figure 11. The farm owner paying his harvester, book of hours, 1525

Sales pictures showed different postures from gift scenes. (I use them here not as reports of actual behavior, but as suggestions for norms of etiquette and behavior.) Male workers being paid were relatively erect before their standing masters, though the employees were often bareheaded while the employer had his hat on (figs. 10, 11).[42] In market scenes, the seller might be bending forward slightly and otherwise gesturing to display his or her wares and the buyer might be pointing to

Ioseph estant dans le Puits deuallé,
  Iuda émeu de pityé fauorable
  A ses consorts(& bien)ha conseillé:
  De ne l'occir de mort tant miserable.
Ains pour venger leur courroux implacable
  Aux Payens l'ont à prix d'argent vendu:
  Ainsi luy est pour son dict veritable,
  Ingrat guerdon & seruage rendu.

Figure 12. Judah selling his brother Joseph to the Ishmaelites, 1564

Figure 13. A woman purchasing fish in Jacob Gerritsz. Cuyp, *Fish Market,* 1627 (Dordrechts Museum)

√√ ⎤

an item, but here again the two parties mostly held themselves at the same level in bargaining or paying, even when their clothing indicated divergent social status (figs. 12, 13). In a 1553 Bible picture, a sitting Esau sells his birthright to a standing Jacob, who hands him a plate of pottage with one hand, while shaking his twin brother's hand with the other (fig. 14); perhaps the handshake was a gesture accompanying major sixteenth-century sale agreements, for it is also found in an Antwerp painting by Sebastian Vrancx showing a man agreeing to buy a row of casks from a wine merchant.[43]

Whatever the case, the postures of the sale mode suggest participants who have or have had equally binding and simultaneous commitments; stakes that were measured and known (even though these were sometimes argued about, as in Bible pictures of the vineyard workers of Matthew 20 objecting to their pay[44]); and a bargain that could be repeated another day but that could also be conclusive, leaving everyone *quitte* (quits).

The gift mode and the sale mode diverged in regard to measure. In gift exchange—at least as an ideal type—there was some incommensurability in value and indeterminacy in time. One did not always know when the return on the gift

GENESE XXV.

Jacob fut doux & simple de nature,
Mais Esaü, robuste personnage:
Qui lui vendit sa primogeniture,
A l'appetit dun petit de potage.

Figure 14. Esau selling his heritage to Jacob for a mess of pottage and shaking hands to close the deal, 1553

would come: sixteenth-century courtesy books reminded readers that they must return their benefits neither too soon "out of pride" (it would make the donor feel the gift had been forced), nor too late (it would humiliate the first giver), but "to wait for the appropriate time and place."[45] The gift rhythm of obligation and gratitude was in principle unending. In contrast, after sales and payments, an ending—being quits once and for all—was a possible outcome, and the ending was not always a happy one. Charles Du Moulin quoted an old proverb to this effect: "If I've lent to an ingrate, I don't get it back. If I get it back, I don't get it all. If I get it all, from a friend I've acquired an enemy." Better to end on good terms: "she left very satisfied [bien contente]," Jean de Gennes wrote in his accounts after paying Janecte Duval her year's wages, two shirts and two headcloths at the end of her term; "We remained quits and good friends," Claude de La Landelle wrote in his accounts after paying his bonnetmaker for several items.[46] Indeed, the intermingling of gifts and sales was intended to allow friendly endings or to guarantee continuity in a sales/payment relation.

To be sure, the indeterminacy in the gift register could bring its own disruptions. "Petit disner longuement attendu / N'est pas donné, mais cherement vendu," went the popular ditty: "A little dinner, awaited too long / Is not a gift, but a costly sale."[47] And there could be trouble at the gift/sale border in regard to office in government and church. These disturbed borders we will look at later. For the moment, the serving woman has received her pins, the journeyman his wine, the seigneur his deer, the peasant neighbor her cider, the noble patron his hunting bird, the professor his sweets, the physician his gloves, the scholar his book, the courted lass her jewel or flower. And for the moment, they have accepted these gifts and been grateful for them.

5

Gifts Gone Wrong

Ingratitude, thou marble hearted fiend,
More hideous when thou show'st thee in a child
Than the sea monster!
— King Lear to his daughter Goneril

 hus far, gift systems have appeared as ordering devices, easing social relations, marking status, helping people to stay connected, as one citydweller put it, "like stones in a good building joined together by cement." Gift modes and market modes have remained in creative tension with each other, and the entanglement of volition and obligation in inter vivos donations has not deterred the recipient from gratitude.

But gifts can go wrong, and sixteenth-century people were often fretting about it. At the king's palace at Fontainebleau, courtiers were reminded by paintings of Pandora that a gift box contained mixed blessings, while pictures of the Judgment of Paris warned them that the gift of a golden apple could lead to a Trojan War. (Readers will recall that the goddess of Discord got Athena, Aphrodite, and Hera quarreling by throwing a golden apple into a banquet with the label "to the fairest"; that the three goddesses prevailed upon Paris to judge them, each promising him gifts; and that he chose Aphrodite because she offered him the most beautiful woman in the world, namely, a certain Helen, wife of Menelaus.) In country huts, peasants exchanged knowing proverbs about the narrowness of gift circles: "One barber shaves another"; "One hand rubs another." [1]

Troubles came in part from inevitable tensions in gift systems, as the ancient quarrels suggest. Gifts call forth ingratitude the way markets call forth monopolies. But sixteenth-century France placed strong strains of its own on gift systems, deriving from an intensified culture of obligation. The gnaw of obligation ate into the psychological economy of people in many social echelons, from well-off peasants on up. We will examine its sources in this and subsequent chapters in family life, in the required favors of social advancement, in the political practices of the French monarchy, and in the prescriptions of religion. The ordinary course of making presents had its perils, but how was one to respond if one was an inferior in a hierarchical world, trying to make a return to or catch the attention of a superior? "To father, to master, to God all powerful, no one can return the equivalent," went the popular proverb, making clear that exact accounting was not possible: "A pere, a maistre, a Dieu tout puissant, nul ne peut rendre l'equivalent." [2] To some, this adage was soothing, to others discouraging. Meanwhile, on Europe's distant margins in the eastern woodlands of America and in Brazil, another kind of asymmetrical gift-giving was going on to which Europeans applied a very different evaluation of gratitude. But let us start our tale in the troubles of the household.

Possibilities multiplied for the marriages and careers of children in sixteenth-century France, and at the same time parents worked more energetically than ever to plan and shape the family's future. From the farm of the propertied peasant to the townhouse of the wealthy merchant to the aristocrat's chateau, fathers and mothers schemed about whether son Louis should be a farmer or a priest, a lawyer or a physician, a captain or a courtier, and whether daughter Marguerite's marriage should be to a near neighbor or should create a distant alliance. If children seemed to have more choices in the expanding urban economy and state-building polity of the day, then parents had to exert more control over them: to guarantee family survival and to hope for family advancement. Ideally, as described by a Lyon textile merchant in recounting the activities of the men in his family, fathers "sought the advantage" of sons and oldest brothers of younger brothers "in sending them to study . . . and then in accord with the [child's] natural qualities, placing them in households where they could advance." Then the sons and younger brothers were "not ungrateful and sought the advance" of the next generation.[3]

Convergence between the wishes of children and the wishes of parents might be achieved peaceably by the older generation consulting with the younger, a policy encouraged by humanist educational tracts. Convergence could be achieved by coercion, as in the 1557 royal edict requiring that women under the age of twenty-five and young men under the age of thirty have their parents' consent for their marriages to be valid. And then convergence could also be achieved by gifts: by the promise of gifts, by the hoped-for gratitude and sense of obligation from gifts, by conditions placed on gifts, and by the fear that gifts would be withheld. So we see in Lyon how parents and other kin used will-making to influence behavior. A boat maker makes his grandson a universal heir, but disinherits him if he "becomes naughty and lives badly" and refuses to stay with his uncle. An unmarried Tuscan merchant residing in Lyon withholds a bequest to one sister if she lives with the wrong relative, and cuts another sister off from any inheritance "because she married without [his] consent and against [his] will." The widow of a royal notary and rural judge chooses her granddaughter from her first marriage as her universal heir over her son from her second marriage — thereby reversing the ordinary gender preference of the time: her son had not only sued her, he had also been "disobedient and mistreated her, insulting her in public several times, shouting to people coming out of Vespers, 'There's the dirty wicked brothel-keeper [*maquerelle*]. Get her! She has the sickness of Saint Jean!' " (She nonetheless left him a small bequest of fifty livres from her rather substantial estate, perhaps in hopes of shutting him up after her death.) [4]

Most telling are the wills that tried to protect family aspirations and direct the religious choices of children. In 1542 a printer's wife sets up as co-heirs her current husband and her daughter from her first marriage, and then dictates to her Lyon notary, "My daughter Catherine is a follower of the heretical Lutheran sect . . . and is living in Geneva [indeed, her daughter was the young widow of one of the most important early Protestant printers in France] . . . I forbid her to receive any of this inheritance until she is reduced to union with our holy mother church, lives like a true Catholic Christian, and leaves Geneva for Lyon or some other place not suspect of Lutheran heresy." (It may have worked: in a new Catholic will five years later, the second husband who had deceived and beaten her is disowned and Catherine is her mother's universal heir.) [5]

From Geneva in 1577, a refugee Lyon merchant makes his son Guillaume his universal heir, "but only so long as he comes to live in Geneva, according to the holy Reformation . . . But if he continues in his debauchery and bad family life, preferring . . . to detach himself from the true Christian religion in which [we] raised him, he receives only 100 livres and [my] wife Fleurye is [my] universal heir." Associated with the increased "liberty" of sixteenth-century parents in determining the movement of property (to cite once again lawyer de Rubys) was a sense of the strong expectation of what their children owed them. [6]

Parents certainly hoped that their children would follow their provisions and live in accord with one another and with surviving spouses. As the Duke and Duchess of Montmorency put it in dividing their extensive properties among their ten children: "We wish to cut away the roots of disagreements and disputes, which often come about among brothers over the goods left them by their parents." Over in Geneva, a blacksmith's widow suggested that her son, daughter, and son-in-law give each other receipts once various payments are made "so that good peace and friendship prevail among them." A Lyon notary was more stringent: the inheritance to his wife and bequest to his rural brother were on condition that they not quarrel about the distribution of family properties. Peasant fathers in Languedoc and Gascony were more realistic yet: they made their sons their heirs while giving their widows full governance of their goods, and then spelled out what heirs must give widows "if they can't get along": a certain room or rooms for her own, a certain amount of grain, wine, and oil each year, and a garment, shoes, and stockings every other year.[7]

And still quarrels broke out. Sometimes there was litigation, and things were patched up. Other times there was serious rupture. In 1542 after the death of her husband, the widowed Duchess de La Trémoille wanted to continue living with her mother-in-law and her eldest son and his family at the castle in Poitou for the rest of her days, and sent away all but fifteen of her servants so as to placate her son and keep down the expenses. Her son wanted her out—"to enjoy his rights and what belonged to him"—and when she would not leave, he isolated her in the castle without firewood. "This is a strange way for a son to treat a mother," she said. "This is not in your contract," he answered. After much quarreling about a monetary settlement and an accusation by her son's agent that "she did not love her children," she finally agreed to move away. Her son put his gentlemen at the castle gate to prevent her taking any furniture and had her coffers opened in the town square to see if she had concealed any goods that did not belong to her.[8]

The bestower of these blessings did not witness them, for François, the late Duke de La Trémoille, had departed the scene. But even when donors were still alive quarrels broke out and made them regret their gifts. We can follow these conflicts in regard to the inter vivos donations, the donations among the living, whose paths we have traced in a peaceable mode. French law permitted the giver to revoke a donation when the recipient could be proven ungrateful, and together with their notaries disappointed donors wrote down stories of ingratitude.[9]

A much talked-about case of revocation in the late 1540s and afterward concerned the jurist Charles Du Moulin. In 1547, the same year he published his book on contracts, usury, and donations, Du Moulin revoked a gift made some sixteen years before to his younger brother Ferry. Their father had died and made Charles, the eldest son, heir to his properties and goods. At the time of his donation to Ferry, Charles explained, his head was wrapped up in his legal studies with no thoughts of marriage. He had given his brother a substantial part of his inheritance on condition that Ferry take care of the property and provide their sister's dowry when she was old enough to wed. He, Charles, had gone on to be a loyal brother, supporting Ferry at his studies in Orléans and Paris and introducing him to his post as barrister in the Parlement of Paris. And what did he get in return? Ferry sold the resources put aside for his sister's dowry and siphoned off the income from their father's estate for his own profit, leaving the property in disrepair. Even worse, he had gone around Paris spreading atrocious lies about his older brother, turning his friends against him, and throwing him into melancholy. In the meanwhile, Charles had married and had children of his own. Now, "for reasons of ingratitude," he took back his earlier gift.[10]

It took four years and a suit before the Parlement of Paris for Charles Du Moulin to get his gift back. Charles published an account of their quarrel, angering Ferry all the more, and the enmity between the brothers lasted for life and passed on to the next generation. In 1572, when both brothers were in their grave, Ferry's daughter and her husband were accused of murdering Charles's daughter to get revenge and seize the keys to the manorhouse that had once been a gift.[11]

Not all gifts-gone-wrong ended up in bloodshed, but they could entail bodily harm and gross insult. This was the claim of one Jean Colombier, an old unbeneficed priest living in Condrieu, a little town along the Rhône River. In the 1560s, Messire Jean had given all his goods to his nephew Antoine and his nephew's wife on condition that they support him for the rest of his life. Instead, when he came to their house from his religious duties with money, they took it from him. When he came with none, they insulted him: "Haven't you earned anything? Dirty pig, get out of here [Va, vilain pourceau]." "You're no longer worth anything but being put into a sack and thrown into the Rhône." (The priest did not accuse his nephew and niece of heresy, merely that they shouted he was one of the "race of priests.") And, Messire Jean maintained, they hit him and left him to go about Condrieu covered with lice and begging for food and a place to stay. Finally, another nephew, Pierre, took him in (one wonders why it took so long), and in July of 1568 Messire Jean revoked the earlier donation on the grounds of "ingratitude, beating and threats" and made a new one, with the same services expected, to Pierre.[12]

Many more such examples of revocation could be given.[13] Readers familiar with civil suits may find such cases commonplace. The "ingratitude" of Ferry Du Moulin and Antoine Colombier will seem just another illustration of the timeless propensity of people to quarrel and use the resources and language of the law to get what they want.

This may be true, but there is also something historically specific about such quarrels in sixteenth-century France. I have suggested a connection between new possibilities for children, a new "liberty" of parents to plan for a family future, and heightened expectations about what parents could expect from children—expectations reproduced when children grew up to be parents or aunts and uncles themselves. Christian gift theory and the Three Graces taught that the giver must always give without requiring return, while the recipient must always feel grateful and be impelled to give in turn. The wills and donations often anticipated and even spelled out the return rather than leaving it to the leaven of gratitude. The 1539 requirement that all inter vivos donations be recorded in a contract—and of course revocations as well—intensified the planning process. In a setting where obligation-anxiety was high, it is not surprising that there was disagreement about expectations and that cries of ingratitude were bandied about.

Shakespeare's *King Lear* can offer us a sixteenth-century comment on the underlying emotional economy of these quarrels: a play about inter vivos donations revoked, wrongly given and wrongly received. The practical conditions that Lear sets upon his gifts of sovereignty and territory are already fraught with danger— that is, that he would keep his title and prerogatives and visit each daughter for a month with his hundred knights—even with daughters less heartless than Regan and Goneril. But the love test—"Which of you shall we say doth love us most? / That we our largest bounty may extend / Where nature doth with merit challenge"[14]—is impossible to pass. Cordelia does not mind telling her father:

> I love your Majesty
> According to my bond; no more nor less . . .
> You have begot me, bred me, loved me; I
> Return those duties back as are right fit,
> Obey you, love you, and most honor you.[15]

What she objects to is, on the one hand, the boundlessness of Lear's demand, its limitless obligation ("Haply, when I shall wed, / That lord whose hand must take my plight shall carry / Half my love with him, half my care and duty"[16]), and Lear's imagining, on the other, that the quantity of one's love could be put fully into words and then matched neatly with the opulence of a gift. Gift relations founder on exclusivity and such strict commensurability: Two Graces rather than Three.

The family was not the only arena for gift trouble. Where advancement and reputation depended so much on favor, obligation-anxiety was aroused in many milieus, even among friends and virtual peers. In his 1516 translation of the New Testament from the Greek, Erasmus published a note eulogizing the eminent French humanist and Hellenist Guillaume Budé, but also took issue with Budé's translation of a passage from the Greek in the opening lines of the Gospel of Luke. A friend brought Budé the book fresh from the printer, and he immediately wrote Erasmus to thank him for the gift of his praise.

I assure you, dearest of men, that you are to receive not less than what you have done for me. For on this point I could not endure to give way to you, and not recompense on equal terms a friend who had done me service and . . . had made the name Budé immortal . . . I feel you have landed me in a tight place with this encomium, in which you have made me an elephant, as they say, instead of an ant. You know, I imagine, that if I pay adequately and in good faith what I owe—and I owe you everything in the way of exorbitant praise—I should immediately be thought to be returning one favor for another, at least among those who know what you have written, which means everybody . . . If, on the other hand, in order to avoid this I touch on your praises, copious as they are, cautiously and with circumspection, I must inevitably be thought very mean, and grossly unfair towards you who deserve so much. So this is the kind of dilemma you have put me in by starting this wholly admirable practice of obliging a friend, when I ought to have forestalled you and landed you with the problem, since you would have been much cleverer at finding a solution for the difficulty. All the same, I hope . . . to invent a satisfactory way of getting quit somehow of this obligation, but to be quit once and for all is more than I expect in my whole lifetime, for really the debt is larger than everything I possess. All the same, I would take on anything, rather than incur such a great burden of ingratitude.

After this polite but ambivalent play with the formulas of gift friendship, Budé said he was also grateful to Erasmus for correcting his errors of translation from the Greek, but still maintained that he was right and Erasmus wrong. He wondered why Erasmus wasted his great learning on such "trivialities."[17] Both Erasmus and Budé published the letter in a subsequent collection, the first exchange in a long correspondence of learned and quarrelsome friendship.

Much worse, in hurt feelings and in the uses to which language and letter writing had to be put, was having to plead for gifts, a frequent occurrence in relations between client and patron. "I have heard," wrote Jean de Ravenel, high servant to François, Duke de La Trémoille, in a 1540 letter from court,

> that Monsieur the Abbot des Pierres asked in my favor that you give me the guardianship of the park of Châlon and that you answered that you had already given it to Bellemarion's son. This makes me think that I would be wasting my time to ask you for something better, however much I think I merit it, for my fortune is such that whatever I ask you for, I am always refused. This seems strange to me, seeing that for more than a hundred years, my ancestors and I have been in the service of your house without ever having received any reproach. Not so long ago at the battle of Pavia, my brother died in the service of your late father (may God absolve him) and if I hadn't taken sick en route, I would have done my duty there as well. When it pleases you, Monseigneur, give this consideration.[18]

François died two years later and may not ever have considered it.

The literature on the courtier—a popular genre in France and throughout Europe—was full of reference to the presents one must distribute to make one's way in a great or princely household and to the cost to one's virtue and one's self in seeking favor. Antonio de Guevara's *Le Favory de court* (The court favorite), translated from the Castilian for French readers in 1556, began with the gloves, belts, and bonnets that the would-be courtier had to distribute to the pages and maître d'hôtel to get a good seat at the table; continued with the convivial tone one must take toward the men standing guard at the doors of the great and the gifts and étrennes one must provide them; and went on to the banquets and feasts the courtier must mount for his honor. "And at the end one has spent much more than one had planned, and has to borrow."[19]

More unsettling was the dissimulation of the would-be courtier, as Guevara pointed out in his rhetorical counter-book, translated from the Castilian in 1543: *Du Mespris de la court* (On contempt for the court). The courtier sits around chatting with others all day, laughing and being amusing, when inside he feels mortal enmity. "Isn't it too much dissimulation to do honor to him whom you would like to lead to the gibbet—and all for ambition?" This view was elaborated in a remarkable and paradoxical work a few years later, *Le Philosophe de court* (The philosopher of the court) by Philibert de Vienne, a barrister in the Parlement of Paris. Where does this life of accommodation lead? he asked. Liberality, good appearance, civility, grace, and decorum are required "to please others," even if it means losing the self. "We dissimulate, we accommodate ourselves to everyone . . . to win their benevolence." "The gentleman courtier is not subject to himself [le gentil-homme Courtisan nest point subiet à soy]. If he must laugh, he laughs, if he must be sad, he weeps . . . In short, he is ready to do anything to please others, even if his feeling is totally otherwise." [20]

Dissimulation was hardly special to the gift mode. Lying about weights, measures, and the quality of goods went on in the trades. Deception was part and parcel of politics even at its most coercive. But in the sixteenth-century quest for patronage and its rewards, the requirement to be pleasing and gracious was continuous, not intermittent. A gracious, friendly, or benevolent manner was thought intrinsic to the gift mode: the strain on participants could be considerable.

Several decades after Philibert de Vienne, another man of the law, Michel de Montaigne, reported his feelings and judgments more sharply concerning the pressures of gift and obligation in the pursuit of economic survival and social advancement. Montaigne is, of course, an unusual figure in his articulated sense of autonomy and expressiveness. He is not quoted here as "typical" of sixteenth-century sentiments: indeed, Pierre de Ronsard, poet of kings and dreamer of a lost Golden Age, basked in the light of patronage and favor.[21] But Montaigne was a keen observer of his times and of himself and a prober of the deep rigors in gift relationships.

In his essay "On Vanity," which first appeared in the 1588 edition of the *Essais,* Montaigne has been talking about how his house and property in Gascony had so far escaped the sacking and bloodshed of the religious wars.

I've escaped, but it displeases me that it's more by luck or even by my prudence rather than by justice, and it displeases me to be outside the protection of the laws and under any other protection but theirs. As things stand, I'm living more than half by the favor of others and that's a hard obligation. I don't want to owe my safety to the goodness and benevolence of the great. I don't want my legality and liberty to come only at their will.[22]

Montaigne then leaves the violence of war and goes on to describe his reactions to the bonds of gift and obligation in everyday life.

I believe that one must live by law and authority, not by reward and grace . . . I flee from submitting myself to any kind of obligation, especially one that attaches me by the duty of honor. I find nothing so costly as that which is given me, for then my will is mortgaged by a title of gratitude. I'd rather buy a [royal] office than be given one, for buying it, I just give money. In the other case, I give myself. The knot that ties me by the law of honor seems much tighter than the knot of civil constraint. I'm throttled more gently by a notary than by myself.

Montaigne goes on to congratulate himself that he is relatively free of such ordinary entanglements and of their rhetoric. "From what I know of the science of benefit and gratitude, which is a subtle science and very much in use today, I don't see anyone more free and less indebted than I am up to now. What I owe, I owe to our common and natural obligations . . ." Quoting Virgil, Montaigne adds,

" 'And the gifts of the great are not known to me.' " He, Montaigne, is beholden only to God, by whose grace he enjoys a blessed freedom.[23]

Elsewhere, in an essay on Cicero, Montaigne talks of his unwillingness even to write in the prostituted language of courtesy and compliments, to offer service and affection, to take leave and to thank.[24] His letters of recommendation for others turn out dry and unsatisfactory. He hates to feel he might be a flatterer. And how should he weigh any praise of himself if it comes from somebody who has an obligation to him?

In fact, Montaigne was not as free of the world of favor as this self-portrait suggests. From 1557 to 1570, he had been judge in the Parlement of Bordeaux, a post that must have involved some favor-seeking by him at least at its start and some favor-seeking toward him by the man to whom he sold the office at its end. In 1577, he was named *gentilhomme de chambre* for Henri de Navarre, and in the next years served as go-between for Henri and moderate Catholic forces in the southwest. In 1580 he was elected mayor of Bordeaux, a responsibility that sent him to court several times on town business. Montaigne was writing about the public world of benefits and favors as a participant as well as an observer.

He was also involved in other forms of gift exchange. During his 1580–1581 voyage to Italy, he accepted wines, books, and dinners offered to him and his party as travelers, and at a spa near Lucca, after spending several weeks at the baths, he gave a festive ball with prizes for all the local women. Two of his essays he dedicated to women friends, and he found an appropriate language of appreciation with which to salute them.[25] The first edition of the *Essais* he presented to Henri III in person, and when Henri said the book pleased him, Montaigne got around the "prostituted language of courtesy" by his quip: "Then, Sire, I must please your Majesty, for my book . . . is nothing more than talk [un discours] about my life and actions." (Similarly, Montaigne lightened the embarrassment of having to kiss the pope's foot during his audience with Gregory XIII by his comment afterward: "the pope raised his toe a little.")[26]

More important, perhaps, Montaigne set up a privileged realm for gifting in the bequest of one beloved friend to another, a subject to which I will return later. For now, Montaigne has described for us the emotional and intellectual wounds possible from the public social gift relations of his day. The clarity of contract, the impersonality of just law, and the economy of honest and intimate speech are what he celebrates against the ambiguities, dependencies, and exaggerations of unceasing obligation.

Where are the women's voices in these complaints about the gift mode? We have seen women everywhere active in gift-giving: circulating food, clothes, and jewelry among their peers and kin; making inter vivos donations; and sending benefits, presents, and alms up and down the social scale. We have heard women making accusations of ingratitude or being accused of that "unnatural" sentiment, disinheriting children, and revoking or putting conditions on their gifts.

But we have not heard them speaking more generally about the costs and strains of the gift register and its practices. In the courtier treatises written by men, women with their cosmetics and coquetry stood for a perfect dissimulation, all the more reprehensible because carried on with little sense of wrongdoing. Though women could also condemn the ruses of court life—"the false face of the Court and its disguises I reject," wrote the literary Marie de Gournay in 1626—this was not a central refrain in their complaints. As for Montaigne's cry against the unending obligations of the gift mode, it was infused with a sense of autonomy quite distinctively masculine in the sixteenth century. He claimed to pass beyond other men, who drew their authority from some "particular and strange marking," such as their vocation. "I am the first [to communicate to others] by my universal being, as Michel de Montaigne, not as a grammarian or a poet or a jurist."[27]

Women in sixteenth-century France were unlikely to describe themselves in this way. As the poet Louise Labé reminded her readers, women had to struggle simply for the liberty "to apply themselves to the sciences and other learning." However adept they might be at making gold thread, preparing linen, running a printing atelier, administering a farm, or teaching a little school, they were rarely seen to have "a particular and strange marking." Their vocation was marriage, or alternatively for Catholic women, the religious life. One was not simply "Michel de Montaigne tout court," but the daughter of so-and-so, the wife and then widow of so-and-so. Even Marie de Gournay, the intellectual friend of Montaigne's last years and his literary executor, defined herself as the "Daughter" of Montaigne and him as her "Father by alliance." Where women's being was thought universal, it was not a sign of self-possession, but of a subject status, of being given away.[28]

Concern for autonomy was not, then, a woman's path to a general critique of endless obligation in the gift mode. In fact, women engaged in a public quest for favor for themselves less often than men. Women were beggars seeking alms at the bottom of the social hierarchy; they were patronesses dispensing benefits and presents at the top as queens and princesses, and in the middle, say, as hotelkeepers sustaining their circle of "gossips." There are, of course, individual cases of women seeking office or public favor for themselves via the gift mode: Louise Bourgeois maneuvering for the office of royal midwife in part through the intervention of grateful mothers she had delivered; the Lyon publisher Antoinette Peronet, dedicating a translation of a text by the Stoic emperor Marcus Aurelius to the governor of the Lyonnais in hopes for his protection during the troubled times for "poor widows with orphans" like herself; a noblewoman at court competing for attention of the queen.[29]

On the whole, however, women sought public favor not for themselves, but for members of their family: husbands, brothers, and especially sons. Jeanne du Laurens tells in her family history how her mother, Louise de Castellan, "spared nothing in her power" to train and advance her eight sons after the death of their physician father in Arles in 1574. Father Louis had set a good example, "frequently giving banquets for the teachers from the college so that they would go out of their way for his sons." Once the young men had doctorates, the widowed Louise visited potential patrons and employers. Alerted by her physician son that a canon of Saint Trophime of Arles had a mortal illness, she hastened over to remind the canons of the merits of her theologian son Julien and his services to the cathedral and "used other compliments to induce them to her will." Though Louise was much opposed to simony and would not have paid for her son's benefice, the "other compliments" surely included the customary banquets. Brother Julien got his canonry, and the weight of future obligation fell on him, not on her.[30]

Women's dedications in printed books, few in number though they are in the sixteenth century, can suggest general attitudes among educated women. No discomfort was expressed about gift processes or their vocabulary. What was on the dedicators' minds was their authority as women speaking in public. As Marie de Gournay put it in her 1595 preface to Montaigne's *Essais*, even the stupidest of men could get away with dismissing a woman's opinion by the mere phrase, "But it's a woman talking" ("C'est une femme qui parle"). Women writers often relieved this anxiety by dedicating their books to each other, or simply to "toutes honnestes Dames."[31]

Especially revealing are women's dedications to royal figures. In 1541 Hélisenne de Crenne presented her French translation of the first four books of Virgil's *Aeneid* to François Ier. Her dedicatory epistle uses the traditional commonplaces of female unworthiness while praising the king extravagantly:

Premeditating this [translation], I was seized with an extreme timidity, which hindered me from carrying out this arduous enterprise. I remonstrated with myself that the insufficiency, weakness, and ineptitude of my style made it inappropriate to present the work to your sublime and exalted excellence, so singularly adorned with learned splendor . . . acquired from delicious acquaintance with Minerva . . . who has endowed you with historical knowledge, lively [skills of] observation, sovereign eloquence, a magnanimous heart, a political life, and generous habits.

Remembering that François Ier was magnanimous and benign, Hélisenne de Crenne decided, despite "the incapacity of her fragile mind," to put this book in his royal hands.[32]

This ornate and convoluted dedication was precisely the kind that Montaigne found obnoxious. But it also contrasts with the direct and feeling prose of Crenne's dedicatory letter to honest and noble ladies, written about the same time for her *Angoisses douloureuses*. There she expects her woeful tale to arouse the "compassion natural to women."[33] Crenne shifted easily from one gift relation to another.

Where then did these women writers locate unbearable pressure in social relations? Not so much in the endless obligation and associated falsehood engendered in the gift mode and threatening the authentic self—though women sometimes felt this—but rather in the requirement of endless obedience that could arise in any mode of exchange. Excess here threatened the female self even in the borders allowed to women in the sixteenth century.

The women's complaint is found in stories rather than in treatises or essays. One witness is Griselda as her tale is told by Christine de Pizan in her *Book of the City of Ladies,* Christine reworking her version from Petrarch's *De Oboedentia ac Fide Uxoria Mythologia* (Fable on wifely obedience).[34] Gualtieri, the handsome marquis of Saluces, begins his relation with the poor peasant Griselda by getting her father's assent to his marriage and by bestowing wedding gifts on her: robes and jewels befitting a noble woman. To his first tests of her constancy and patience—the pretended killing of their daughter and son on the false grounds that his barons and subjects did not want the children of a peasant to rule over them—she responds that the children are his to do with as he wishes, as is her own life. Though she quietly makes sure that the children will be properly buried, she betrays no outward sadness or any emotion at all as they are borne off.

The marquis's next test involves goods and status, as he tells her falsely that his subjects cannot bear his having a peasant wife and that he must put her aside for a noble woman. Griselda strips off all the garments he has given her, returns rings, jewels, and ornaments, and says she has always been aware of the contrast in their status. "I am ready to return to my father's house." She leaves dry-eyed and calm, dressed only in a shift and accompanied to her paternal hut by weeping lords and ladies, who disapprove of their ruler's behavior.

Summoned back to court by Gualtieri supposedly to make arrangements for his wedding feast, Griselda greets the alleged bride—actually her own daughter—with a glad face and is taken with her beauty. She then speaks her mind again to Gualtieri: "I would . . . give you only one bit of advice: that you neither trouble nor needle her with the torments which you inflicted upon your first wife. This woman is younger and has been raised more delicately so that she probably cannot bear as much as your other wife did."

Whereupon the marquis, overwhelmed with pity for all the suffering he had brought upon Griselda and with admiration for her virtue, revealed his feelings: "There is no man under the heavens who has come to know the love of the marriage bond through so many trials as I have with you . . . You alone are my wife, I want no other and will have no other." Discovering her daughter and son are alive and before her, Griselda expresses emotion for the first time—joy and happy tears. "Restored to greater authority than ever before and richly fitted out and bejeweled," Griselda lived together with the marquis in joy and peace, her village father now part of the court as well.

The story of Gualtieri and Griselda tells of gifts gone wrong, showing the gift register shifting into coercion. The raiment and jewelry were not fully given at the start, but simply lent or reallocated for Gualtieri's purposes. Griselda was not surprised when the marquis wanted his "property" back. The repeated ordeals tested her not for constancy of gratitude, which she never expressed, or for constancy of love, which she expressed only in regard to the beginning of their marriage, but for constancy of obedience. Christine de Pizan uses Griselda as an admirable counter-example to the accusation of female fickleness, but she also characterizes the marquis as "strange," his harsh behavior showing the extremes to which men will go in their insistence on obedience. Griselda complies with sober recognition of the realities of power, of which she herself apprises Gualtieri in her two speeches. She shows no outward feeling until she discovers her children are alive: is this Christine de Pizan's way of suggesting a protection of the inner self against the costs of obedience?

At least as troubling as the demands of unending obedience from a husband were those from a mother or a mother-surrogate. Marguerite de Navarre creates such a witness in Rolandine, the heroine of story number twenty-one in the *Heptaméron,* the details drawn from the struggle of the highborn Anne de Rohan with Queen Anne de Bretagne.[35] As a young woman Rolandine was raised at the French court, where she was disdained by the queen, her "mistress," because of a grudge against her father, and where her avaricious father back at his castle was indifferent to her dowry and her fate. Thus, even though some great personages had asked for her hand, Rolandine reached the age of thirty unmarried. Whereupon, after years of uncomplaining retirement, prayer, and pious works, Rolandine struck up a friendship with another unfortunate at court, the illegitimate son of a great nobleman, who had neither riches nor good looks. The queen repeatedly forbade Rolandine to have any communication with the man, and Rolandine repeatedly found clever ways to disobey her. As their friendship ripened into love, the man asked for her hand, to which Rolandine assented, saying that she was obeying God if not the queen and her father, who had "hindered her well-being" and treated her unfairly for so long. For the sake of honor and virtue, however, she had the man agree that they would not consummate the marriage with anything more than a kiss until her father either consented to their union or died.

Rolandine continued to visit with her husband despite all prohibition, until the queen's spies uncovered the secret of the marriage. Rolandine then laid bare her grievance against the irate queen before the entire court: the queen's years of ill-will and persecution, discouraging all suitors and then making a scandal about her virtuous and honorable choice to marry. "You reproach me for a fault before everyone which might better be imputed to you."

Sent back to her father, Rolandine was imprisoned by him in a forest castle for her disobedience. Loyal to her husband even after she learned that he was courting a rich woman in Germany, Rolandine was released from her vows by his sudden death and was welcomed by her father, who admitted to his fault in not dowering her in her youth. Sought by a nobleman of aristocratic family, Rolandine married again and became her father's heir.

Both tales show women's responses to unceasing pressure to obey, one in a setting where gifts are abused, another in a setting where gifts are withheld. Both show how easily women's relations, whether with husband, father, or mother figure, can fall into coercion. Both accounts help us imagine the feelings that accompanied the quarrels, accusations, and revocations found in women's wills. For Montaigne, one might never be quits of the demands of gratitude. For Marguerite de Navarre, coercion might rob gratitude of its force.

In his celebrated essay "Des Cannibales," Montaigne described the Tupinamba of Brazil as still living by the laws of nature:

a nation . . . in which there is no kind of exchange [trafique], no knowledge of letters, no science of numbers, no title of magistrate, no political superiors, no contracts, no inheritance, no property division, no occupations other than leisure, no respect for kinship beyond that common to all, no clothing, no agriculture, no metal, no use of wine or grain. The very words that signify lying, treachery, dissimulation, avarice, envy, detraction, pardon are unknown.[36]

Thus Montaigne imagined a society in which all the elements of gift and reciprocity of his own country were missing. Though he did not add "gratitude," "obligation," and "ingratitude" to his list of unknown words, his account of what he had heard from a trustworthy visitor to those lands includes no behavior connected with such feelings.

In fact, Montaigne's report is not accurate in regard to exchange, and much less insightful than his comments on the Brazilians' reciprocal custom of roasting and eating the flesh of longtime enemies captured in war. It does sustain, however, his efforts to remove the pejorative elements from the notion of "savage" and to use the so-called New World to raise questions about the Old. As such, it contrasts with descriptions of gift exchange in contemporary travel accounts, which affirm European superiority and yet unabashedly cast Europeans in an ungracious and deceptive light.

In their earliest voyages across the Atlantic, the French had decided what would constitute appropriate objects for gifting. In 1504 in Honfleur, Captain Gonneville loaded the hold of the *Espoir* with textiles—hardy linen and woolens, along with a few fancier pieces for someone important—and especially hardware: axes and other tools, knives, combs, mirrors, and glass beads. Verrazano had a similar collection of textiles, small metal goods, mirrors, little bells, and beads when he and his French crew sailed up the coast of North America twenty years later.[37] In his voyages from 1534 to 1540, Jacques Cartier packed garments rather than textiles to give as gifts to Amerindian rulers; some of them were used to clothe the Iroquoians whom he seized to take back to France. Especially, as he and his men moved up the Saint Lawrence River, they gave combs, knives, axes, rings, and glass beads— what Cartier referred to disparagingly in his reports back in France as "works of little value," "little goods," "little presents" ("petitz présens de peu de valleur"), but which, he said, the Iroquoian men and women received with dancing and shouts of joy.[38]

The same tale of unbalanced gratitude was told by the Protestant Jean de Léry about his mid-century stay of ten months among the Tupinamba of Brazil, published years later in 1574. Léry's tone is more surprising since his travel account is much richer and more thoughtful in ethnographic observation than Cartier's. He wrote appreciatively of some features of Tupinamba life, such as their presents of food to their neighbors and their gracious hospitality to friendly visitors, including foreigners like the French. Still, Léry described such a visit in terms of amused superiority:

One day when I was in a village, my *moussacat* (he who had received me into his house) entreated me to show him everything I had in my *caramemo,* that is, my leather sack. He brought me a fine big earthen vessel in which I arranged all my effects. Marveling at the sight, he immediately called the other savages and said to them, "I pray you, my friends, consider what a personage I have in my house, for since he has so many riches, must he not be a great lord?"

And yet, as I said laughing with a companion of mine who was there with me, what this savage held in such high esteem was in sum five or six knives with different kinds of handles, and as many combs, mirrors, and other small objects that would not have been worth two testoons in Paris . . . They love above all those who show liberality. Since I wanted to exalt myself even more than he had done, I gave him freely and publicly, in front of everyone, the biggest and handsomest of my knives, which he set as much store by as might someone in our France who had just received a golden chain worth a hundred crowns.[39]

Let us focus for a moment on the European meaning of such little gifts, especially of the knife (the *agoheda,* as it is called in Cartier's French-Iroquoian glossary, the *taxe miri,* the "little knives," as they are called in Léry's French-Tupinamba dialogue), and other small metal goods.[40] We have heard from Erasmus how knives and other small objects figured in the ordinary gift exchange among friends. And we have seen pins being distributed to village women by Gilles de Gouberville on his saint's day and more generally given as something extra to female servants. Small metal objects were, of course, useful to Europeans. Every man outside the nobility had a knife of some size on his belt (the nobleman had his sword); every working woman had pins and needles on her sleeves.

These small objects served in France as *tokens* or *signs* of an important relation, tokens that sustained trust or good will, and in some cases, as gratuitous *supplements* to existing wages. On the other side of the Atlantic, though, the objects became the *substance* of European gifting and barter with the peoples of the Americas, who were returning to them much-needed food and providing them with essential information about their whereabouts. Thus the customary giving of useful signs of a relationship became the deceptive bestowal of goods the Europeans believed overvalued.

Cartier let this misrepresentation stand. He even received a direct challenge during his second voyage from two young Iroquoians, Taignoagny and Dom Agaya, who had spent a year in France. The Indians were bringing eels and fish to the French and Cartier was returning knives, beads, and "other little things." Whereupon Taignoagny and Dom Agaya addressed their fellows, "What the [French are] giving you is not worth anything [sahauty quahonquey]! You can just as well get hatchets as knives for what you are giving them." Cartier reported this shamelessly, evidently pleased that the Iroquoians were not deterred and the exchange continued as it had begun.[41]

Léry also let the misrepresentation stand, but without Cartier's superciliousness. He at least noted—as Cartier did not—some of the uses to which the Tupinamba happily put the French goods, the women stringing the glass beads on their arms, the men using axes to cut wood, the boys replacing the thorns on the ends of their fishing lines with iron fishhooks. He also reported two instances of bargaining when the Tupi astutely ranked the iron objects.[42] Nonetheless, we have already heard him laughing with a fellow Frenchmen about the naiveté of his Tupinamba host.

In France, fooling about the value of a gift and making fun of the expansive gratitude of a recipient were insulting actions or worse. In the New World, the first generations of French travelers found them acceptable. In Europe, people warned each other, in a prudent adage that went back to the *Iliad*, "not to give away gold for bronze," "a mad exchange" in Homer's words. In the New World, they were happy to benefit by letting the Indians make "a mad exchange."[43] The indigenous peoples of the Americas were not merely strangers and non-Christians; these traits by themselves did not deter the French from sumptuous and courteous diplomatic exchange with the Ottoman sultan in these very years. (A few years after Cartier reported to François Ier that he had given chief Donnacona two brass pots, eight hatchets, and other "little works" to console him for being kidnapped, the French ambassador to Constantinople was asking François for 67,500 livres to pay for the gold and silver vases and silk and scarlet robes needed to please the sultan Suleiman.[44]) The Americans, by contrast, were "savages," unenlightened about the true value of things as Europeans saw it.

"Savages" were not qualified for full reciprocity according to European rules. Accordingly, Cartier and even Léry were reluctant to characterize themselves, the French, as "grateful" to the Amerindians for their gifts. Early in his second voyage, Cartier and his men were welcomed by Iroquoians bringing them eels, fish, cornmeal for bread, and big melons. Cartier received them as best he could, "and to express his thanks [pour faire sa congnoissance] gave them small presents of little value." This is one of the few occasions where the French captain was characterized for European readers as grateful. That sentiment was rarely reported, not even when the Iroquoian chief Donnacona presented the French with his daughter and two young lads "out of love and as a sign of trust." When Donnacona sent over a marvelous remedy for an illness that had reduced many of the French to despair, Cartier was grateful to God but not to Donnacona or the women who brought him the leaves.[45]

Léry described the Tupinamba as "not ungrateful," always remembering who had given them a gift and what it was and appearing prepared to give something in return. "Courtesy" was the appropriate French response: after a Frenchman has eaten, rested or slept at a Tupi dwelling, "if he is courteous," he will present little gifts to his hosts. Léry also assured his readers that he could "entrust" himself to Tupinamba allies, more surely than to some of the disloyal Catholics in France:

> Just as they hate their enemies so mortally that when they have captured them, without any discussion of terms, they slay and eat them, so, on the contrary, they love so dearly their friends and confederates (as we were to the Tupinamba nation) that to keep them safe and spare them any hardship they would have had themselves cut into a hundred thousand pieces.

But Léry was never "grateful" to the Tupinamba, not "obliged" or inspired by their gifts to go on gifting. Much of the time he referred to French-Tupinamba exchange in the language of trade or barter even while he quoted the Indians as using the verb *amabe,* "to give." Though other features of Brazilian life made Léry think anew, he seems not to have asked himself whether the Tupinamba gift system had a distinctive structure of its own.[46]

One day, walking with some Amerindians in a great forest, delighting in the green foliage and the bird songs, Léry burst into singing Psalm 104. Stirred to joy by the sound, one of the Amerindians asked what it meant, and after Léry explained, gave him a prized piece of game, saying, "Here, because you have sung so well." Even then, Léry did not say he was grateful.

This picture would change somewhat in the seventeenth century, when fur traders, governors, Jesuits, and Ursulines of New France established long-term gift and trade relations with the Amerindians.[47] Iroquoians and Algonquians became knowledgeable about European practices and bargained astutely; the French and especially the Jesuits tried to imitate the remarkable rhetoric with which the Indians presented furs and wampum necklaces. There were still troubles in this later period, but now the Europeans looked down at the "savages" for their extravagant openhandedness among themselves and their incessant requests for gifts from the French. The Amerindians in turn told the French they were avaricious, loving themselves and their own things more than other people.

In the sixteenth century, gifts went wrong in the New World in a way that underscores the limits of reciprocity in the Old World. Anguish about gift relations in France grew out of ambiguities central to that mode, reinforced by its operation in a hierarchical society: How to get the gifts one deserved? How to limit the sense of obligation imposed by gratitude? Trouble came also from the coercion of donors, parents, and other givers forcing recipients beyond the bounds of gratitude.

In the Americas, the issue of force was in the open, magnified by the claims to superiority made by the "civilized" Europeans over the "savages." In both Québec and Brazil, French men were in situations where fighting rather than gifting would have been their customary reaction. But they were outnumbered, and dependent on their "inferior" hosts. The Amerindians were also suspicious and some-times hostile. The lord Donnacona told Captain Cartier that he was sorry to see the French always carried weapons, while he and his men carried none. "That's our custom in France," responded Cartier. In Brazil, Léry was terrified of the cannibalism that he witnessed, and, despite his comments about trust, told of times when he suddenly feared that Tupinamba were going to kill and eat him.[48] Under such circumstances, the field of force was constantly threatening the rhythms and sentiments of gift exchange. Different though they were in so many ways from Europe, the fragile gift relations along the Saint Lawrence and the Amazon help us understand the disruption of reciprocity along the Seine, Loire, Dordogne, and Rhône.

6

Gifts, Bribes, and Kings

And thou shalt take no gift: for the gift blindeth the wise, and perverteth the words of the righteous.

—Exodus 23:8 (AV)

Some complain that they are not rewarded by the king according to their merit . . . They should remember that the king holds his crown not from us, but from God and the ancient law of this kingdom . . . We must not take it as an insult if he prefers others to us.

—Speech of Chancellor l'Hôpital to
the Estates-General of Orléans, 1560

ifts were everywhere in the movement of French politics, justice, and appointment in the sixteenth century, and they raised important questions about how to tell a good gift from a bad one and about the nature of political reciprocity in a monarchy. In cities and towns, there were not only presentations to the king at his first entry after coronation, but any accession to office of an important official—the king's chancellor, the governor, the lieutenant-governor, the seneschal, or any magistrate—called forth a municipal gift to do him honor, "to make him a friend of the town" ("pour faire amy de la ville de luy"), "to recommend the town and its affairs to him." Wines of the region, olives, sweets, spices, candied fruits, cheeses, grains, game, fish, heavy wax torches, silver and golden cups, golden chains—whatever the town could rightly afford found its way to the officer's dwelling. If he visited the town, the gift was repeated. Rodez offered its famous cheese (Roquefort) to the seneschal of Rouergue and his court every Christmas, and on good years to every judge in the Parlement of Toulouse as well. In addition, gifts were made when any specific issue was at stake. In the 1540s the consuls of Lyon sent fine jellies to their representative at the royal court "for presents" while he pressed for lower taxes and for the elimination of a new registration procedure for documents. When it was a question of exemption from

Figure 15. Peasants lining up at the lawyer's office with gifts of food by Pieter Brueghel the Younger, ca. 1615 (Art Gallery of South Australia)

a military subsidy, a purse of three hundred crowns was given to the governor of the Lyonnais so he would write a letter to the king.[1]

Individuals gave presents for political business as well as towns. When Nicolas de Herberay sought a royal privilège for the printing of his new translation of *Amadis de Gaule,* he, of course, took two books to present to the chancellor's secretary. Any publisher had to do the same. Sire Gilles de Gouberville never rode to see any officer at Valognes, the administrative center near his seigneury, without game in his pouch: half a kid for the tax collector; a whole kid for the main judicial officer; two partridges for the record keeper for a copy of materials relating to some litigation he had pending (beyond the three sous paid to the clerk who did the actual copying), and more.[2]

Gift-giving around law cases was customary and widespread. Villagers showed up at their lawyer's study with rabbits, eggs, and chickens. It would have been unthinkable for them to arrive empty-handed. City dwellers brought their attorneys geese and hares "the better to be served." Wealthy Parisians and Toulousans made inter vivos donations to their barristers hoping to inspire them to ardent pleading. A satirical painting circulating in Poitiers in 1577 depicted a lawyer taking money and a hare from a villager with both his hands while a helper pumps gifts into him from behind. In the early seventeenth century, Pieter Brueghel the Younger showed the office of a country lawyer with a lineup of peasants bearing chickens and eggs (fig. 15). As for the judge in a case—whether the judge in a local court or the judge in a high court of Parlement assigned to investigate and make recommendation in a case—both parties in any litigation were likely to offer him presents, ranging from food and game to golden objects.[3]

These various gifts existed within a universe of popular discussion that was alternately approving, tolerant, and critical. Current proverbs suggested that this was the way things were, like it or not. "Empty hands, empty prayers." "By gifts and presents, one gets to the end of one's affairs."[4]

As far as the French law went, gifts to do honor to new officers were perfectly acceptable, however much they were intended to bring favor upon the donor. Indeed, the consuls of Lyon were baffled in 1541 when the new chancellor refused to accept a golden cup, and sent Portuguese gold to one of his familiars to persuade him to accept it. Governors and other high officers were not to compel the king's subjects to make them presents, as a 1560 royal edict spelled out especially in regard to regions where there were provincial estates. Chancellery secretaries were instructed not to take anything beyond fixed fees for signing and delivering royal letters. Yet gifts to the secretaries were customary and there is little evidence of prosecution.[5]

Where the law changed in the course of the sixteenth century was in regard to gifts to judges, a change as much related to the king's efforts to control his judicial officers and win their loyalty as it was to popular complaint. Up until 1560, the law forbade judges to accept any presents from litigants in a current case under penalty of loss of their office and, for the parties, loss of their case and other punishment, *except* for gifts of food, wine, and other perishables. (This is an ancient exception going back to Roman times). Then by the Edict of Orléans in January 1561, the law was modified to read that all gifts including food were prohibited, except game taken from the forests of the seigneurs who were presenting it. This led, as one critic noted, to litigants hastening to the nearest market to buy game and then lying to the judge about its origin. Finally, in 1579 the Ordinance of Blois forbade any gifts whatsoever from parties in a current case.[6]

Did this legislation affect practice very much? There was already prosecution and punishment of money gifts to judges in the Parlement of Toulouse in 1494 and again in 1528, and in 1540 the Parlement of Normandy was disbanded for a time for disorders including complaints about "taking presents."[7] In 1559, a case was brought against Gilles Becdelièvre, a judge responsible for criminal cases in the *présidial* court of Rennes in Brittany.[8] Among the complaints against him was that he was insisting upon judging all the cases himself, overworking the record keepers and secretaries, keeping the accused in prison too long, and slowing down the administration of justice. The main charge against him, however, was that he took money and other gifts (one witness spoke only of bread and sugar) to deliver certain judgments, or as one accuser put it, "I gave money to the judge so as to get him to order an arrest of a certain person . . . I gave the judge eight crowns to corrupt him." Or in the words of another, "I was advised by some prisoners to give a present to the judge [faire ung present au Juge]." The judge was allegedly given gold coins, either directly in his hands or left on the corner of his table, and the givers specified what action they wanted him to execute. "Go, go, my friend," the judge was supposed to have said while covering six crowns with paper, "I'll take care of your dispatch."

Becdelièvre claimed these were all lies coming from dubious witnesses who had themselves been "corrupted by money and other gifts" from the prosecutor, who coveted his post. How could he have committed such acts in his office, whose door was always open and with people always coming in and out?

In fact in 1560 Becdelièvre was acquitted after a witness confessed he had been paid and given "dons" for false testimony, and the judge received damages and back salary. But the case demonstrates that prosecution sometimes occurred and shows us how people talked about bribery ("corrupting the judge"; "give a present to the judge") and what gestures and actions were associated with it. Noël du Fail, one of the judges in the case, later used some of its motifs, such as the money at the end of the table, in his widely read book of legal stories.[9]

There is very little evidence, however, that the gifts of food and game stopped even after the 1579 Ordinance of Blois. A few years later in Limoges, so the story went, a hotelkeeper announced to his guests that the hare they were eating cost one hundred réals. It seems that the judges in the présidial court preferred money to game. When presented with a hare by a litigant, the judge had his wife sell it right back to the presenter, who would give it to other judges and then sell it to another litigant for presentation. The hare made the rounds of the court, and finally, when it threatened to spoil, came into the hands of the hotelkeeper.[10]

Sixteenth-century France was debating a central issue. In a world of gifts that created "friendships" and grateful obligations, where did bribery begin?[11] There was not even a special word for bribery in Old Regime France. In England, "bribe" had negative meanings in Chaucer's day and by the early sixteenth century meant a gift to corrupt judgment or extorted for political favor (we see it so used in Shakespeare's plays, for instance *Measure for Measure* and *Julius Caesar,* and Chancellor Francis Bacon was charged with "base bribery" in 1620–1621).[12] In France "bribe" meant and still means a little morsel of bread. The phrase "pot-de-vin," which came by the nineteenth century to refer to something illicit (but still not as clear-cut as the English "bribe"), was in the sixteenth century an amount of wine that one might buy at supper at an inn, or that might be used for the friendly drink between traders clinching a sale agreement, also called "le vin de marché." Thus, in France, one just used the words "dons" or "présents" and had to decide by context and performance whether the gift was a good one or a bad one.[13]

On one side, there were judges who claimed that the presents were small, that they were offered by both parties in a suit, that it would be contemptuous and inhuman not to accept them, and (as Chancellor Bacon was to say later in his trial in England) that they had no effect on the rectitude of their judgment. In *Le Tiers Livre,* François Rabelais offered portraits of two judges who fit this image. One was Bridoye, the judge of Myrelingues, who decided all cases by throwing the dice. Rabelais made it clear that constraining justice was bad: Bridoye's jurisdiction had formerly been in the bloody hands of "a Tribonian," "a miscreant . . . as avaricious as he was wicked, who sold laws, edicts . . . constitutions and ordinances for hard cash to those who offered the most." But in Bridoye's practice, little gifts had no serious consequence for the outcome. He simply piled all the papers produced by the plaintiff at one end of the desk, together with the "sugar candies and spices" (*épices* being a customary money payment from both parties to the judge, a payment that had once been a voluntary gift of sweets and spices from the winner in a case and that could still be stretched further into a gift), and all the matter, candies, and spices produced by the defendant at the other end. Then he threw the dice. In forty years no one had ever appealed Bridoye's decisions, so fair had they seemed except the last one, and that was because, with his aging eyesight, Bridoye had misread the dice.[14]

Judge Bridoye also praised the peasant Perrin Dendin, "an honorable man and good farmer," who arbitrated more quarrels in Poitou than all the local courts put together. No pig was slaughtered in his district without his being given roasted morsels and sausage. Dendin simply waited until the disputants were all exhausted and penniless from quarreling and then "at a banquet, feast, wedding party, baptismal or churching feast or in the tavern"—that is, in the very setting for gifts and reciprocity—he reconciled them and had them all drink together. The journal of the Sire de Gouberville (himself a reader of Rabelais) shows him playing a similar role of arbitration, gift-reception, and festive reconciliation, the dinners taking place at his manor house rather than at an inn.[15] Rabelais attacked avaricious professional judges more than once—the "géants dorphages," living off of presents, their document bags always open for venison; the "chats fourrés," the cats in robes trimmed with judicial ermine, surrounded by game, velvets, and satins, and living off "corruption"—but the local judges, the Bridoyes, Dendins, and Goubervilles were not corrupt.[16]

On the other side, there were those who thought the temptation of gifts and obligations so strong that no matter how small, they destroyed the possibility of fair judgment. This argument was advanced in the wake of the Edict of Orléans by Jean de Coras of the Parlement of Toulouse in his *Petit Discours des parties et office d'un bon et entier iuge* (Discourse on the duties and office of a good judge)—published not long after his book on the Martin Guerre case. Judges, he said, echoing Exodus 23:8 and Deuteronomy 16:19, must "abhor every hope of gifts and presents whatsoever, which trouble the understanding . . . , blind the eyes of judges, divert them from the right path and lead them in the ways of injustice." We are stipended by our prince, our wages paid regularly every quarter. Besides that we collect "épices" from the litigants after our judgment. How can we think we need our kitchens furnished by rich and poor alike with venison, game, and other eats? Our obligation, Coras argued, is only to the rectitude and equity commanded by God and the laws. Moreover, accepting gifts teaches a wrong lesson to litigants about the workings of justice. If they lose, they have contempt for a judge so debauched as to accept their presents and claim they have given him more than they have. If they win, they attribute it not to God's providence, but to the virtue of their gifts.[17]

It is surely significant that Jean de Coras was a strong supporter of royal sovereignty, developing that concept forcefully in his 1560 *De Iuris Arte,* well before the *Republic* of Jean Bodin. Eliminating gifts meant tightening the judges' ties to the monarch as against their competing ties to local aristocracies.[18] It is also perhaps significant that Coras was a Protestant, but his sentiments were taken up later in a powerful metaphor by the Catholic president of the Parlement of Paris, Guy du Faur de Pibrac: touching gifts by a judge was like the fisherman touching the torpedo fish. First it made the fingertips go to sleep, then the whole hand, and little by little the rest of the body.[19]

Such sentiments were dispersed to a wider audience in France through popular prints. A mid-century emblem book portrayed an admirable group of judges as described by Plutarch from an ancient painting at Thebes (fig. 16): they sit around the president of the court, who is blindfolded so he will not be improperly swayed from just decision, and all of them have their hands cut off so they can take "no money or other presents."[20] Hans Holbein's *Les Simulachres . . . de la mort* (Pictures . . . of death), sent throughout France in edition after edition from 1538 to 1562, showed a corrupted judge of his own day. Here, and in other pictures of bribery, the poor litigant is not offering a gift, but stands ignored and disconsolate. The judge has his hand open to the rich one, who pulls coins from his purse (figs. 17, 18). ("I've heard it said that he extorts from the poor and lets evildoers off for money," a witness testified in the Becdelièvre case.[21]) There are three men in the picture besides Death, who has come for the judge, but only two are making an exchange. As with the family gifts gone wrong, the gift of bribery can not engender gratitude, has no freedom of movement, and is too much tied to its solicited return.[22]

If the quarrel over "corrupt" gifts made people think more deeply about the nature of reciprocity in the republic, the quarrels about royal gifts posed questions about how much obligation subjects could place on a ruler. Not that this was a new issue in the sixteenth century, but it became especially acute when simultaneously monarchs were claiming more sovereign authority and subjects more rights of control. The argument was acted out in part in two gift arenas: royal entries and the acquisition of royal office.

Sometime after a king's advent to the throne and coronation, he and his court would make a formal entry into Paris, Rouen, Lyon, and other of his good towns. A ceremony going back to the fourteenth century, the entry was at its most elaborate and expansive in the sixteenth century. For months the town was astir with preparations: artisans making floats, pictures, and statues; tailors and seamstresses making outfits; musicians rehearsing; poets preparing verses and speeches; a master of ceremonies organizing parade routes, water jousts, fireworks, banquets, *tableaux*

AND. ALCI. EMBLE. LIB.

In senatum boni principis.

Effigies manibus truncæ ante altaria diuùm
  Hic resident, quarum lumine capta prior.
Signa potestatis summæ sanctiq; senatus
  Thebanis fuerant ista reperta uiris
Cur resident? quia mente graues decet esse quieta
  Iuridicos, animo nec uariare leui.
Cur sine sunt manibus? capiant ne xenia, nec se
  Polliatis flecti muneribúsue sinant.
Cæcus at est princeps, quòd solis auribus absque
  Affectu, constans iussa senatus agit.

Figure 16. The judges of Thebes with their hands cut off and a blind president in their midst, 1536

Disperdam iudicem de medio
eius.

AMOS II

Du mylieu d'eulx uous osteray
Iuges corrumpus par presentz.
Point ne serez de Mort exemptz.
Car ailleurs uous transporteray.

E

Figure 17. Bribing the judge, from Hans Holbein, *Les Simulachres . . . de la mort,* 1538

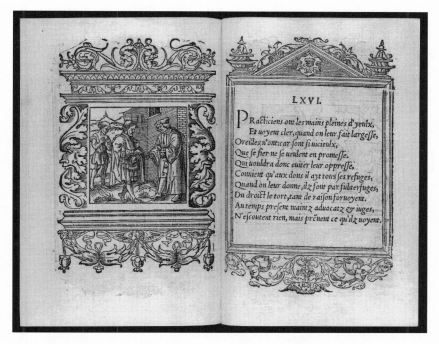

Figure 18. Bribing the judge, from Guillaume de La Perrière's emblem book, 1540

vivants, and presentations. During the days of the entry itself, the king, queen, and court were viewed by the town, and the men of the town of all estates paraded before him (women might mime on the floats, but were spectators for the procession). The city was offering itself to the king, and in the midst of this spectacular hospitality, it gave concrete gifts to him and his queen as well: golden or silver statues, presented in jeweled velvet wrapping. In 1548, Lyon gave Henri II a golden king to whom the goddesses of Faith and Liberality presented a kneeling lion. In 1549, Paris gave Henri II a silver statue linking his predecessors—Louis XII, François Ier—and himself.[23]

In return, the king thanked the city graciously, pardoned most prisoners in the jails, created new guild masters in cities with sworn crafts, and then touched the many people gathered to be cured of the king's evil, that is, scrofula. By late medieval custom, the king would also perform two other actions of constitutional importance for urban political life: he would confirm all the privileges and titles of the town, and he would assent to the remission of a tax or taxes levied by his predecessor. As the work of Lawrence Bryant has shown us, it is precisely in these two areas that a shift was taking place by the reign of Henri II: a shift made at the royal initiative and expressing the movement from a concept of reciprocal authority (authority shared with cities, estates, and corporate bodies) to a concept centering authority in the prerogative of the king.[24]

Already by the late fifteenth century, the confirmation of privileges would take place first in a private session at court, to be publicly reconfirmed at the time of the royal entry. This was practical when the entry might occur many months after the king's accession. But under Henri II, the ceremonial balance became weighted toward the first occasion. Thus deputies from Lyon were sent to court at Paris in the spring of 1547 to swear faith, homage, and loyalty to the new king and to ask for the confirmation of the town's privileges, exemptions, and liberties. The king responded, "As long as the inhabitants of Lyon are good and loyal subjects toward me, I will treat them as a good prince," and confirmed the grants of his predecessors. Fifteen months later at the royal entry, if Henri II repeated that confirmation, it was so downplayed that it received no mention either in the town records or in the published report of the entry.[25] Thus the king enhanced the sovereign quality of his act by preferring to make it a response to subjects come to him in obedient homage rather than a response to subjects receiving him with gifts and didactic hospitality, which might seem to oblige him.

The Lyon notables would doubtless have preferred it otherwise, as would those of Paris and Rouen. Both at court and during the entry, the Lyonnais tried to tell the king what they wanted, that is, what behavior, changed policies, or grants would make him "a good prince." Accompanying the presentation of the king's golden statue was an eloquent speech, in which attacks on monopolies in the alum trade and the salt trade were inserted along with loftier considerations. The goddess Liberality gesturing on the golden statue would remind the prince of the return for which the Lyonnais hoped.[26] They went right on talking to the king even when he was not a good listener.

Among the most important requests made of the king were those concerning taxes. Only four days after the death of François Ier, the town councilmen of Paris were asking Henri II to remit the forty thousand livres tax his father had levied on them. Lyon's representatives, swearing homage to the king a few months later, sought relief from several tariffs that were harming trade at their fairs. Then during the 1548 entry itself, the Lyon councilmen asked for exemption from the tax for army expenses levied annually on all the walled towns in the kingdom: Lyon's quota that year was 67,500 livres. Behind the scenes, the Lyonnais expostulated with the king's privy councillors and collectors about how much the city had paid in the past six years for the army and how much it was now laying out for the royal entry — the bill came to at least sixteen thousand livres — but in vain. The published description of the Lyon entry concluded, "His Majesty left to return to Fontainebleau with the queen as pleased and satisfied with the duty shown by the town as any virtuous and benign prince could be," but the 67,500 livres tax stood, to be paid in full and on time. Five months later, the king had the Lyon notables who had welcomed and gifted him placed in prison for ten days until they found a way to raise the tax money.[27]

The Lyon entry of 1548 is a small episode in a long process: the principle of taxes as grants to the king made by his subjects assembled at the Estates-General was supplanted by the principle of taxes as impositions simply declared and continued by the king for the needs of his government. But the process was contentious all the way and fought on many fronts. The Estates-General of 1484 had insisted on the practice of consent and had also made a "gift" of three hundred thousand livres to Charles VIII for his "joyous accession" to the throne. In the course of the sixteenth century the "joyous accession gift" was extracted from cities and officeholders as a royal right, but the Estates of 1560–1561 and 1576 were called in part to consent to taxes.[28]

In one line of thought, payments to the king were constructed in the mode of gift or the mode of contract, or a mixture of the two. Writing in 1584, Judge Jean Combes, one-time lawyer in a royal tax court, observed that the kings who had found it "easy" to collect new taxes were those who had sought the advice of the Estates, which "recognizing the graciousness of the good king, . . . responded that they were ready to live and die with their king and help and serve him with body and goods." If it was true that in France "where the king's will is, there is the law," it was also required that "there be mutual friendship between king and his subjects." In the other line of thought, payments to the king were constructed in the coercive mode. In the words of jurist Charles Loyseau at the opening of the seventeenth century, to conserve the public good the king had a right to have access to the purse of his subjects whether they approved it or not, "like a sick person who is given medicine against his will."[29]

The last royal entries in France were for Louis XIV. They were wholly centered on the person of the absolute king, a tribute of humble and obedient subjects to the glory of the ruler who would bring peace and harmony. Reciprocity and royal obligation have been drained away, though Louis XIV did pardon prisoners and touch for scrofula before the ceremony was done.[30] In the sixteenth century, despite conflict about the king's share, the gift elements in the entry sustained the notion that the king was obliged not just to God but to his people, and in ways that his people might define.

The quarrel about royal offices was especially lively in the sixteenth century because there was an increase in the number of things the king could give away. Now the king, by the 1516 concordat with the pope, had the right to nominate abbots and bishops in the Gallican Church, and now he had new courts—such as the présidial courts set up in 1552—which he could staff. Further, the use of payments for office increased, raising questions about the suitability of those who purchased them. Not that this was a new practice, as lawyer Jean Savaron reminded readers in *La Vénalité des offices:* the "presents" sent to the Merovingian kings for confirmation of office were already ominous, and in the ninth century, Charles the Bald was accused of granting office only "for the price of money." But by 1615, when Savaron was taking stock, the sale of office by a money-hungry monarchy had become so widespread that cries for reform were rife.[31]

Such a situation pitted the expectations of subjects against the claims of royal power. Were recipients to get gifts of office because they merited them or simply because it was the king's pleasure? Was the king obliged to acknowledge the subject's merit or could he follow his own royal will?

The lawyer-humanist Guillaume Budé came down firmly on the side of merit in *De L'Institution du prince* (The instruction of the prince), composed in 1519 for François Ier and finally published in 1547. The king should be liberal in his gifts — liberal and just. Distributive justice meant that honors, offices, and benefits should go only to learned and virtuous persons who had contributed to the common-weal — Budé thought they would be men of good letters like himself — and not to ambitious favor seekers:

> When learned and virtuous men, who have deserved well of the republic and the fatherland [ont bien merité de la Republicque et de la Patrie], are preferred and have their just part of the goods and honors that [the king] distributes, then liberality is joined with justice . . . When it's done otherwise, then liberality becomes injustice.

Bestowed on the unworthy, liberal gifts led to ungrateful servants who sought only their private ends. Kings had the authority by themselves to give offices to those whom they found "good and appropriate," but they should seek advice so as to make the right choice.[32]

In his *Republique,* fifty-five years later, Jean Bodin made explicit the tension between the king's power to give as he wished and his subjects' qualities and claims. Some people maintained that the greatness and liberality of a prince could not be recognized if he gave only to those who deserved it. Bodin, insistent clarifier of the notion of sovereignty, reported this argument and took it seriously, more seriously than Budé. He started off by dividing the king's gifts — offices, honorable charges, benefices, monies, tax exemptions, ennoblements, legitimations of children born out of wedlock, and the rest — into two categories: "les loyers," "rewards," given for merit, and "benefits," given by royal grace. The king in his liberality must first attend to those who have deserved it ("ceux qui ont merité") before turning to the others. But as Bodin worked through the argument, he was reluctant to concede that the king's gifts should ever be made to those who did not deserve them. As he put it,

> Some say that the grandeur and liberality of a prince can not be demonstrated if he gives only to those who merit it. Indeed, magnificence is seemly for a great prince and it should not be found wrong if he takes a singular pleasure in raising a little journeyman to the status of a high seigneur provided that the little journeyman has something in him that merits it. For if the prince elevates an unworthy man above respectable people or puts him at the rank of great personages, he does a favor for one, but insults everyone else.[33]

Bodin was setting down what he believed to be the conditions for a stable monarchy and, in the midst of the wars of religion, he was acutely aware of the sources of sedition: gifts to the unworthy caused jealousy and quarrels and ultimately rebellion.[34] Moreover, Bodin recognized how deeply contemporary notions of "worth" and "merit" were connected with social position. A nobleman believed himself likely to have more merit than others simply because he was a noble. Sixteenth-century tracts stressed the importance of education in bringing out the virtue required for true political service, but defenders of the *noblesse de race* argued that birth enhanced the potentiality for that virtue. Some said that noble youths would be inspired by the examples of their ancestors; some said that a noble father would inevitably educate his son so as to produce meritorious action; some said that the wide capacity for virtue was in the noble "seed" or stock itself. Those a notch below on the social scale—the newly ennobled or the wealthy commoner—challenged the nobles' claim to superior virtue, merit, and educability, but then used a similar range of arguments to justify themselves being chosen for royal office over "persons of obscure and low condition."[35]

For Bodin, then, the sovereign had large scope in bestowing (or withdrawing) gifts of his own accord, but he should be responsive to certain qualities in his subjects and in the social order. The king's distributive justice must be "harmonic," acknowledging the hierarchy of merit with gifts appropriate both to status and to talents.

The king, who wants to treat his subjects as a good father does his children, is not bound by human laws, but nonetheless he does lay down laws and ordinances concerning the appointment and dismissal of officials. The honors and salaries of office will not be distributed to everyone, but only to those who deserve them . . . The royal treasury to the most loyal, arms to the bravest, justice to the most upright . . .[36]

At the same time, the king must take birth and riches into consideration, favoring nobles over commoners, though not so exclusively that the "flames of jealousy" would be ignited:

The wise King must govern his kingdom harmonically, gently mixing together nobles and commoners, rich and poor, but always in such a fashion that nobles have some advantage over the commoners. For it's very reasonable that a gentleman equally excellent in arms and law as a commoner be preferred in the charges of justice or war, and that a rich man, equal in other things with a poor one, be preferred in posts that have more honor than profit, while the poor have offices with more income than honor.[37]

Elsewhere Bodin made even more concessions to the social order. Rather than affirmative action for nobles and the rich only when they were equal in talents to others, he advised in a section included only in his Latin edition that

[The prince should] divide the honors and preferments of the State unto the richer and nobler sort, albeit that they be not men of so great experience as are some of the poorer and baser sort, so as to prevent stirs and seditions . . . provided always that unto them which of themselves are not of sufficient capacitie be . . . associated men of good experience in their charge, so as to cover and supplie the defect of the others.

Bodin also thought, perhaps naively, that men with inherited wealth would be less tempted by bribes than poorer men.[38]

The actual practice of gift-bestowal in sixteenth-century France was rife with contradictions for observers like Budé and Bodin, and satisfied neither king nor subjects. Consider the appointment of a judge in the Parlement of Rouen, an honorable office and perfect example of one of Bodin's "loyers" or "rewards." By the 1540s, every new judgeship involved a payment to the king, described as a loan to help the monarch in his urgent necessities. (A similar characterization was used in payment for offices in the Parlement of Paris in the early 1520s.) The fiction of eventual repayment was stoutly maintained in these early years: the purchase of office was not a market transaction but a friendly loan. In addition, every new judge had his nomination urged by important legal figures and by members of the high Norman aristocracy, whose recommendations were essential but who themselves hoped for subsequent services from the judge. The king's final letters making the gift of office then added merit: "good and praiseworthy report has been made to us" of the new judge's "sense, sufficiency, loyalty, integrity, practical wisdom, learning, experience in judicial matters, and sound diligence." The new judge would have to demonstrate to the Parlement of Rouen his training in and knowledge of the law, his moral integrity, and his rhetorical skills before he could take his oath of office.[39]

Virtually any royal office was obtained through a like mixture of payment and patronage, and the royal letters always insisted on the merit and deserving qualities of the recipient—even during the reign of Henri III when the crown quite openly sold offices to the highest bidder. Indeed, the 1579 Ordinance of Blois required such a report. The register of the king's "gift of office" ("don de l'office") in the Lyonnais throughout the century shows the language of entangled considerations. From royal sergeant and concierge in the royal prisons to tax collector and judge in the Lyonnais royal court, the king has good report of or perfect confidence in the "good sense, sufficiency, loyalty, probity (*preudhommie*), experience, and great diligence" of the officer, with "learning" and "experience" added where appropriate. In many cases, the source of the good report is mentioned: François Charlin is praised by noble Adam Deschaves, first barber-surgeon and *valet de chambre* of the king, as he is made royal barber in the Lyonnais in 1546. Payments are included only occasionally in the body of the letter. In early 1556, Néry de Tourvéon paid four thousand golden crowns to become criminal judge in the Sénéchaussée of Lyon, a goodly fee for a high post, but other times the price is marked in small letters in the corner of the page or found in another royal account entirely.[40]

The quarrel about the king's gifts—about whether the king was obliged to recognize merit and status in his gifts or was a free and supreme donor, who could give them to whom he wished and could sell them if he wished—remained unresolved in France. Indeed, the quarrel is a period marker for the whole Old Regime.

In the sixteenth century, gifts-gone-wrong set up a serious predicament. On the one hand, people relied on gift-systems to create solidarity with each other, to mark and soften relations, to acknowledge services, to get goods around, and to seek protection, alliance, and advancement. On the other hand, gift relationships were the source of intolerable obligation and of accusations of corruption. For some, the language of gift courtesy was adulterated or mendacious, and the meaning of words like "service," "merit," and "reward" strained. In family life, patronage, and the state, coercion was recasting gift relations so they led to mistrust and strife. By requiring payment for royal office, the monarchy was introducing a sale mode into an already contested gift mode for distributing the honors, benefits, and profits of the republic.

But what did a society, so committed to the rhythms of gift and obligation, do about gifts gone so badly wrong? Stop all gifts? Unthinkable. Sort out good reciprocity from bad? But how?

The story of the "misanthrope" Timon of Athens was known from Plutarch, Lucian, and other sources among the educated in sixteenth-century France. As elaborated by Shakespeare, the overly lavish giver Timon turns bitter when, bankrupt, he is deserted by all his flattering clients and retainers. Once Timon had proclaimed with all courtesy, "We are born to do benefits." Now from his cave, he declares to bandits, "Each thing's a thief":

> The sun's a thief, and with his great attraction
> Robs the vast sea; the moon's an arrant thief,
> And her pale fire she snatches from the sun;
> The sea's a thief, whose liquid surge resolves
> The moon into salt tears; the earth's a thief,
> That feeds and breeds by a composture stol'n
> From gen'ral excrement—each thing's a thief.
> The laws, your curb and whip, in their rough power
> Has uncheck'd theft. Love not yourselves; away,
> Rob one another.[41]

Montaigne, in a brief essay of ironic fancy, wrote on how "the profit of one is the damage to the other." Farmers do best in their business when grain is dear, architects when houses are ruined, physicians when people are sick, judges and lawyers when people quarrel, ministers of the church when people are caught in vice or die. Even our inner thoughts are mostly nourished at the expense of those around us. Nature herself has connected the birth and increase of one thing to the decline and corruption of another.[42]

Was it still possible to believe in the fruits of human reciprocity or to enjoin with Jesus, "Freely ye have received, freely give"?

7

Gifts and the Gods

he Lord was a party to all gifts, as the original supplier of everything humans have, as a spectator to all gift transactions, and sometimes as a recipient. The gift flow here was a privileged one: it could provide a model and offer prescriptions for exchange within society at large. Gift connections within religious institutions also had a special status, setting a tone for the offering of presents in other situations. Religious action and metaphor helped define wider patterns of human reciprocity.

As with models, so with breakdowns. Uncertainty and conflict about reciprocity flooded religious debate in sixteenth-century France. The pressures of obligation, weighing down gift relations in so many areas, found anguished expression in Protestant criticism of Catholic paths to salvation. In a profound sense, the religious reformations of the sixteenth century were a quarrel about gifts, that is, about whether humans can reciprocate to God, about whether humans can put God under obligation, and about what this means for what people should give to each other. The religious quarrel stands on its own and is argued in its own terms, but is parallel to the quarrel about the king's obligations to his subjects just described. In this chapter, I describe four different ways of constructing mutual obligation as they emerged out of sixteenth-century reflection on the human relation to divine and sacred things. Could they provide an answer to the despair of "Each thing's a thief"?

The Catholic gift system was based on the ancient notion that sacred things, the gifts of God par excellence, could not be sold. Over hundreds of years payments were often made for clerical offices and for entry into religious orders, but they were just as regularly denounced as the sin of simony. The idea remained firmly in place in teaching and canon law that the church was an institution in which gifts flow. The theme was illustrated in a 1570 book of *Figures* from the New Testament (fig. 19). The ex-magician Simon tries to purchase the apostles' power to pass on the Holy Spirit by the laying on of hands. "Man without conscience," Peter reproaches Simon in the accompanying verse, "since you've presumed to have the gift of God by your money and your fortune, may money be your perdition."[1]

The characteristic of the Catholic system was a complex and articulated reciprocity, in which many items were presented, from candle wax to faith. There was exchange between the living and the dead. As we have seen, food was left for ghostly souls on the Day of the Dead (2 November); ghosts visited and warned the living; prayers were said for souls in Purgatory. Saints were given statues and candles; they interceded with God for humans.

There was exchange between laity and clergy: the lay people gave chalices, vestments, banners, and money; the priests returned prayers and liturgical intercession through the mass. A sign that money for a private mass or an anniversary mass could be perceived as a customary gift rather than as a straightforward purchase was the different amounts given each time. An anniversary mass at the Church of Sainte Croix in Lyon might be said for two sous, ten sous, or twenty sous, and where "pity" prevailed, for nothing, as when a poor person was prayed for. René Benoist, doctor of theology at Paris, claimed that the tithe was a kind of gift, an offering or oblation of first fruits made by lay people to God through the person of his priests. The act of offering would dispose the peasants to receive more goods from the Lord, both spiritual and material: "God makes those prosper who pay tithes voluntarily and with a good heart." The clergy should then use the tithes well, not for worldly things, but for God's glory, the repair of churches, the support of worship, and aid to the poor.[2]

Gifts moved in many channels around the clergy itself. More important than payments to a distant pope were the many exchanges among people in religious orders and among clerics within a diocese, a city, a chapter, or an order. To woo a priest into resigning his benefice in one's favor and then to reward him when he had done so, one offered him dinners with wine, made him "loans," and founded masses for him to say. Entering a new curacy, a priest customarily sent wax for candles to the religious patron who had named him. Any new canon or priest founded masses within his chapter, "moved with devotion" at being received by his fellow priests.[3] Men from these chapters and from male religious houses visited each other in procession and prayed together at certain feast days each year, sometimes transporting important sacred relics, sharing meals, and giving each other small amounts of money—a system of liturgical hospitality.[4] Women's religious houses, cloistered as they were supposed to be, sent each other relics and devotional books

Simon presente aux Apostres de Christ
 Argent, à fin d'auoir mesme puissance
Qu'eux de donner aux gens le sainct Esprit
Par le toucher des mains: à luy s'auance
Sainct Pierre & dit, Homme sans cõscïece,
Puis que d'auoir tu as presomption
Le don de Dieu par argent & cheuance,
Soit ton argent à ta perdition.

Gg 4

Figure 19. Simon trying to buy the gifts of the spirit from the Apostles, 1570

by messengers: in 1517, "for the greater glory of God," the nuns of the Benedictine order of Montmartre in Paris bestowed on the Benedictine nuns of Saint Pierre at Lyon a piece of ear and three ribs from Christians martyred long ago on their hill. Secular clerics had confraternities just among themselves; common banquets and a common treasury helped reduce quarrels and encouraged them to be "brothers," supportive of each other and holy worship.[5]

Secular clerics remembered each other in their wills, making gifts to choir boys, to their chapter, to their church for repairs, to their successors in holy office, and to relatives who were priests and nuns. (The wills also reveal the same petty indebtedess among clerics that was common among lay friends and neighbors.) Amé Baronnat, choirmaster of Saint Paul's in Lyon, had paid for the rebuilding of the church and its granary in the wake of the wars of religion. After his death, "to keep the memory of his gift alive and not be stained by ingratitude, the greatest of all vices," the chapter had his name mentioned at the altar after the Memento during every parish mass.[6]

Confraternities existed especially among the laity, drawn from persons in the same trade, parish, village, or city. They ranged in size from twenty to several hundred; most had around forty to sixty members contributing to the common treasury. Here prayer was shared as well as a specially blessed loaf of bread (*pain bénit*) after a common mass, quarrels were arbitrated, help was given when one was ill, funerals were arranged, and food and drink were taken together at the annual banquet.[7]

Lay people and clerics also provided gifts to the poor, often in holy settings: gifts of food to the hungry at the house door or at the confraternity banquet, alms to beggars at the church door, clothing for the poor who bore torches at the funeral, dowries for poor girls, and dinners and sheets for the sick at the hospital, to give a few examples. Always there was the hope that grateful recipients would feel obliged to pray for the souls of donors.

Finally, there were gifts to God, from whom all gifts came. Alms to the poor were often described as simultaneously offered to God as well. The meritorious act of the donor could thus come to God's attention and perhaps play some role in the Christian's salvation. The gold, incense, and myrrh presented by the Magi to the infant Jesus in worship of his divinity (Matthew 2:1–12) were much represented in painting and discussed in a tradition going back to the Church Fathers. This commentary spiritualized the gifts rather than calling on Christians to reenact them literally: myrrh, for instance, stood for faith in the resurrection. The gifts at the Feast of Kings were, as we have seen, sweets and other foods passed on to neighbors, with the sacred resonance muted by the merriment of banquets and dancing.[8]

The central symbolic event here was the sacrifice of the mass. Sacrifice, pondered by Christian theologians over the centuries, has been discussed by anthropologists and anthropological historians as an offering that relates humans and gods in supremely important ways. Gods are honored, thanked, and shown the awe in which they are held; humans are pulled together in communion and commensality. But also sacrifice is needed by both sides: "the gods require it," as Henri Hubert and Marcel Mauss said in their 1899 essay on "The Nature and Function of Sacrifice." The human gifts sustain the gods; "if nothing were reserved [and given over] from the harvest, the grain god would die." Inga Clendinnen describes the Mexica earth gods of the early sixteenth century as "hungry" for the human flesh that itself had been nourished by the fruits of the earth. Mexica sacrifice was the fulfillment of an "involuntary debt" to the gods "by returning earth-fed flesh and blood to the earth." [9]

Humans need the sacrifice as well, to guarantee their continued nourishment (as with the Mexica) and to propitiate the gods and deflect their anger. The sacrificial victim is given over to the powerful gods to "ransom" or "redeem" the sacrificing humans: "there is no sacrifice where some idea of ransom is not present" ("il n'y a pas de sacrifice où n'intervienne quelque idée de rachat"), maintained Hubert and Mauss. They went on, in phrases that anticipate Mauss's more general essay on *The Gift* twenty-four years later, to structure sacrifice as strict reciprocity. "If sacrificers give something of themselves . . . it is in part to receive. The sacrifice . . . is both a useful act and an obligation. Unselfishness is mixed with self-interest [Le désintéressement s'y mêle à l'intérêt]. That is why it has been conceptualized so often as a contract." [10]

Is this how sixteenth-century Catholics experienced and thought about the sacrifice of the mass? Let us move through the performance of a parish mass to identify the themes of gift and return. An offertory procession preceded the canon of the mass. The lay worshipers brought candles, wine, bread, and alms to the altar for use by the clergy and the poor. They kissed the linen cloth covering the chalice and said French prayers linking their offering to the Lord: "[Accept] the small gift that I give you . . . for all my misdeeds, as you took the gifts of Abel."

Then the sacrificing priest performed the acts that changed the substance of the bread and wine into the true and actual body and blood of Christ, which would be offered to the Lord. Gift language continued throughout. In the name of Jesus Christ, God the Father was asked to bless and sanctify the sacrifice being prepared. The bread and wine were called "these gifts, these presents, these holy and incorrupt sacrifices" ("haec dona, haec munera, haec sancta sacrificia illibata"). They were offered by the priest on behalf of the whole Catholic Church, that is, both the faithful actually present for the mass and other living Christians as well as the saints in paradise and the contrite dead in Purgatory. God the Father was asked to receive the oblation in reconciliation (*ut placatus accipias*); to look at the Host and wine, themselves gifts from him, with a favorable and serene eye; to find them agreeable "as it pleased thee to find agreeable the gifts of Abel thy just lad, the sacrifice of our Patriarch Abraham, and the pure host offered to thee in holy sacrifice by thy high priest Melchizedek." [11]

The hoped-for return was described in the language of supplication. At the *Memento Domine,* when the names of special people were uttered along with reference to the faithful present at the mass, the sacrifice was offered "for their preservation, the redemption of their souls, and their hope for salvation." At the *Hanc igitur,* God was asked to keep those presenting the oblation in his peace and deliver them from eternal death. At the elevation of the Host, the French prayer recommended to the lay woman in a 1520 text suggests how the individual worshiper could construct the return:

Oh, eternal God the father, I present this holy sacrifice to you . . . and I request of you in virtue of this blessed sacrifice that it please you to pardon all my sins and give me the grace to do your holy will in all things.[12]

The requests continued. At the *Memento etiam,* God was asked to better the lot of the faithful already dead but not yet in heaven, and then, as the worshipers struck their breasts as sinners, the priest prayed that one day they, too, would be admitted to the company of the saints in Paradise. Finally, just before his communion, the priest bowed and begged the Lord to have him take the body and blood of Christ so worthily that he would by this deserve the remission of all his sins and be filled with the Holy Spirit.[13]

Sixteenth-century Catholic commentary on the sacrifice of the mass built upon medieval thought and developed further in response to caustic Protestant attack. The Jesuit Antonio Possevino, an important preacher in Lyon and Paris in the 1560s, explained that a sacrifice was something consecrated and offered up to God to appease his wrath and indignation and to give him reverence and honor. The mass, prefigured in the Jewish sacrifices of oxen and calves, fulfilled the Old Testament promise of salvation (figs. 20, 21, 22). Its end, in Possevino's words, was "to make us by a holy and blessed fellowship to be coupled and joined with God," or, in the phrase of the Jesuit Émond Auger, "to keep all faithful Christians in a body of friendship and peace." René Benoist, preaching to the parishioners of Saint Eustache in Paris, added that Christ was sacrificed to God his father in the mass for the remission of sins of the living and the dead and to deepen the memory of his Passion.[14]

Nowhere in this vernacular theological writing was God the father "obliged" by the sacrifice he has been offered; nowhere was he "grateful" for these "gifts and presents"; nowhere was divine return a simple consequence of the mass itself. Indeed, Bernhard Jussen has explored the semantic field around "gifts to God" in twelfth-century texts and found that *munus* (gift) was not associated there with *remuneratio* (remuneration, gift-return), but rather with *cor* (heart), expressing the concern about giving to God with the right attitude and feeling, as in the offerings of the Magi. God rewarded good deeds done to other people rather than reciprocating gifts given to him.[15] So, too, right feeling was urged in sixteenth-century instruction: to hear the mass with good devotion, the lay woman was enjoined to think on the sufferings of Christ, "feeling them profoundly in your heart until you weep." Esprit Rotier, longtime inquisitor and preacher in Toulouse, stated flat out that though the mass was a sacrifice, the Church had no intention "to give ran-

A Catholic View of the History of Sacrifice
by Thomas de Leu, late sixteenth century

SACRIFICIVM
Sub Lege Naturæ

Statinatque homo creatus fuit, naturali ipso instinctu, patrem Creatoremque suum agnoscere amare, varijsque honoribus venerari cœpit: primus enim sibel victimas Deo immolauit. deinde Noe: post hunc Abraham. Denique omnis posteritas varijs sacrificiorum generibus supplicauit. Vnde spes, et diuinitatis timor et reuerentia in vniuerso mundo occreuit.

Figure 20. *Sacrifice under the Law of Nature*

A Catholic View of the History of Sacrifice
by Thomas de Leu, late sixteenth century

Figure 21. *Sacrifice under the Law of Moses*

A Catholic View of the History of Sacrifice
by Thomas de Leu, late sixteenth century

Figure 22. *Sacrifice under the Law of the Gospel*

som and satisfaction for our faults [de rachepter et satisfaire pour noz faultes], but rather to reconcile us to God the father and restore us to our baptismal grace, lost by our wrongdoing." [16]

Nonetheless, the mass was a source of grace, and confessors and preachers taught that attendance at it in the right spirit of penitence and devotion brought immediate effects or effects in the near future. God forgave one's venial sins and the mortal sins one had forgotten about and the penalty for them was wiped away. Contrite souls in Purgatory, remembered during the mass, were released to heaven: "Never is a mass said but that some soul is pulled out of Purgatory" went the popular adage. (This may be true, the Franciscan Jean Benedicti affirmed in his book for confessors, but he warned that it might not be the same soul one had been praying for.) After offering the sacrifice of the mass with a devout heart, one was stronger in will and body, able to resist bad passions, drained of concupiscence, girded against the temptations of evil spirits. It could even help digestion in the popular view: "Saint Ambrose says that food is significantly more profitable to the body after mass."

The sacrifice of the mass was also a resource for many precise current needs: for pregnancy and safe delivery, for safe traveling on the sea, and for protection from fevers, storms, and animal plague, to name a few listed in a 1510 missal. If the outcome was favorable, the worshiper could think "these gifts, these presents" to God the father had helped. Some Christians believed the consecration and sacrifice so sure in their power that they slipped herbs and papers with words written on them under the altar cloth "in hopes of some work of Magic." [17]

To Protestants, the mass seemed simply an effort to put up ransom to God, to oblige the Lord by a gift. To most Catholics, learned and unlearned, that characterization was too rigid. Similarly, the Hubert-Mauss generalization about sacrifice left out the ambiguities and asymmetries present in the Catholic case. God the Father was being appeased and reconciled, not further obliged by the replaying of Christ's sacrifice. The Lord's reaction to human requests accompanying the sacrifice was determined by many things, some inscrutable. One did not even know for sure why he had rejected Cain's offering of grain and accepted Abel's sheep (Genesis 4: 2–7). Still, the mass did establish *a model of close gift reciprocity* between humans and God the Father, the forces of exchange moving back and forth across the same field, and its frequent repetition nourished the human hope for divine favor.

Where did the Catholic gift system seem in trouble to its practitioners in the sixteenth century? Where was it vulnerable to criticism from Catholic reformers? First, in the frequent slippage of customary gifts into required payments: the age-old problem of simony, intensified by the Protestant charge that priests were traffickers in sacred things. In the Catholic view, it was legitimate for a chapter of canons to distribute grain or money to priests after they had said mass each day, for "the laborer is worthy of his hire" and wages were in order. But was it legitimate for lay people to give money to a preacher for his sermons or to a priest for hearing confession or for saying mass? The Jesuits thought not and forbad their members to accept all such payment, while the Franciscan Benedicti judged it simony only when the money was required.[18]

An episode in Lyon in 1572 illustrates Catholic uncertainty on the matter. The Jesuit Antonio Possevino had been preaching Lent in the Church of Saint Nizier to the enthusiastic response of the lay parishioners. The vestry was taken aback, however, when Possevino asked them to cease their "ancient custom" of collecting money for the preacher from those listening in church. He had taken a vow to receive nothing for his sermons. The vestrymen explained that the parish had no other revenue for such occasions, and dropping the collection would cause difficulty for later preachers. Possevino then assented, saying it was reasonable to do this for preachers from the "poor mendicant orders," but that it must be announced that the present collection was being made not for him but for the poor.[19]

A second defect in the Catholic exchange system was its narrowness, the tightness of its reciprocity. The generosity circled round in limited groups, to one's own kind, one's fellow clerics, one's spiritual brothers and sisters, one's relatives, one's servants. "One barber shaves another." The favors stayed too close to home.

This limitation, too, Catholic reformers tried to remedy, as Saint Francis and his followers had tried to do centuries before. Erasmus placed mercy and pity above sacrifice, which he defined loosely as any form of legalistic observation. Gifts should go out to the poor, he said, rather than to church buildings for more sumptuous ornament. New urban welfare institutions were founded in Paris, Rouen, and Lyon, where gifts went into a central civic poor fund and then were redistributed to the needy. City fathers had diverse worries in making these changes, including fear of uprisings and eagerness to rid the streets of beggars, but they were sometimes supported by Catholic reformers. "What is a city but a great monastery?" Erasmus had asked in 1518. Six years later his fellow humanist Juan Luis Vives proclaimed, "Let Christian charity diffuse itself throughout the whole state, making one harmonious household with common interests among them," and issued a practical proposal, *On Assistance to the Poor,* for the town of Ypres; the reforming priest Jean de Vauzelles played a similar role in Lyon in the 1530s, affirming in one of his sermons, "It is to the living and not to the dead that are owed the alms that resurrect." The circle of those receiving aid was now much wider, though it stopped at the city walls and did not extend to healthy beggars. Connection was still possible between donors and recipients under the new welfare regime, but it was more distant than with alms handed out at one's door or in a neighborhood or parish setting. In Lyon during the annual Easter procession of those on the city's relief rolls and the hospital orphans, the poor were to pray for their benefactors, while the watching donors were to be "moved to devotion and charity" so as to make further contribution.[20]

These changes never fully supplanted the older forms of charitable relief, and were sometimes actively opposed by more traditional Catholics. A city like Toulouse never took well to the centralizing features of the new poor funds.[21] In any case, the changes were mere adjustments to a Catholic system etched deep with reciprocity and marked by a liturgy of sacrifice.

One response to a tight system of reciprocity is to reject it in the name of human relations in which there is no property at all. Where all is shared, there are no gifts. We might call this our second model of alliance and obligation, the model of fusion or boundarylessness. Among Catholics, the experience of fusion was found in mystical writing, as with Teresa of Ávila in the late sixteenth century: there the union joined Christian and the Lord rather than people. For powerful descriptions of human fusion, we can turn to Michel de Montaigne and to an early Protestant teacher, Robert Olivétan, both of them reacting to unsatisfactory systems of obligation and exchange.

Montaigne's essay "On Friendship," first published in 1580, describes his six-year relation with Étienne de La Boétie, who had died some seventeen years before. They had met by chance at a town banquet when they were both young judges in the Parlement of Bordeaux, and had taken an immediate liking to each other. Their communication had been total and complete, said Montaigne, and their friendship of a higher order than even the best described by Cicero.

In this friendship I speak of, our souls intermixed and confounded themselves one in the other, with so universal a commixture that they erased the seam that joined them together . . . In this noble commerce, offices and benefits (which nourish other friendships) were not even taken into account, so complete was the fusion of our wills . . . The union of such friends, being truly perfect, makes them lose the feeling of duty [toward each other] and detest and drive from use between them words of division and diffence: such words as benefit, obligation, gratitude, entreaty, thanks and the like. All things being in effect common between them—their will, thoughts, judgments, goods, wives, children, honor, and life—and their fitting together as one soul in two bodies . . . , they can neither lend to each other nor give anything to each other.[22]

We have seen earlier, in his essay "On Vanity," how Montaigne discharged the tension of obligation in public life by the relief of contract (or at least he did so in his writing, if not always in his practice). Here, in his essay on La Boétie, Montaigne dismisses the rhythms of gift friendship and obligation in favor of a transcendent intimacy, a seamless union. This is clearly not a long-term social solution to the strains of human reciprocity, for the release is possible only for a limited time and with one person: "for this perfect friendship is indivisible, each gives himself so fully to his friend that there is nothing left to give out elsewhere."[23]

The death of La Boétie brought division, and the break finally introduced a gift into their friendship. La Boétie made Montaigne heir of his library and all his papers, and Montaigne responded by publishing his friend's sonnets and political writings. Montaigne's own *Essais* were in part an effort to continue the conversations started with La Boétie, but now shared with the whole body of readers.

In his own last years, Montaigne had a friendship once again, this time with Marie de Gournay, a young literary woman—"a very holy friendship, a kind of

friendship to whose heights we do not read that her sex has yet been able to rise."
Here, with a young woman not his wife, there could be no fusion, but rather the
relation of a "Daughter" to a "Father by alliance," to use Marie de Gournay's terms.
Montaigne left the final revised copy of his *Essais* to Marie de Gournay to publish, which she did in 1595 and subsequent editions. So the gift came alive again,
bearing fruit not in a favor returned directly to its donor, a path which Montaigne
detested, but in the future time after his death.[24]

Montaigne's example on human friendship late in the century helps us understand the targets, the mood, and the aspiration behind a remarkable text on sacred
matters written years earlier by Robert Olivétan: the 1535 dedication of the first
Protestant Bible in French, of which Olivétan was the translator. Born in Picardy,
Pierre Robert Louis Olivétan tasted "the pure religion" during his university years
in Orléans and Paris, and by 1528 was a refugee in Strasbourg studying theology and
Hebrew. A few years later he was keeping school in Neuchâtel and writing manuals for the instruction of children and good Christian men and women. In 1533,
he moved up into the Alps to bring the new teaching to the children of the Waldensian communities, hidden away for centuries with their parchment vernacular
Bibles, heretics as seen by Catholic authorities, but true carriers of Christian faith
as seen by the Reformers. In the mountains Olivétan finished his translation of the
Holy Scripture into French, the Old Testament from the Hebrew, the New Testament from the Greek. The Waldensian elders made a gift of some five hundred
golden crowns (écus)—no small sum—to pay for the publication.[25]

In June 1535, the last pages of the folio Bible came off the presses of Pierre
de Vingle, alias Pirot Picard, in Neuchâtel. Several years before, Vingle had left
his atelier in Lyon, already a source of evangelical publication, for the purer air
of Neuchâtel. For this, his most holy task, he assembled an editorial group of
learned young enthusiasts, including his fellow Picard Olivétan and the young Jean
Calvin, who had been studying Hebrew in Basel. The dedication—or rather anti-
dedication—was sent by "P. Robert Olivetanus, the humble little translator, to the
church of Jesus Christ, Salutations."[26]

He is not going to present this book to some prince, king, or emperor, in expectation of liberal reward. Nor will he seek safe conduct for it from some "Very
Illustrious, Very Magnificent, Very Excellent, Very High, Very Powerful, Very Magnificent, Very Victorious, Very Holy Name." Dame Custom had importuned him
to provide some lordly guide for his translation but he will not subject himself to
her. This book is different from all others. It cannot be offered, as authors usually
do, in "cunning exchange for rich gifts and plentiful grants."

Rather, "to you, O poor little Church of the true faithful, having the knowledge of God by Jesus Christ, his son, our only Lord . . . I, your friend and brother
in Jesus Christ, address this precious treasure." He has found it in old Hebrew and
Greek coffers and cupboards and repacked it in a good French purse. "And this
offering is rightly due you, for it contains all your patrimony, all your proprietary

right, all that belongs to you . . . the word of Truth, the word of life, the word of God."

Olivétan then uses a phrase drawn from the conventions of gift exchange — "Accept . . . O poor little Church, this gift that I present you . . . with the joyous affection with which it is sent" — only to break into a lyric celebration of a relation that *transcends* dedication, a relation beyond reciprocity:

This good is yours [ce bien est tien], and when I give it to you, it still remains mine entirely, so fecund and felicitous are the sources of this estate . . . O this salutary possession of grace, which brings the same joy and delight to the person who gives and the person who receives! What other gift could human beings give to another without fearing some damage? . . . What a good face we usually put on when we give, coloring the words in our mouth to express our good will, when there is always in some corner of our heart a timorous prudence which cries out, "Watch out what you're doing, beware lest you miss the thing you're giving away with such prodigality."

Now this work is of a very special nature . . . for it is made only to be given and communicated to another . . . It enriches those to whom it is given and impoverishes not at all the givers, who rather think themselves to have made a great gain when they find the occasion to give it away.[27]

Olivétan's letter captures the experience of a painless giving and receiving of sacred culture, innocent of danger and loss. No sense of oppressive obligation is created because, endlessly fertile and buoyed by grace, the biblical book is made to be passed on. Olivétan has constructed an open social situation in which the barrier between self and others is let down. In the realm of good news from God, in the realm of sacred communication, there is, at least for a moment, no property.

Jean Calvin, too, was present in the 1535 Protestant Bible. He precedes Olivétan's anti-dedication with an anti-privilège, turning inside out the usual printer's request for exclusive right to publish a book for a certain number of years. Calvin's letter is written to all princes, kings, and emperors saying that this translation needs no worldly privilège. Its privilège comes direct from the King of Kings, and it is granted to all people everywhere. For too long the Bible has been monopolized by the wicked Catholic clergy, and now it must be presented to everyone in a language they can read. Then after Olivétan's anti-dedication, Calvin sends a letter to "the people of the alliance of Sinai," that is, the Jews, "our neighbors and conjoined to us in God." He calls upon them to move beyond the commandments of the Law and accept the faith and the promises of the New Testament. "The Kingdom of the Messiah, the son of David, has no end . . . the New immortal men, created according to God, must be citizens of the New and eternal Kingdom." He prays that salvation through Christ be accepted by everyone, Jew and Greek (Romans 10:12) so that "the temple and city of Jerusalem, this celestial land, may be built."[28]

Calvin's mood approximated that exhilarating fusion expressed at the climax of Olivétan's letter, and added to it a millennial tinge. For both of them, God's gracious Word, embodied in a book and text, lifted humans into a liminal space beyond boundaries, gift exchange, and reciprocity. But as with the seamless union between Montaigne and La Boétie, which left no energy over for other people, this ecstatic joining of the faithful could flare up only for a moment and be rekindled only now and again. Otherwise there would be no energy left over for the more detached work of constructing the doctrine, liturgy, and institutions for the Reformed faith.

Building a new religion involved destroying the old. Pierre de Vingle's presses were again of service in 1533, when he published *Le Livre des marchans* (The book of the merchants) by the French emigré and proselytizer Antoine Marcourt. Much reprinted in the sixteenth century, *Le Livre des marchans* was a funny polemic, accusing the Catholic clergy of being not merely "gret marchauntes, but furious theves," "terryble marchauntes . . . who sell God and devyll." The merchant's estate is an honorable one when practiced in "temporal and civyll welth," but "accursed and detestable in divine and spirytuall lyfe." Marcourt itemized the things the clergy sells: the souls of the living and the dead, the times of the day and the days of the week, ceremonies and songs. He went on to compare them unfavorably to lawful merchants, who seek only a moderate profit on their sales. And what civil merchant would sell just the *sight* of an object, the way the clergy do, or keep both money and merchandise, the way priests do when they sell the lighting of a candle to some "poore foole" and then blow it out and sell it again to someone else? Most civil merchants have a specialty, like cloth, "but these have ravyshed at once al thinges for to set all unto sale, their occupyenge conteyneth a whole world."

Marcourt played off the clergy's sales not so much against a gift mode, but against commerce rightly conducted. (Merchants were also among his hoped-for converts.) Marcourt did remind readers that Christ "commanded [us] to give for nothing what he gave," but his focus was less on safeguarding what should be given in spiritual exchange against sales than on restoring what should be free and belong to everyone in spiritual life against violent usurpation. The clergy's lucrative sales are based on an original theft, and they are backed by the "great and rude tyranny" of excommunication and the trickery of appearing to be be poor.[29]

Jean Calvin went well beyond the image of the clergy as thieving merchants when he published his *Christianae Religionis Institutio* in 1536 and its French translation a few years later. In that great work and its subsequent enlarged editions, in his sermons, and in his biblical commentary, Calvin denounced reciprocal notions that he found at the core of Catholic theology. The whole Catholic apparatus of gift and obligation he tried to dismantle, recasting reciprocal relations in terms of gratuitousness wherever he could.[30]

Calvin started from the same donation as the Catholic theologians: all our gifts come from God, and the greatest is the gift of Jesus Christ, his natural son.

God's promises are made to humankind out of gratuitous goodness, "bonté gratuite," "bénignité gratuite." He alone has taken the step toward alliance and has
in no sense been obliged by our merits, which, if examined, could never win us
salvation.[31]

What was Calvin to do with all those troubling Bible quotes that refer to eternal life as *loyer* or *merces* (wages or reward) or similar words—statements such as
"The recompense of a man's hands shal God give unto him" (Proverbs 12:14, I
use here the translation published in Geneva in 1560 by English refugees[32]); "He
that feareth the commandement, he shal be rewarded" (Proverbs 13:13); "Rejoyce
and be glad, for great is your rewarde in heaven" (Matthew 5:12); "And everie man
shal receive his wages, according to his labour. For we together are God's laborers"
(1 Corinthians 3:8–9)? Undaunted, Calvin reinterprets them as a free gift the Lord
makes to humans. Words like "loyer" here do not mean we have done works for
which we have won salvation. Rather it refers to a remuneration for the sanctified
life by which God himself conducts the elect, a compensation for the miseries of
the world and the feebleness of the flesh. Lest people still think that "the salary
promised by the Lord must be measured by merits," Calvin cites the simile from
Matthew: the kingdom of heaven is compared to the father of the household, who
sent everyone out to work in the vineyard, but then paid them exactly the same
amount no matter how many hours they had worked. When the laborers protest,
the householder answers "Is it not lawful for me to do as I wil with mine owne . . .
So the last shal be first, and the first last: for manie are called, but fewe chosen."[33]

Calvin concludes, "Let it be decreed in our hearts that the Kindgom of heaven
is not a wage for servants [salaire de serviteurs], but an inheritance of children [héri-
tage d'enfants], enjoyed only by those whom God has adopted for his children."[34]

Calvin's metaphors of "adoption" and "inheritance"—found also in Scripture
and in Catholic theological writing, and of overriding importance in the expression of the Geneva reformer—would have been heard by his readers in the context
of sixteenth-century family experience. Legal adoption was little practiced in early-
modern France outside the circle of urban artisans, who wanted children and for
whom neither land nor "blood" needed protection from outside claims or contami-
nation.[35] Adopted children with full inheritance rights were a rarity. For ordinary
children, inheritance was commonplace, and, as we have seen, it could engender
both gratitude for what children got and anxiety about the possibility of their exclusion. Calvin's God is an absolutely free donor, constrained by no customary law
dictating division of patrimony and unconcerned about "meritorious" children. In
this inheritance, the judgment is final and there are no absolute rights to dowries
or to a legitimate fraction of the inheritance (as existed in both French family laws
and in Genevan law of the Reformed regime[36]), no quarrels are allowable, and
no superior courts exist which will allow an appeal. Yet the "inheritance" metaphor suggests that God's grace and salvation in some sense belong to the adopted
Christian; it sustains hope that the gift will come.

The word "adoption" also helps us understand the meaning of the French term used consistently by Calvin to describe God's connection with humans, both the children of Israel and the faithful Christians: "alliance." "That special alliance by which God adopt[ed] the race of Abraham," "the spiritual alliance that God set up with his Church," and "the gratuitous alliance of his mercy" are among many examples. In his day the word referred not only to a connection established for social or political or economic purposes, but also to an association made for friendship and kinship, as in families creating an alliance through marriage. When Montaigne "adopted" Marie de Gournay as his special literary friend, she became his "fille d'alliance." "Alliance" is a more flexible term than the legalistic "contract" or "convenant" or *pactus,* or even than *foedus,* the term that Calvin himself used in his own Latin. These last three words were used in the movement toward a "covenantal theology," already beginning to stir in the thought of Ulrich Zwingli and Heinrich Bullinger, which would develop in the late sixteenth century among the Puritans and which would moderate much Reformed theology in the mid-seventeenth century. In covenantal theology, though divine grace is supreme, there is a notion of conditions—God promises to do something conditional on a human response—and conditions can then seem to bind in both directions.

Calvin would not admit even the slightest suggestion that God was obliged to anything outside: the Lord's promises and decisions always flowed entirely from himself. In imagining the earliest alliance, Calvin liked Bible quotes that involved a simple and unilateral naming of a relation: "I wil be your God and ye shal be my people," "Je vous seray pour Dieu, et vous me serez pour peuple" (Leviticus 26:12). "This alliance is made gratuitously from the beginning and remains so always."[37]

What do humans do with God's gift of grace? To start with, Calvin makes clear that grace is not a *thing* given us: "grace is not infused in us" the way Catholic theologians teach, "justice is not infused in us." The gift is rather a predisposition, an orientation within Christians as a result of hearing and accepting a divine promise. Humans do not return the gift directly to the Lord: "God can receive no benefit from us."[38] This teaching goes well beyond the consoling advice of the popular proverb, "To father, to master, to God all powerful, no one can return the equivalent." With Calvin, no return is possible, and any effort to make it will lead to the endless obligation of righteousness by works that Luther had decried. What Christians do with God's gifts is obey him, love him, be grateful to him, act always for his honor and glory, and exercise good works toward our neighbors.

The restructuring of the human relation to God emerges strikingly in Calvin's condemnation of the sacrifice of the mass. In the first age of the Israelites, sacrifice was commanded by God. As Calvin says in his commentary on the sacrifices offered by Cain and Abel (Genesis 4:3–4), "God commanded the ancient Fathers to make sacrifice for two reasons: first, so that the exercise of piety would be common to everyone in that they thus professed themselves to belong to God and express gratitude to him for all things; and, second, to warn them that they need some purification before they could be reconciled with God." About Noah's sacrifice of one of every clean beast and fowl after the flood (Genesis 8:20), he remarks

that sacrifices were instituted so humans would get the habit through them of celebrating God's goodness and rendering him thanks. But even then, the real event
of the sacrifice was not the external ceremony, but the inner faith and spiritual in-
vocation. Thus the Lord accepted Abel's sacrifice of cattle and refused the grain
of Cain not because there was anything wrong with the offering, but because he
knew that Abel had faith and Cain did not. Thus the "savor of rest" ("odeur de
repos") smelled by the Lord from Noah's sacrifice (Genesis 8:21) did not appease
him by its smell—"the stinking smoke of entrails and of burned flesh"—but by
Noah's acknowledgment of all he had received from God's mercy.[39]

All this changed with the voluntary and holy sacrifice of Jesus Christ. With his
innocent death, the son of God had redeemed humans once and for all; through
his blood he had reconciled God to humankind. The old animal sacrifices were
clearly superseded, but the new sacrifice of the mass was a scandal. It detracted
from Christ's full redemption; it was a wrongful way to propitiate God, to appease
his wrath, and to try to satisfy him for human sins.

Calvin and his fellow pastors denounced the mass on several grounds and
scoffed at transubstantiation as an impossible doctrine with no support from Scripture.[40] Here we focus only on the implications of that criticism for models of reciprocity. Calvin compared the mass to the Lord's Supper (the Cène), newly instituted in Geneva. In the liturgy of the Lord's Supper only one gift is mentioned,
that given by Christ of his body and blood, really present and spiritually communicated to the Christian with faith, a gift leading him or her toward eternal life. The
sacrament is a witness to the "alliance of grace" between God and fallen man, and
the grateful believers ask the Lord only that the memory of redemption through
Christ be ever imprinted in their hearts. In his commentary on the Lord's Supper,
Calvin inserts some moments of lyrical fusion, reminiscent of the shared union of
the Olivétan Bible. "In this sacrament, we recognize Jesus Christ to be so incor-
porated in us and we also in him, that all that is his we can call ours and all that is
ours we can name his." But this climactic blending is part of a longer movement
in which the sacrament attests to or seals a divine promise, received by the believer
in gratitude.[41]

Calvin makes the contrast between the two liturgies:

In the Cène, our Lord has left the memory of his passion engraved and imprinted. For the
Lord's Supper is a gift of God, which must be taken and received with thanksgiving. On
the contrary, the Sacrifice of the Mass is a payment to God, which he receives from us in
satisfaction. As much as there is a difference between taking and giving, so much is there
a difference between Sacrament and Sacrifice. And certainly it is an unhappy instance of
human ingratitude that where man should recognize the largesse and liberality of divine
goodness with thanksgiving, he wants to make God believe he is obliged to him . . . To
think we could oblige him is a diabolic presumption.[42]

"As much as there is a difference between taking and giving [prendre et donner],
so much is there a difference between Sacrament and Sacrifice." The phrase sug-

gests Calvin's rupture with current notions of gift reciprocity. In his classic study *Le Vocabulaire des institutions indo-européennes* (Vocabulary of Indo-European institutions) of 1969, the French linguist Émile Benveniste showed the profound connection between "taking" and "giving," between "prendre" and "donner" in Indo-European languages. The words are closely allied linguistically, the border between them is fluid, and Benveniste used the English words "to take" and "to take to" as illustration of the connection. Noting the open boundary between other paired opposites that refer to exchange, such as buying and selling, giving and receiving hospitality, Benveniste suggested that the history of language lent weight to Marcel Mauss's model of the gift calling forth a counter-gift.[43]

Calvin's leap here shows how in fact new distinctions can be made in language: overly direct reciprocity—gift/counter-gift—was precisely what he did not want in his core image of human relations with God. But in snipping the age-old tie between "giving" and "taking," he had left himself with a formidable task in recasting human obligation.

He started with the word sacrifice. Unlike Erasmus, who displaced it as secondary to mercy and pity, Calvin held on to the word, but reinterpreted it in a metaphorical way, far removed from any liturgical performance with a sacrificing priest, a consecrated offering, an eating, and a witnessing audience. Human lives are the stuff of sacrifice: praising God is sacrifice; human obedience to the Lord is sacrifice; using one's spiritual gifts to serve others is sacrifice. "In the important sacrifice, we are consecrated in body and soul as holy temples for the Lord . . . We and all our works should be dedicated to him so that everything in us can serve his glory and exalt his magnificence." As for the command of Deuteronomy 16:16–17 that no one appear before the Lord empty-handed but "each give as he is able, according to the blessing of the Lord," Christians fulfilled it by giving alms to the poor, "a token of their gratitude" to God.[44]

The gift flow thus is downward from the Lord and outward from us. Can we visualize it in part as a child receiving an inheritance in gratitude and then passing it on to his or her own children? (The Protestant noblewoman Charlotte d'Arbaleste wrote of it this way as she addressed her memoirs to the son she and Philippe du Plessis de Mornay had brought into the world. Her son had drunk in the fear of God with his mother's milk. "It is no small blessing to be born of Christian parents, who precede us in the fear of God and through whose persons we have, so to speak, received the 'arrhes' of his mercy, which lasts for a thousand generations."[45]) In contrast with the Three Graces or Mauss's image of the spirit of the gift carrying with it an element that wants to circle back finally to the donor, we have here a spirit of the gift that wants to move through time, through history, never reversing its direction.

What then of reciprocity in gift relations among people living at the same time? Calvin did recommend some reciprocity here, but of a general and diffuse kind, rather than organized in specific and concentrated clusters. In the Lord's Supper, the common spiritual banquet, "we oblige ourselves to each other mutually . . .

to all the offices of charity." If there is this special tie among Christians, still all humans share a nature "formed in the image of God" and "we must embrace in a feeling of charity all men generally, without excepting any one, without distinguishing between Greek and Barbarian." [46]

Turning in more detail to gift relations, Calvin swept away most of the Catholic special systems. No more exchange between the living and the dead, as Purgatory disappears. No more systemic exchange between laity and clergy; all believing Christians are priests and now pastors are paid regular salaries. No more confraternities circulating gifts among the brothers and the sisters; Christians have no particular fellowship other than their parish. Fewer things can serve as gifts, as candles lose their religious role, and fewer holy days exist that might occasion special gift exchange. The relations of charity are all-important, and here Calvin (following an age-old tradition) does allow the Christian to favor one group first, to help its members more "familiarly": "les proches," those near to us, that is, those closest to us in kinship, friendship, and neighborhood. They are seen more often, and it is not an offense to God to serve them more.[47]

Beyond this, Calvin offered three great rules, all of them to do with giving and none with taking. First, we act charitably toward all human beings "without looking to see if they are worthy or unworthy," without considering whether they merit our help our not. If we looked at them too closely, we might "often be more inclined to hate them than love them." Remember what would happen to us if God looked at us closely and asked what we deserved. Rather we see in others the image of God, and then serve and love them even if they have done nothing to deserve it.

Second, act charitably with a joyous face and kind words and do not try "to subjugate a person to whom you have done a benefit by making him obliged to you." Calvin used an interesting and not wholly conventional body metaphor here to strengthen his point: "when one part of the body is being restored or renewed by the other parts, we do not insult it by insisting that it be especially obliged to work for the other parts because they are currently working for it."

Third, we are not discharged from our duty when we have helped one person. We are in debt to those near us for all we can provide. Our gifts stop only when our faculties fail.[48]

In short, Calvin's theology refused to conceive of human solidarity in terms of any measured reciprocity. His model was the opposite of the situation where "one barber shaves another." He talks only of the obligation to give to the limit of one's faculties and without regard to the inevitably disappointing merits of others.

The rules for taking from one's fellow humans are much less fully developed in Calvin's thought. He considers gift-reception incidentally to a larger theological point: "if someone given usufruct of a field tried to usurp title to it as his own property, wouldn't he deserve by such ingratitude to lose possession of the field?" One should receive gifts in thankfulness, acknowledge one's benefactor with praise, and not abuse the gift or misrepresent its origin.[49] Any other action inspired by a gift he does not discuss. All Christians have a mutual obligation to each other in Calvin's theological vision, but he does not build into it a patterned structure, a rhythm of giving and receiving. Humans are left free and uncharted with their gifts.

The shaping effect of this theology on language and practice in the Reformed city of Geneva, and its partial realization over the decades in ecclesiastical, welfare, and political institutions we can consider only briefly. Genevan law put stringent limitations on gifts and festivities at the time of childbirth, baptism, engagement, and marriage, much stronger than the sumptuary legislation on banquets in Catholic France. This legislation, backed up by inquiries from the Consistory, was in part inspired by hope for seemly comportment in a godly city, but it was also an effort to transform the relations accompanying gift exchange. Women were forbidden to bring the usual sweets when they came to see a new mother and visiting days were curtailed; at the baptism, the amount spent on gifts exchanged between godparents and parents was fixed, and by the mid-seventeenth century any such presents were prohibited. For a time after 1581, engagement feasts were entirely banned; the government relented in the seventeenth century as long as there were no more than ten people and the gifts were not bejeweled. Wedding feasts were especially contained, and bride and groom were ordered to make no gifts to anyone but each other—and then with presents that were not excessive.[50]

Town elections in Geneva in the early sixteenth century were always occasions for what was called "brigue," intrigue hatched at banquets given by the candidates, where gifts were distributed and promises made of appointment to office after election. The issue came up sharply between 1538 and 1540 and again in the mid–1550s, when candidates elected to the Council through "banquets, gifts, and subornation" (to quote a contemporary) voted against Calvinist-style Protestant policies. All such practices were forbidden—indeed, any banquet not devoted to strictly family matters was prohibited for six weeks before elections—and Genevan electoral politics changed somewhat in tone after 1555 from populist excitement to sober sermonizing and controlled voting assemblies. In case any councilman or judge was tempted to accept gifts, in 1604 a painting of the judges of ancient Thebes, with their hands cut off, was added to the very walls of the council chamber.[51]

Meanwhile the welfare system in Geneva expanded impressively in the course of the sixteenth century. Deacons were established as officers with the holy duty of tending to the poor. Care of orphans and other indigent persons, bread doles for poor householders, and other activities were centralized in a new Hôpital Général, set up by local Protestants before Calvin's arrival in 1535 and supported by him subsequently. Special relief funds were established for the influx of refugees from France and Italy. The residents of the Reformed city, both old natives and recent arrivals, responded to these institutions with substantial bequests. Calvin himself chided wealthy givers if they tried to dominate poor recipients. The new Calvinist ethos tried to push against particularistic forms of gift reciprocity—where the possibility of immediate obligation was great—to encourage instead more general forms moving through the whole community.[52]

Calvin's gratuitous vision had only partial impact on the practices of everyday life in Geneva—what vision ever does sweep the field?—and the repeated prohibition of "brigues" in the seventeenth century indicates that gifts and banquets had revived in politics. Still, we may wonder whether the cutting back on certain forms of patronage and on informal neighborhood gifting did not leave the field open, on the one hand, for the intensification of obligation within the internal realm of the immediate family and, on the other, for the expansion of the less ambiguous and more detached networks of legal contract.

A decade after Calvin published the first edition of his *Institutes,* a physician, ex-Franciscan, father of three children born out of wedlock, and recipient of benefits from more than one enlightened bishop published in Lyon *Le Tiers Livre* (The third book) of his great ongoing novel. In it François Rabelais provides us with a fourth model of human recipricity in the form of a debate betwen Panurge and Pantagruel. Panurge had come into Pantagruel's life disheveled and penniless after adventures as a captive among the Turks. Pantagruel, still in his student days in Paris, had taken a liking to Panurge from the start and after hearing Panurge state his situation in many languages, the prince had asked him to stay in his company: they would become "a new couple in friendship." Panurge is a trickster figure, an incarnation of Mercury, master of eloquence, god of merchants, and god of thieves. He puts his talents to use in the opening of the Third Book as he responds to Pantagruel, now grown beyond the brave antics of his early days to a good and wise prince.[53]

After conquering the kingdom of Dipsodie, Pantagruel settles some of his loyal Utopian subjects among the Dipsodians and treats them all well, establishing once again (as in the conduct of Grandgousier toward the conquered Canarrians) that a conquered land is won over by "good laws, gracious gifts and benefits" and not by tyranny and pillage. He then gives a section of Dipsodie—the chatelainy of Salmiguondin—to Panurge to rule. Whereupon Panurge spends three years' worth of revenue in two weeks full of merry banquets and joyous feasts open to any lass or lad who comes by, and in other recognizably improvident activities, such as cutting down trees and buying dear and selling cheap. Pantagruel gently chides him and remarks that if he keeps on this way, he will never get rich.[54]

"Rich!" exclaims Panurge. His goal is not wealth, but living joyously. He shows how virtuous his behavior has been: a source of distributive justice in feeding hungry young people and of commutative justice in buying dear, and useful in cutting down dark forests, which are just a hideout for murderers, counterfeiters, and other troublemakers.

"But when will you be out of debt?" asks Pantagruel.

"At the Greek Calends," replies Panurge—meaning "Never," for there were no Greek Calends and the phrase had been used in ancient times to describe people who would never pay their debts. As a further "never," he adds the solipsistic and impossible image that he will be out of debt "when you are your own heir." He then launches into a comic encomium of lending and borrowing as a set of relations that keeps the whole world together in peace and harmony. Debtors and lenders depend on each other and wish each other long life so they can get what they need or are owed. The planets, sun, and earth would fly apart if they did not lend to each other. Human beings would not run to help each other in case of fire or flood, for they would have no interest in keeping each other alive. And within the human body, what a racket (*quel tintamarre*), would go on without these relations. The head would not lend sight to the eyes to guide the feet and hands. The feet would not deign to carry the body. The heart would get irritated with working, and the lungs would neither send it air, nor the liver send it blood. (Recall Timon of Athens talking in his bitter solitude of the sun as a thief, while Calvin imagined the strong body parts as helping the weaker without requiring return.) With nothing borrowed or loaned, says Panurge, the body would perish.

But what harmony when each person lends and each person owes. No war, no usury (all loans in Panurge's panegyric are without interest), no litigation, charity will reign. "Among humankind, Peace, Love, Delight, Faithfulness, tranquility, banquets, feasts, joy, jubilation; gold, silver, petty cash, chains, rings, and merchandise will skip from hand to hand." In each part of the body, the blood will do its work, and the other members will provide what they must "in gratitude" ("en reconnaissance"). Husbands and wives will pay the marriage debt to each other and perpetuate the human race.

Panurge has mostly used the language of interest-free loans, or "friendly loans" as they were called, rather than of gift and return-gift, but he has set up the argument so that the principle of reciprocity over time applies to both registers. His narrative is about sustaining mutual indebtedness, not about ending it; similarly in gift relations, gratitude and obligation are supposed to keep objects and services moving. He even mixes in the words "gratitude" and "charity."

Pantagruel listens patiently to Panurge, but then says, "Preach from now to Pentecost . . . but you won't persuade me by your fine speech to have debts. The Holy Apostle says, 'Owe nothing to anyone but love and mutual affection.' " With this quotation from Paul (Romans 13:8), Pantagruel deflates Panurge's extravagant metaphor of reciprocity and goes on to describe the day-to-day realities of literal loans. Lenders are disliked and feared. Debts and lies usually go together. Loans have to be made from time to time, to be sure, but should be made sparingly, when someone who has worked as best he or she could has nonetheless fallen on hard times.[55]

Some commentators on this exchange today see Rabelais as giving all the sound arguments to Pantagruel. Panurge is a fast talker who jumbles together different neo-Platonic ideas, misapplies examples, and generally makes a fool of himself in a self-interested effort to justify his irresponsible spending.[56] But Panurge's daring use of a single metaphor to find a universal principle of human solidarity—François Rigolot has called it a "universal syntax"[57]—has something compelling about it.

Throughout his novel, Rabelais allows his clever trickster Panurge to lie, to boast, to be a coward and vindictive; yet sometimes he has insight into the true state of things, or his behavior reveals something profound about the human predicament. There is surely some self-knowledge in Panurge's description, following fast on the encomium to borrowing-and-lending, of why he wants to marry and what he fears from marriage. Panurge is not just a foil for Pantagruel, then, but a necessary companion and friend.

Rabelais has created in *Le Tiers Livre* an ongoing debate between two views of reciprocity, between what I am calling here, in a somewhat "ideal-type" analysis, a "Catholic" view and a "Reformed" view. Panurge is right in seeing exchange and reciprocity—giving and taking, borrowing and lending—as central to human solidarity. That kind of reassuring structural exchange was going on in Rabelais's world all the time, some of it a source of amity and order, as we have seen. But Panurge's view also has its limitations. Loans and obligations lead not only to lies, but to disruptive quarrels and worse. The system of reciprocity that Panurge has described is narrow: one individual to another, one part to another, the debts known though not perhaps the time of repayment, but still without the ambiguities, uncertainties, and indirections that keep gift systems from turning into bribes or oppression.

Thus Pantagruel clears the air and clears the accounts with his Pauline: "we owe nothing to anyone but love and mutual affection." In fact, he promises to pay all of Panurge's back debts for him. But between the sweep of Pantagruel's broad gratuitous principle and the few precise situations where charitable loans are prescribed is a vast space of relationship that must be filled with choices and with rituals and patterns of giving and taking.

Panurge is not satisfied with Pantagruel's answer and not even with the cancellation of all his debts. He begins to thank Pantagruel in the exaggerated language of gratitude and obligation—"You do me benefits more than belong to me, more than I deserve, more than my merits justify"—but he says he is troubled by being free of debts. It will leave him isolated and unwanted (indeed, one of the reasons he wants to marry is to live with creditors and a companion both[58]). When people fart in Salmiguondin, they say, "That's for those who are quits." He is sure he would not survive long without lending and borrowing, giving and taking. Pantagruel insists that they change the subject, but it is not certain that he has won the argument.

"Catholic" reciprocity, "Reformed" gratuitousness. The comic teaching of Rabelais is a double one: we tack between the pole of obligation and the pole of the gratuitous. This teaching evokes gifts of speech always in play, a debate among friends, an argument that can enrich those to whom it is given while impoverishing not at all their giver.

Conclusion

ifts have come in many guises in the pages of this book, and I have sought to show their inner spirit, the relations they engendered, and their outward forms in sixteenth-century France. Gifts marked the times of year and of the life cycle; they sustained connections among friends, neighbors, kin, and coworkers at all levels of society; they softened oppressive relations across lines of class and status. They brought added confidence and trust to trade arrangements, and were everywhere present to ease the way in social advancement and political transaction. Giving goods and services always drew on manners, from the humility of the alms recipient to the polite praise of the dedicator and the graceful phrases of the bestower of a jewel. The gift mode brought courtesy.

It also brought quarrels, jealousy, and the burden of obligation. Gift paths and circuits could be narrow and exclusive. The gift register is inevitably a contentious one, so this book has argued. In societies like sixteenth-century France ("early-modern," "Old Regime" societies), gift-trouble comes not so much from the impact of money, markets, and sales as from arguments about power and reciprocity in families, royal politics, and religion.

Religion was a privileged realm for experiencing and defining both the gracious and the grievous features of the gift mode. Thus my narrative opened and closed with God's gifts. The Protestant Reformation was not "caused" by conflict in family and political life, nor was it a "reflection" of the same. Rather, similar patterns of giving and receiving and of thinking about obligations and reciprocity were at work in all three arenas, and their interplay strengthened the pressures of obligation as a cultural mood. Some people and groups thrived in the crisscross of reciprocity, some did not. But the issues it raised nourished long-term political reflection about the obligations of kings and the claims of subjects, and prompted both Catholic reform and Protestant innovation.

Several gift-trails were not followed in this study. The role of gift systems in the world of artists and natural philosophers, described so well in Italy by Alexander Nagel and Paula Findlen, was not examined.[1] Evidence for France would surely complement in important ways my discussion of gifts and fees to purveyors of knowledge, the professors of theology and medicine, and the healers.

Gender and gift obligation, too, could be considered further, especially in regard to the symbols, supplications, and doctrines of religion. As we have seen, women were active givers and recipients of presents of all kinds, reveling in certain kinds of gift performance (such as bequeathing their intimate clothing to servants, friends, and kin) and developing less fully other forms of exchange (such as the gifts of political patronage)—but still sharing with men much of the gift terrain and the quarrels about family gifts. The difference between men and women lay especially in their response to the gratitude-obligation sequence. For those men who chafed at the humiliations of begging favor and at the dissimulation and extravagant language of request and thanks, and whose conscience felt "throttled" (to use Montaigne's word) by the seemingly limitless requirements of gratitude, the gift register threatened their autonomy and dignity. The circle of literary women whom we could follow used gift etiquette when they needed to and did not appear troubled by the demands of reciprocity, particularly with other women. Their complaint was about unceasing external demands for obedience, which made gratitude lose its spark and broke the chain of reciprocity.

What kind of model for religious reciprocity would a sixteenth-century French woman generate? And would she have had a distinctive view regarding the sacrifice of the mass and the Lord's Supper? Religious publications from Catholic and Protestant women in sixteenth-century France do not address theological doctrine and liturgy directly. Rather they take the path of spirituality, as in the manuscript *Voyage spirituel* of Gabrielle de Bourbon, or of ardent personal prayer, as in Marguerite de Navarre's *Miroir de lame pecheresse* (1531), or of moral teaching, as in the emblem book, *Emblemes, ou devises chrestiennes* (1571), written by the Protestant Georgette de Montenay. One may note, however, that the great Catholic female religious figures—Teresa of Ávila in the sixteenth century, Marie de l'Incarnation in the seventeenth century—sought fusion through mystical union with the Lord and/or through frequent communion. In their behavior, obedience to God and their convent superiors was not passive, but an exercise in spiritual heroism that won admiration. Here obedience enhanced rather than disturbed gratitude.[2] The evangelical poetry of Marguerite de Navarre also had a mystical strain: "Faith that we must have to be worthy of the gift from on high, Faith, which unites by ardent Charity his humble servant to her Maker."[3]

On the Protestant side, Katharina Schütz Zell (ca. 1498–1562), recently studied by Elsie McKee, was writing theology in Lutheran Strasbourg. Zell's meditation on the Lord's Supper moves rather quickly from a prayer that Christ "may abide in us and we may abide in him and not die" to the charitable actions nourished by the "bread and . . . cup of thanksgiving": "as Christ there gave himself for us and set his soul to death for us, so also we may offer ourselves for all people and brothers." McKee stresses the centrality of ethical action in Zell's thought: the command to love the neighbor was as important as the cardinal doctrines of Protestant faith, more important than in the thought of contemporary male clerics except her own husband. Similarly, in her Christian emblems, Georgette de Montenay condemns Catholic idolatry by picturing a nun kneeling with money bags before the statue of a golden calf—"idolatry is avarice"—and insists in her emblem on Charity (fig. 23), "Who says, 'I have faith,' without charity, boasts falsely that he is a Christian." Montenay omits entirely the characteristic emblem-book representation of the loyal, prudent, silent wife, and instead shows Christian men and women helping each other up the mountain of Christian learning.[4]

Both Catholic and Protestant women writers disobey the cardinal command to be silent. The Catholic women get around the tight bonds of reciprocal obligation by spiritual fusion. The Protestant women relieve the uncertainties of utter gratuitousness by their strong stress on love of the neighbor. These women's texts surely have much more to yield on the theory, symbolic meaning, and practice of gifts.

The gift modes in non-Christian societies would also warrant further study, both to compare systems and to explore French relations across cultural divides. The exchange of ambassadorial gifts between the French king and the Ottoman sultan has been briefly mentioned, but beyond this, Ottoman objects and manuscripts were sought in the west as signs of beauty, curiosity, and wished-for domination. Did they get there by gifts, purchase, or seizure? French travelers to the lands of the Grand Porte, such as Pierre Belon, Guillaume Postel, and Nicolas de Nicolay, included some description of gift forms: the presents at a boy's circumcision, the gift flow at weddings, the types of charitable donation, from street alms for water carriers to gifts made to large hospitals and hostels. Here the French were willing to grant the Turks some praise—"it is impressive to see what their charity looks like," commented Postel—though they were far from understanding, and probably even experiencing, the workings of hospitality in Islamic societies. Trade relations between Christians and Muslims were extensive, but gift relations may have seemed fraught with danger.[5]

Jewish gift systems and views of reciprocity are yet another case. Inside Jewish communities, intense gifting went on: holiday gifts at Hannukah and Purim; major and widely discussed exchanges at the time of marriage (more important than at the time of death); lavish gifts to rabbis; and charitable gifts, from inviting poor Jews and scholars to Sabbath dinner table to presenting candles and Torah covers to the synagogue to funding dowries and hospital care. As with the Christians, Jewish gifts brought quarrels (including quarrels about rabbis who refused to accept gifts), and rabbis drew upon extensive Talmudic commentary on presents and reci-

En contemplant ceste femme, voyez
Que charité est vne œuure excellente.
Qui dit, J'ay foy, sans charité, croyez
Que faussement d'estre Chrestien se vante.
Charité (dy-ie) de foy viue naissante:
Non celle-la d'vn Turc, ou infidele.
Car c'est peché, quoy qu'elle soit duisante,
A tout Chrestien qui n'attent salut d'elle.

Cest

Figure 23. A Protestant woman's view of the link between faith and charity, from Georgette de Montenay, *Emblemes, ou devises chrestiennes,* 1571

procity to arbitrate them. Much of Jewish gift activity was unknown to Christian observers, though Jews had a general reputation of generosity toward their own (as contrasted with usury toward the stranger). Contemporary Jewish thought on obligation and the gratuitous, written in Hebrew in rabbinical responsa (opinions on cases of religious law) and treatises, was also hidden away from Christian scholars, who tended to dismiss Jewish reflection out of hand as "legalistic."

Within France itself in the sixteenth century, Jews lived ordinarily as Marranos; exchange between Christians and openly practicing Jews at that date took place in the papal enclave around Avignon, in nearby Alsace, or in towns in Italy and Germany. There were certainly sales between Jews and Christians in Avignon, but gift bestowal seems to have been limited to only a few occasions, as in the offering of a present by the Jewish community to local officials. By old custom in many parts of Europe, the *shtadlan,* the Jewish officer entrusted with representing the Jews to the outside world, presented such a gift to Christian authorities to ensure continued protection and prevent harm to Jews. The Court Jews, who became so important in central Europe in the seventeenth century as lenders and military suppliers to princes and emperor, also donated objects to royal art collections. Already in 1600, Mordecai Meisel, financier of Emperor Rudolf II, presented the emperor on behalf of the Jewish community of Prague an amulet of gold and precious stones, on which was engraved the Temple candelabrum—a symbol of importance to both Jews and Christians—encircled with a Hebrew prayer for Rudolf. The Jewish bankers of Metz in the seventeenth century, who were also suppliers to Louis XIV's army, may have made such gifts to the Sun King.[6]

Sometimes rulers and magistrates responded to gifts from Jews with the required protection. But Christian authorities may have been reluctant to feel gratitude toward Jews and thereby engender obligation toward them, just as sixteenth-century French travelers were reluctant to do toward the Amerindians.

I have described the deceptiveness in the "little gifts" of the French to the Indians as another version of the coercive behavior troubling the gift register back home. It was more allowable along the Saint Lawrence and the Amazon because it was "savages" who were being tricked. Did it perhaps have long-range consequence for the conduct of sales back in France, eroding the moral economy and habituating people to the possibility of greater distance between seller and buyer?

Gift-systems have contracted and expanded over the centuries since Montaigne and Marie de Gournay exchanged and passed on their gifts of learning, and the "spirit" of the Western gift register—the critical role of gratitude—has been redefined as well. Important elements in this shift, such as changing notions and practices in regard to property, contract, and purchasing,[7] I cannot linger on here. But like Marcel Mauss so many decades ago, I can conclude with some moral concerns that connect this book with other gift studies of my own day.

Economic market theory has seemed insufficient as a description of human motivation and conduct in exchanging goods and services, as a picture of how systems actually regulate themselves, and as a prescription for public policy. (The theory generated by command or coercive economies has done no better, ignoring or misinterpreting the extensive presence of gifts in exchange, the significance of informal markets and sales, and the role of voluntary organization.) In recent years Amartya Sen has shown with compelling clarity that the "maximalization of utility" and self-interest theory are inadequate grounds on which to base economics, and welfare economics in particular.[8] But already in 1944, Karl Polanyi's *Great Transformation* was composed "to dislodge the notion—so widely and implicitly held—that markets are the ubiquitous and invariable form of economic organization [and] that any economy can be *translated* into market terms." Polanyi insisted that there was more than one way to conceptualize the modes by which people exchange goods and services with each other. He called them "patterns of integration": reciprocity, redistribution, and market exchange.

Once the market blinders are removed, a move like Polanyi's is likely. Economist Kenneth Boulding made it in the years between 1947 and 1968, with his concept of three kinds of "social organizers," "the threat system, the exchange system, and the integrative system," with markets and bargaining being part of exchange, and gifts and grants part of integration. In 1968 anthropologist Marshall Sahlins portrayed a "spectrum" of reciprocity, as we have seen, whose poles are negative and generalized and whose midpoint is balanced reciprocity. My historical and social perspectives led me to the three modes or registers used in this book—gift, sale, and coercion—forms of human relation, each with their own conventions, which can be put into play in many different situations and can interact and overlap.[9] All of these approaches are in contrast with that enunciated several years ago by Jacques Derrida, who makes an absolute distinction between the exchange and calculation of "economy" and the pure gratuitousness required of all gifts, which renders gifts "impossible."[10]

One consequence of neglecting the "gift mode" is that we may not notice how frequently it appears in the world around us, beyond the recognized but limited categories of philanthropic contribution and anniversary or holiday gifts. It is easier to be attentive to gift behavior in the sixteenth century, when people talked about it so much, from learned treatise and sermon to popular proverb and gossip. In our own time, not only is the voluntary or nonprofit "sector" significant,[11] but also, as Kenneth Boulding pointed out, many transactions in national and international economies are "grants," where a would-be recipient seeks funds and perhaps is "awarded" them, with various conditions of performance ("service" in the old days) expected. Eventually, the recipient acknowledges this aid with thanks. The seeking of scholarships and fellowships—from application and letters of recommendation to reception and expression of gratitude—is a gift performance par excellence. On the whole, we have thought rather little about the "gratitude" and fruitful action expected to be produced by gifts, in contrast to the sixteenth century, where these were, if anything, overanalyzed and fretted about. Perhaps "gratitude" has something to add to our cooler and preferred term "responsibility."

Conceiving the gift as a limited and/or occasional category also may lead us to underestimate the potentiality both for trouble and for renewal from gifts. I have suggested that the gift mode always brings with it the possibility for conflict and ingratitude, and that certain historical circumstances add to this instability.[12] Gifts went wrong in the sixteenth century, but at least people spent much time arguing about what might constitute a good gift and what a bad. Jean Starobinski, in a beautiful study, has shown a similar debate in the eighteenth century between those indulging in sumptuous spectacular liberality and those favoring rational careful donation for the purposes of distributive justice.[13]

Today, too, gifts sometimes have bad or mixed consequences, and such a situation can be reacted to by gift supporters rather than simply used by critics as ammunition against gift alliance. "Subjugation" and "corruption" through gift relations are still part of our twentieth-century scene, albeit in a world with different assumptions about hierarchy in family and society and the legitimation for government. Back around 1949 or 1950, the French writer-philosopher Georges Bataille reflected on the "gifts" of the Marshall Plan in a way that rarely appeared in print at the time (and his thoughts were not themselves published till years later). In a theory of a "general economy" inspired by the reading of Mauss's *Essai sur le don,* Bataille asked whether "being [perhaps] 'in the world's interest' at the outset, [the Marshall Plan] will be warped in the direction of the American interest." He concluded that Cold War resistance by the Soviet Union and other "working class agitation" would have positive effects for the contribution of the Marshall Plan to the standard of living in Europe: they enhanced the need for American intervention but at the same time "reduced the risk that the intervention might turn into a conquest."[14] Bataille's frank weighing of pros and cons strengthens rather than weakens the gift register.

We daily read charges of political corruption going on in both newly established governments and those of long standing. Contemporary theorists usually interpret "corruption" as a product of modern states, with their bureaucratic and rational organization, whose codes are violated by persons lacking integrity or by persons accustomed to societies where gifts are simply accepted in political life. But, as we have seen, "corruption" was already an issue for sixteenth- and seventeenth-century France (with medieval antecedents), as well as for seventeenth-century England and Florence: in all these places corrupting presents were legislated against even while the gift flow was preserved as a necessary part of courteous and decorous political life. Arguing about good gifts and bad gifts today might be a helpful addition to a discourse constructed around public interest and private interest. Indeed, legal scholar John Noonan has suggested ways to identify and evaluate bribery based on two thousand years of ethical debate.[15]

A revived hope for "the possibility of altruism" has also called attention to the gratuitous end of the gift register, and even led to a collection of essays by economists entitled *Altruism, Morality, and Economic Theory*. A trigger to this reflection was Richard Titmuss's book of 1972, *The Gift Relationship: From Human Blood to Social Policy*. Titmuss compared two systems of acquiring blood for transfusions: the commercial system in the United States, where blood was bought, and the voluntary system in Great Britain, where blood was donated. Great Britain had a relatively low rate of contaminated blood (hepatitis was the contaminant at that pre-AIDS date), rather little wastage of blood, and a low cost to the patient; the United States had a relatively high rate of contaminated blood and wastage in a costly system.

Reacting to this book, the distinguished economist Kenneth Arrow acknowledged the existence of "a large class of unilateral transactions," of which the donation of blood, philanthrophy, and certain government expenditures were examples. Arrow still had much confidence in commercial markets, but added that the social irresponsibility of the seller (as in, a blood-seller being untruthful about whether he or she had hepatatis) might well promote economic inefficiency. He went on:

Like many economists, I do not want to rely too heavily on substituting ethics for self-interest. I think it best on the whole that the requirement of ethical behavior be confined to those circumstances where the price system breaks down . . . Wholesale usage of ethical standards is apt to have undesirable consequences. We do not wish to use up recklessly the scarce resources of altruistic motivation . . . .[16]

The Gift in Sixteenth-Century France has taken a different approach in several ways. First, gift-giving was supposed to be a gracious, courteous, or friendly transaction, in which the obligation for return was not made explicit and gratitude was expected, but it was not necessarily or always an ethical register. For that matter, buying and selling were not just experienced as totally self-interested exchange either, partly because gifts were often associated with commercial transactions. Gifts were sometimes calculating, as we have seen, and practical folk wisdom assured the donor that the return would in fact come. The habit of mutual reciprocity could reinforce peaceableness in a community, though on occasion gifts promoted competition and quarrels. But sometimes presents were made with the gratuitous spirit for which the Lord was the supreme model, that is, with a free generosity and with little or no thought of return to the giver. And the flame of gratitude could keep such a spirit moving. The gratuitous or "altruistic" gift (to use a word invented in France in the nineteenth century and then passing to England) had its greatest force when coupled with innovation. The French Protestant Bible of 1535 was born out of that fertile energy.

The translator Olivétan presented this book as the most felicitous of gifts, made only to be given and yet never exhaustible. Here is a sense of plenitude very unlike Arrow's sober observation that gratuitousness is scarce, and indeed unlike Derrida's claim that the true gift and gratuitousness are impossible. In a spirit like Olivétan's, Rabelais invited readers to come to the wine barrel of *Le Tiers Livre:* no matter how much they drank, he would always refill it. His cask was inexhaustible, a perpetual spring, a true cornucopia. Christine de Pizan figured Plenty through the gifts of Ceres and the charity of a woman who breast-fed her starving mother in a Roman prison. Pizan envisioned some bounds to Plenty (she had been an actual mother, after all), but Ceres was to be thanked for teaching men and women how to cultivate the land so their numbers could multiply and the Roman daughter was depicted living out a cycle of replenishment, "giving back to her mother in her old age what she had taken from her mother as an infant."[17]

Today, too, we can see this yearning for plenitude, this intuition of abundant generosity available in the world and in our own selves as givers and receivers. It fueled Georges Bataille's pursuit of the laws of general economy, as he described all nature and life as growing in exuberant excess, which finally must be expended "in gift-giving, in squandering without reciprocation." It has fueled Lewis Hyde's study of gift exchange as "an 'erotic' commerce," creating involvement and union, and the reflection of Eudora Welty and Ronald Sharp on friendship as a "magnet," attracting people and texts one to the other. The intuition of perfect fullness is fleeting, however. Rabelais concluded about his never-dry wine cask that "good hope lies at the bottom, as in Pandora's box," thus showing the bad comes with the good. And Bataille recognized how close war was to gift-giving as an outlet for excess.[18] Still, the dream returns of a world restored, replenished, even expanded in generosity, to which we aspire even as we bury our dead and welcome the newborn to the banquet of life.

NOTES
ILLUSTRATION CREDITS
ACKNOWLEDGMENTS
INDEX

Notes

ABBREVIATIONS

AChL	Archives de la Charité de Lyon
ADA	Archives départementales de l'Ariège
ADHG	Archives départementales de la Haute-Garonne
ADIV	Archives départementales de l'Ille-et-Vilaine
ADM	Archives départementales de la Manche
ADPA	Archives départementales des Pyrénées-Atlantiques
ADPC	Archives départementales du Pas-de-Calais
ADR	Archives départementales du Rhône
ADSM	Archives départementales de la Seine-Maritime
AEG	Archives d'État de Genève
AHDL	Archives de l'Hôtel-Dieu de Lyon
AML	Archives municipales de Lyon
AN	Archives nationales
BML	Bibliothèque municipale de Lyon
BN	Bibliothèque nationale de France

INTRODUCTION

1. François Rabelais, *Gargantua*, chap. 50 in *Oeuvres complètes,* ed. Mireille Huchon (Paris: Gallimard, 1994), 132–34. Daniel Ménager, "La politique du don dans les derniers chapitres du *Gargantua*," *Journal of Medieval and Renaissance Studies* 8 (1978): 179–91.

2. Marcel Mauss, "Essai sur le Don. Forme et Raison de l'Échange dans les Sociétés archaïques," *L'Année sociologique,* n.s., 1 (1923–24): 30–186; reprinted in Marcel Mauss, *Sociologie et Anthropologie,* 2d ed., introduction by Claude Lévi-Strauss (Paris: Presses Universitaires de France, 1980), 145–279. The English translation done by Ian Cunnison in 1969 has been superseded by Marcel Mauss, *The Gift: The Form and Reason for Exchange in Archaic Societies,* trans. W. D. Halls, foreword by Mary Douglas (New York and London: W. W. Norton, 1990). For my quotations, I give the pages both in *L'Année sociologique* and in the Halls translation, which on the whole I am following. Mauss, "Don," 32–33; *Gift,* 3.

3. Mauss, "Don," 45–58, 71, 126–39; *Gift*, 11–17, 23–24, 46–53. At one point, Mauss goes beyond functionalism to describe the gift economy as "incompatible" with modern commercial and production markets: "it was too dependent on chance, was overexpensive and too sumptuous, burdened with consideration for people, incompatible with the development of the market, commerce, and production, and, all in all, at that time was anti-economic" ("Don," 140; *Gift*, 54). Given Mauss's deeper beliefs about gifts, this statement must be infused with irony.

4. Mauss, "Don," 40, 160–67; *Gift*, 7, 65–70. On Mauss's political and social thought in the 1920s, see the excellent biography of Marcel Fournier, *Marcel Mauss* (Paris: Fayard, 1994), 399–461, and Marcel Mauss, *Écrits politiques,* ed. Marcel Fournier (Paris: Fayard, 1997). Among many recent readings of Mauss's work, see Maurice Godelier, *L'énigme du don* (Paris: Fayard, 1996), part I, "Le legs de Mauss," and Wendy James and N. J. Allen, eds., *Marcel Mauss: A Centenary Tribute* (New York and Oxford: Berghahn Books, 1998).

5. Marshall Sahlins, *Stone Age Economics* (Chicago: Aldine Publishing Company, 1972), especially chap. 4, "The Spirit of the Gift," initially published in 1968–69, and chap. 5, "On the Sociology of Primitive Exchange," initially published in 1965.

6. Annette B. Weiner, *Women of Value, Men of Renown: New Perspectives in Trobriand Exchange* (Austin: University of Texas Press, 1976), chaps. 9–10. In a later work on Pacific communities, Weiner focused on possessions that are "inalienable," that is, are kept within families, are never exchanged, and are the source of social distinction and power (*Inalienable Possessions: The Paradox of Keeping-While-Giving* [Berkeley and Los Angeles: University of California Press, 1992]). Of course, to sustain and reproduce that power, these possessions must ultimately be given to heirs of the next generation. Weiner argues that with their stress on reciprocity and exchange, anthropologists have neglected inalienable possessions. Historians, on the contrary, are familiar with inalienable possessions and have been more likely to neglect exchange. The relations between husbands and wives, the construction of power, and gifting are among the many themes in Marilyn Strathern, *The Gender of the Gift: Problems with Women and Problems with Society in Melanesia* (Berkeley: University of California Press, 1988). Strathern points out that objects do not automatically carry their gender with them; they become "male" or "female" depending on "how they are transacted and to what ends" (xi).

7. Claude Lévi-Strauss, *The Elementary Structures of Kinship,* trans. James Harle Bell, John Richard von Sturmer, and Rodney Needham (Boston: Beacon Press, 1969), chap. 2, especially pp. 55–63. Maurice Godelier follows the evolutionary view to some extent in *L'énigme du don,* at least in regard to western societies: "the gift exists, but is freed from all responsibility to produce and reproduce fundamental social relations. The gift has become . . . the expression and instrument of personal relations situated beyond the market and the state." He suggests, however, that with the demise of the communist dream, there has been a "return of the gift" in a call for western capitalist states to give generously so as to solve social problems (291–95).

8. C. A. Gregory, *Gifts and Commodities* (London: Academic Press, 1982). Nicholas Thomas, *Entangled Objects: Exchange, Material Culture, and Colonialism in the Pacific* (Cambridge, Mass.: Harvard University Press, 1991), quotation on p. 205. The Kwakiutl potlatch is another example of a gift form that expanded after contact with Europeans and the introduction of European commodities. Not only did Hudson's Bay Company products, like blankets, and other European trade items become part of the festive bestowal of goods, but with population loss (due to diseases caught from the Europeans) many hereditary

chieftainships became vacant and potlatching increased to fill these positions. See Aldona Jonaitis, ed., *Chiefly Feasts: The Enduring Kwakiutl Potlatch,* with essays by Douglas Cole et al. (Seattle: University of Washington Press, 1991), 110–14, 135. For an excellent critique by anthropologists of the dichotomies non-monetary/monetary, "traditional"/"modern," and gift/commodity, see Jonathan Parry and Maurice Bloch, eds., *Money and the Morality of Exchange* (Cambridge: Cambridge University Press, 1989), chap. 1.

9. Claude Macherel, "Don et réciprocité en Europe," *Archives européennes de sociologie* 24 (1983): 151–66. Alain Caillé, *Don, intérêt et désintéressement* (Paris: La Découverte/MAUSS, 1994), especially part 2, and more generally Caillé's periodical *La Revue du M.A.U.S.S.* James G. Carrier, *Gifts and Commodities: Exchange and Western Capitalism since 1700* (London and New York: Routledge, 1995), quotation on p. 11.

10. M. I. Finley, *The World of Odysseus,* rev. ed. (New York: Viking, 1965; 1st edition, 1954). Georges Duby, *Guerriers et Paysans, 7e–12e siècle. Premier essor de l'économie européenne* (Paris: Gallimard, 1973), 60–69; English edition: *The Early Growth of the European Economy: Warriors and Peasants from the Seventh to the Twelfth Century,* trans. Howard B. Clarke (Ithaca: Cornell University Press, 1974), 48–57. Finley especially acknowledges the help of the economic historian and philosopher Karl Polanyi. Duby quotes Marcel Mauss on the gift. Another scholar pioneering in the study of gifting in early societies is Aaron Ya. Gurevich. See especially his "Wealth and Gift-Bestowal among the Ancient Scandinavians," *Scandinavica* 7 (1968): 126–38.

11. Duby, *Guerriers,* 300; *Early Growth,* 270. Lester K. Little, *Religious Poverty and the Profit Economy in Medieval Europe* (Ithaca: Cornell University Press, 1978), 8, 212–13, 216.

12. Karl Polanyi, *The Great Transformation: The Political and Economic Origins of Our Time* (Boston: Beacon Press, 1957; 1st edition, 1944), chaps. 4–5. Polanyi used the works of Bronisław Malinowski, Raymond Firth, and other anthropologists to rethink the market as a historical constant. Gareth Stedman Jones, *Outcast London: A Study in the Relationship between Classes in Victorian Society* (Oxford: Clarendon Press, 1971), chap. 13.

13. Gabriel Herman, *Ritualised Friendship and the Greek City* (Cambridge and New York: Cambridge University Press, 1987), 6. See also Ian Morris, "Gift and Commodity in Archaic Greece," *Man,* n.s., 21 (1986): 1–17, arguing for the persistence of gift forms beyond the "clan society" of Homeric times into the "state-society" of Greece in the seventh and sixth centuries. Sitta von Reden, *Exchange in Ancient Greece* (London: Duckworth, 1995).

14. Barbara Rosenwein, *To Be the Neighbor of Saint Peter: The Social Meaning of Cluny's Property, 909–1049* (Ithaca: Cornell University Press, 1989), chap. 4, especially pp. 130–43. See also Ilana Silber, "Gift-Giving in the Great Traditions: The Case of Donations to Monasteries in the Medieval West," *Archives européennes de sociologie* 36 (1991): 209–43, where the author argues that religious donations combined in a new form traits that Mauss thought archaic with traits conceived as modern. The practice of giving gifts to saints through monastic institutions has been examined by Stephen D. White, *Custom, Kinship, and Gifts to Saints: The "Laudatio Parentum" in Western France, 1050–1150* (Chapel Hill and London: University of North Carolina Press, 1988).

15. Linda Levy Peck, " 'For a King not to be bountiful were a fault': Perspectives on Court Patronage in Early Stuart England," *Journal of British Studies* 21 (1986): 31–61 (giving earlier English bibliography, but also connecting her work to Maussian questions); *Court Patronage and Corruption in Early Stuart England* (London and Boston: Unwin Hyman, 1990). Sharon Kettering, *Patrons, Brokers, and Clients in Seventeenth-Century France* (New York and Oxford: Oxford University Press, 1986); "Gift-Giving and Patronage in Early Mod-

ern France," *French History* 2 (1988): 131–51. Alain Guéry, "Le Roi dépensier. Le don, la contrainte, et l'origine du système financier de la monarchie française d'Ancien Régime," *Annales.ESC* 39 (1984): 1241–69. Marcello Fantoni, "Il Dona del Granduca: Liberalità, Potere, Ostentazione" (Laurea diss., University of Florence, 1984–85), citing Mauss and other anthropological work in introduction. Jean-Claude Waquet, *Corruption: Ethics and Power in Florence, 1600–1770*, trans. Linda McCall (University Park: Pennsylvania State University Press, 1991). For the classical world, Paul Veyne has written a major study of the relation of public gift bestowal and power: *Le Pain et la cirque. Sociologie historique d'un pluralisme politique* (Paris: Éditions du Seuil, 1976).

16. Natalie Zemon Davis, "Beyond the Market: Books as Gifts in Sixteenth-Century France," *Transactions of the Royal Historical Society*, series 5, 33 (1983): 69–88. Alexander Nagel, "Gifts for Michelangelo and Vittoria Colonna," *Art Bulletin* 79 (1997): 647–68.

17. *Chiefly Feasts*, 110. Mauss or his sources overestimated the frequency and normality of destruction at least in the Kwakiutl potlatch (Mauss, "Don," 39, 107–8; *Gift*, 6–7, 41–42).

CHAPTER 1. THE SPIRIT OF GIFTS

1. Isaiah 11:2; Romans 12:3; Acts 8:17–21; Psalms 24:1–2; Genesis 22:17–18; Matthew 10:8.

2. Jean Bouchet, *Les Triumphes de la Noble et amoureuse Dame* (Paris: Guillaume de Bossonzel, 1536), 31v–32r. Pierre Coustau, *Pegma* (Lyon: Macé Bonhomme, 1555), 285; *Le Pegme de Pierre Coustau, mis en Francoys* (Lyon: Macé Bonhomme, January 1555/1556), 352–53. "Qui donne Dieu luy donne," in Nicolas Dupuy, alias Bonaspes, and Jean Gilles de Noyers, *Proverbia communia* (Paris: Bernard Aubry, 1513), C 2v. "Qui du sien donne, Dieu luy redonne," in Jean Gilles de Noyers, "Proverbia," in *Thresor de la langue francoyse tant ancienne que moderne* (Paris: David Douceur, 1606), 12.

3. Aristotle, *Nicomachean Ethics,* book 5, chap. 5, 1133a 1–5 in Richard McKeon, ed., *The Basic Works of Aristotle* (New York: Random House, 1941), 1010. "Itaque et Gratiarum templum in propatulo urbis loco constituitur, ut sit remuneratio. Hoc enim gratiae proprium est. Nam ei qui beneficium dederit, referendum beneficium est: et is rursus alterum beneficio provocare debet" (*Aristotelis Ethicorum, sive de Moribus, ad Nicomachum Libri Decem* [Hanover: Wechel, 1611], book 5, chap. 5, p. 206). This work had many Latin editions in France in the late-fifteenth and sixteenth centuries, as well as editions in French and Greek.

4. Seneca, *The Woorke of the Excellent Philosopher Lucius Annaeus Seneca Concerning Benefyting,* trans. Arthur Golding (London: John Day, 1578; facsimile edition Amsterdam: Theatrum Orbis Terrarum, 1974), book 1, chap. 3, pp. 3r–v. Seneca's works were published in France by 1500; among later editions is *Les sept livres traitant des bienfaits,* trans. S. Accaurrat (Paris: G. Cavellat, 1561). Seneca is cited, for example, by Coustau, *Pegma,* 282–85, *Pegme,* 350–53; Giovanni Pierio Valeriano and Caelius Augustinus Curio, *Commentaires Hiéroglyphiques ou Images des choses de Ian Pierius Valerian . . . Plus Deux Livres de Coelius Curio,* trans. Gabriel Chappuys (Lyon: Barthélemy Honorat, 1576), 584. On the Three Graces in Renaissance imagery, see D. T. Starnes, "Spenser and the Graces," *Philological Quarterly* 21 (1942): 268–82; Edgar Wind, *Pagan Mysteries in the Renaissance* (London: Faber and Faber; New Haven: Yale University Press, 1958), chap. 2.

5. Erasmus, *Adages* I i 34, in *Collected Works of Erasmus,* trans. Margaret Mann Phillips (Toronto: University of Toronto Press, 1982), 31:83. Gilles de Noyers, "Proverbia," in *Thresor de la langue francoyse,* 4, 13, 17.

6. P. Ourliac and J. De Malafosse, *Histoire du droit privé*, 3 vols., 2d ed. (Paris: Presses Universitaires de France, 1971), 2: 168–71, 421–34. G. E. Aylmer, "The Meaning and Definition of 'Property' in Seventeenth-Century England," *Past and Present* 86 (February 1980): 89.

7. Nicolas Theveneau, *De la Nature de tous Contractz, Pactions et Convenances* (Poitiers: Pierre and Iean Moynes, 1559), 4–5; Charles Du Moulin, *Summaire du livre analytique des contractz, usures, rentes constituées, interestz et monnoyes* (Paris: Mathurin Du Puys, 1547), title page and 1r. Ourliac and Malafosse, *Droit privé*, 1:111–16; P. S. Atiyah, *The Rise and Fall of Freedom of Contract* (Oxford: Clarendon Press, 1979).

8. Robert Estienne, *Dictionnaire Francoislatin* (Paris: Robert Estienne, 1549), 198, 485–86. *Cronique du Roy Francoys premier de ce Nom*, ed. Georges Guiffrey (Paris: Renouard, 1860), 288; similar use of the two words together in *Le Journal d'un bourgeois de Paris sous le règne de François Ier (1515–1536)*, ed. V.-L. Bourrilly (Paris: Alphonse Picard, 1910), 33.

9. Estienne, *Dictionnaire*, 86, 486. "Cadeau" gets its meaning of "present" only in the eighteenth century.

10. Anne de Bretagne, "Extraits de Comptes," in A. J. V. Le Roux de Lincy, *Vie de la Reine Anne de Bretagne, femme des rois de France Charles VIII et Louis XII*, 4 vols. (Paris: L. Curmer, 1861), 4:166–67. AN, KK133, 2503r. Paul Raymond, "Notes extraites des comptes de Jeanne d'Albret et de ses enfants, 1556–1608," *Revue d'Acquitaine*, 11 (1867): 393.

11. *Le Compost et Kalendrier des Bergiers* (Paris: Guy Marchant, 1493; facsimile ed. Paris: Pierre Champion, 1926), g 7v. Bouchet, *Triumphes*, 36r–37v. Jean Benedicti, *La Somme des Pechez, et le Remede d'iceux* (Paris: Denis Binet, 1595), book 4, chap. 7, pp. 484–90. For an excellent study of medieval concepts of charity, see Miri Rubin, *Charity and Community in Medieval Cambridge* (Cambridge: Cambridge University Press, 1987), chap. 3.

12. Bouchet, *Triumphes*, 37r. Benedicti, *Somme*, book 4, chap. 7, pp. 485–86. Georgette de Montenay, *Emblemes, ou devises chrestiennes* (Lyon: Jean Marcorelle, 1572), 90: disabled beggar on the ground receives alms in his bowl, picture engraved by Pierre Woeiriot.

13. Jean Meyer, "Un témoignage exceptionnel sur la noblesse de province à l'orée du 17e siècle: les 'advis moraux' de René Fleuriot," *Annales de Bretagne* 79 (1972): 325–26.

14. Bouchet, *Triumphes*, 37r–v; Benedicti, *Somme*, book 4, chap. 7, p. 490. On the medieval background to the donor's distinguishing among recipients of alms, see Brian Tierney, *Medieval Poor Law: A Sketch of Canonical Theory and Its Application in England* (Berkeley and Los Angeles: University of California Press, 1959). Painting by Andrea del Sarto for François I, done around 1518 (Louvre). Jean Mignon's "La Charité," in Henri Zerner, *The School of Fontainebleau: Etchings and Engravings* (London: Thames and Hudson, 1969), plate 8. Montenay, *Emblemes*, 59 (engraving by Pierre Woeiriot).

15. *Compost et Kalendrier*, d 2r; Bouchet, *Triumphes*, 32v. Benedicti, *Somme*, book 6, "Traicté des restitutions," 723. Gilles de Noyers, "Proverbia" in *Thresor de la langue francoyse*, 2.

16. Jean d'Arras, *Mélusine . . . Nouvelle édition conforme à celle de 1478* (Paris: P. Jannet, 1854), 59–69. *Cronique du Roy Françoys premier*, 369, 306, 370. Jean Starobinski, *Largesse* (Paris: Réunion des Musées Nationaux, 1994), 19–34.

17. Bouchet, *Triumphes*, 35r–36r.

18. Jean Bouchet, *Le Panegyric du Chevallier sans reproche* (Poitiers: Jacques Bouchet, 28 March 1527/1528), 191r–192r. On Bouchet, see Auguste Hamon, *Un grand Rhétoriqueur poitevin: Jean Bouchet, 1476–1557?* (Paris: H. Oudin, 1901).

19. Bouchet, *Triumphes*, 35r–36r. Cicero, *On Moral Obligation. A New Translation of Cicero's "De Officiis,"* trans. John Higginbotham (Berkeley and Los Angeles: University of

California Press, 1967), book 1, chap. 15, p. 56. Erasmus, *Adages,* I iii 89–90, in *Collected Works* 31:309.

20. Bouchet, *Panegyric,* 16r–v: "Acquiers amys par bienfaictz et largesse / Tu ne pourrois faire plus grand sagesse. / Mieulx vault amy du nombre des loyaulx / Que biens mondains qui sont tant desloyaulx." Gilles de Noyers, "Proverbia," in *Thresor de la langue francoyse,* 2: "Amys vallent mieux qu'argent." Jean Papon, *Premier Tome des Trois Notaires* (Lyon: Jean de Tournes, 1568), 326.

21. Bouchet, *Triumphes,* 35v.

22. Pierre de L'Estoile, *Journal pour le règne de Henri III (1574–1589),* ed. L. R. Lefèvre (Paris: Gallimard, 1943), 48.

23. François de La Noue, *Discours politiques et militaires,* ed. F. E. Sutcliffe (Geneva: Droz, 1967), Septiesme Discours, 208.

24. ADHG, E916, letters of Jean de Coras to his wife Jacquette de Bussi, 1567, reprinted in Jean de Coras, *Lettres de Coras,* ed. Charles Coras (Albi: Imprimerie G.-M. Nouguiès, 1880), 6–12, 15, 18–20. AML, AA4981, letters of Marie Teste from Lyon to her husband Guy de Masso, on mission to the king at Paris, 20 March 1559 [*sic,* for 1569?], 7 August 1572. Natalie Zemon Davis, *Fiction in the Archives: Pardon Tales and their Tellers in Sixteenth-Century France* (Stanford: Stanford University Press, 1987), 44, 174 n. 38.

25. François Rabelais, *Pantagruel,* chap. 9, and *Le Quart Livre,* chap. 13, in *Oeuvres complètes,* ed. Mireille Huchon (Paris: Gallimard, 1994), 246, 249, 570. Bouchet, *Triumphes,* 13r.

26. Erasmus, *Adages,* I i 2, in *Collected Works* 31:31; Erasmus, "Sympathy" in *The Colloquies of Erasmus,* trans. Craig Thompson (Chicago: University of Chicago Press, 1965), 527. ADR, 3E5295, 4 February 1551–52; 3E3908, 51r–54r, 101v–104r, 169v–171v, 209v–210v; BP3655, 20r–21v. In the 1541 will of Jeanne Feste, the wife of a rope maker, a tripe-merchant "son bon amy," is made executor of her will (ADR, 3E3908, 48r–50v); the 1582 will of Françoise Turquet, wife of a financial officer, leaves a dress and a rosary to "sa cousine et bonne amye" (ADR, 3E221, 25 May 1582). These are unusual words in women's wills. Bouchet, *Triumphes,* 41r–v. Classic texts from Aristotle and Cicero in Eudora Welty and Ronald A. Sharp, eds., *The Norton Book of Friendship* (New York and London: W. W. Norton, 1991), 63–79.

27. Bouchet, *Triumphes,* 41v.

28. Bouchet, *Triumphes,* 39v.

29. Proverbs 3:28, 14:20–21; Ecclesiastes 4:4; Leviticus 19:13. Matthew 14:9. Dupuys and Gilles de Noyers, *Proverbia communia,* 101v, 104r; Gilles de Noyers, "Proverbia," in *Thresor de la langue francoyse,* 3, 11. Erasmus, *Adages,* I i 32, in *Collected Works* 31:81–82.

30. Bonaventure Desperiers, *Nouvelles Récréations et Joyeux Devis,* ed. Louis Lacour, 2 vols. (Paris: Librairie des Bibliophiles, 1874), Nouvelle 18, 2:98–99. A. Vachet, "Le Livre de raison d'une famille de robe au 17e siècle," *Revue du Lyonnais,* 5th ser., 13 (1892): 310. Here Louis Fornet urges his heirs to try "to make yourselves liked by everyone and especially by your neighbors, and to achieve this, seek out occasions to serve them. The saying is really true that 'a good neighbor is worth more than a distant relative,' from whom you can expect little service. From a good neighbor you can receive pleasure all the time."

31. BN, MS. fr. 26161, 813r; Nouv. acq. fr. 1441, 8v–9r.

32. Lorenzo Valla, *The Treatise of Lorenzo Valla on the Donation of Constantine,* trans. Christopher B. Coleman (New Haven: Yale University Press, 1922), 27–51.

CHAPTER 2. GIFT PRACTICES AND PUBLIC TIMES

1. N. Vignier, *Les Fastes des Anciens Hebreux, Grecs et Romains, Avec un traicte de l'an et des mois* (Paris: Abel l'Angelier, 1588), 5r–v; Jacob Spon, *Recherches curieuses d'Antiquité contenues en plusieurs dissertations* (Lyon: Thomas Amaulry, 1683), 485–95.

2. Anne de Bretagne, "Extraits des Comptes," in A. J. V. Le Roux de Lincy, *Vie de la Reine Anne de Bretagne*, 4 vols. (Paris: L. Curmer, 1861), 4:160–61. Gilles de Gouberville, *Le Journal du Sire de Gouberville*, 4 vols. (Bricqueboscq: Les Éditions des Champs, 1993–94), 2:63, 147; 3:542. *Livre de Comptes de Claude de La Landelle, 1553–1556,* ed. René de Laigne (Rennes: Société des Bibliophiles Bretons, 1906), 20, 40, 119. Pierre de L'Estoile, *Journal de L'Estoile pour le règne de Henri III (1574–1589),* ed. Louis-Raymond Lefèvre (Paris: Gallimard, 1943), 210, 291–92, 319–20, 344–50, 372, 441, 541; *Mémoires-Journaux de Pierre de l'Estoile, 1574–1611,* ed. G. Brunet et al., 12 vols. (Paris: Librairie des Bibliophiles, 1875–81; facsimile edition, Paris: Tallandier, 1982), 9:192. For the medieval period, see the interesting analysis of the New Year's gifts of Philip the Bold, Duke of Burgundy, by Carol M. Chattaway, "Looking a Medieval Gift Horse in the Mouth: The Role of the Giving of Gift Objects in the Definition and Maintenance of the Power Networks of Philip the Bold," *Bijdragen en Medelingen betreffende de Geschiedenis der Nederlanden* 114 (1999): 1–15.

3. Louis La Trémoille, *Les La Trémoille pendant cinq siècles,* 5 vols. (Nantes: Émile Grimaud, 1892–94), 3:87. Duchess Anne also sent a New Year's gift to her own aunt, similarly seeking good will: "Madamoyselle ma tante, Je crains de vous faire ung si petit prasent que celluy que Je vous envoye pour vos estrannes. Toutesfoys Il est selon la puyssance de personaige, vous suppliant treshumblement, Madamoyselle ma tante, le Recepvoir daussy bon cueur que Je desire tousiours demeurez en votre bonne grace" [Mademoiselle, my aunt, I'm afraid to give you so little a present as that which I'm sending you for your New Year's étrennes. However, that's all that's in my power [to send] begging you very humbly, Mademoiselle my aunt, to receive it with a good heart for I wish always to remain in your good grace] (AN, 1AP251, no. 100).

4. Clément Marot, *Les Estreines* (Paris: J. Dupré, 1541), reprinted in Clément Marot, *Oeuvres diverses,* ed. C. A. Mayer (London: Athlone Press, 1966), 241–63. Charles Fontaine, *Estreines, a certains seigneurs, et dames de Lyon* (Lyon: Jean de Tournes, 1546), described in R. L. Hawkins, *Maistre Charles Fontaine Parisien* (Cambridge, Mass.: Harvard University Press, 1916), 250–51. L'Estoile, *Mémoires-Journaux,* 9:40. Among numerous examples of New Year's dedications to individuals: Laurent Joubert dedicated both his *Erreurs populaires au fait de la medecine* (Bordeaux: Simon Millanges, 1578) and his *Traité du Ris* (Paris: Nicolas Chesneau, 1579) to Marguerite de France, queen of Navarre, both dated 1 January 1578. Joubert was chancellor of the medical faculty of Montpellier and physician to Henri de Navarre, Marguerite's husband.

5. Noël Taillepied, *Histoire de lestat et Republique des Druides . . . Anciens François* (Paris: Jean Parant, 1585), 44r–v, 120r. Roger Vaultier, *Le Folklore pendant la guerre de Cent Ans d'après les lettres de rémission du Trésor des Chartes* (Paris: Librairie Guénégaud, 1965), 93–96. Collection for the aguilanneuf by young men in the bailliage of Berry at New Year's 1536 (AN, JJ249bis, 26r–v). Noël du Fail, *Propos Rustiques. Texte original de 1547,* ed. Arthur de La Borderie (Paris: Alphonse Lemerre, 1878; reprint Geneva: Slatkine, 1970), 75–84, 219–20. M. du Tilliot, *Mémoires pour servir à l'histoire de la Fête des Foux* (Lausanne and Geneva: n.p., 1751), 67–71: 1595 text on the quête de l'aguilanneuf by young men and women in

the diocese of Angers. Arnold Van Gennep, *Manuel de folklore français contemporain*, 7 vols. (Paris: A. and J. Picard, 1946–72), 7:2874–981.

6. Two examples where Christian themes are present: children and pupils sang noels door to door and were given money by Gouberville (*Journal*, 2:240, 321, "Je donné xx s. en liards aulx escoliers qui vindrent chanter des dictiers de Noel céans"; 3:468). In 1587, Henri III held back one hundred crowns from his thousand-crown étrennes to the knights of Saint Esprit and gave them to the Franciscan convent for repairs (L'Estoile, *Journal . . . pour le règne de Henri III*, 482.

7. Du Tilliot, *Fête des Foux*, 69. Vaultier, *Folklore*, 97–98. Van Gennep, *Folklore*, 7: 2875–980. Jean Guéraud, *La Chronique lyonnaise de Jean Guéraud, 1536–1562*, ed. Jean Tricou (Lyon: Imprimerie Audienienne, 1929), 8. Felix Platter, *Beloved Son Felix: The Journal of Felix Platter*, trans. Sean Jeannett (London: F. Muller, 1961), 49, 91–92. AN, JJ249bis, 21v–22r. Jean Deslyons, *Traitez singuliers et nouveaux contre le paganisme du Roy-boit* (Paris: Widow of C. Savreux, 1670).

8. ADR, 15G21, 170v, 259r, 378v–379v; 15G22, 177v; 15G125, 139r–140r. La Landelle, *Comptes*, 145, 147, 148 (payments to a serving boy and to the mother of his innkeeper "pour faire ses Pasques," "pour son confesseur").

9. Gouberville, *Journal*, 2:176. De La Nicollière-Teijeiro, "Compte de la Fabrique de Saint-Jean Martin de Châtenay, 1481–1506," *Revue de Bretagne, de Vendée et d'Anjou* 37 (1875): 184. Paul Paris-Jallobert, "Registre de compte de la paroisse d'Izé des 15e et 16e siècles," *Bulletin et Mémoires de la société archéologique d'Ille-et-Vilaine* 13 (1879): 213. The accounts of René Lecoq, treasurer for the parish of Notre Dame de Vitré, suggest that contributions for *pains bénits* were highest on Easter Sunday (AN, MSS., Nouv. acq. fr. 1723, 120r–133v). Accounts of the fabrique of Angerville-la-Martel record four high points for collections from May 1541 to May 1542: Pentecost 8s. 2d.; All Saints 11s.; Christmas 18s.; and Easter 25s. 6d. (ADSM, G7910). Usual Sunday contribution for Angerville-la-Martel worshipers was 2–3s. A similar picture emerges in the accounts of the parish treasurer of Anglesqueville-la-Bras-Long, 1541–42 (ADSM, G7920).

10. Vaultier, *Folklore*, 59. Jacques Toussaert, *Le Sentiment religieux en Flandre à la fin du Moyen Âge* (Paris: Plon, 1963), 333. Jean-Marie H. Forest, *L'École cathédrale de Lyon* (Paris and Lyon: Librairie Dehomme and Briguet, 1885), 145–46. Christina Hole, *Easter and its Customs* (London: R. Bell, 1961), 27–28.

11. AChL, E4, 141r; E5, 146v. *La Police de l'Aulmosne de Lyon* (Lyon: Sébastien Gryphius, 1539), 41–43. Guéraud, *Chronique*, 113. G. Montaigne, "La Police des Paouvres de Paris," ed. E. Coyecque, *Bulletin de la Société de l'histoire de Paris et de l'Île de France* 15–16 (1888–89): 117.

12. Vaultier, *Folklore*, 60. Van Gennep, *Folklore*, 3:1271–355, especially 1277, 1280, 1283, 1289–315, 1321–22, 1328, 1341–47. Hole, *Easter*, 41–47.

13. ADSM, G7910, accounts of the *fabrique* of Angerville-la-Martel: January 1528/29–January 1529/30: highest collection at Easter, then Christmas, then All Saints, then Pentecost; the same is true for May 1541–May 1542. Jallobert, "Comptes de la paroisse d'Izé," 213–14. Vaultier, *Folklore*, 10.

14. Toussaert, *Sentiment religieux*, 212–13. Jean Delumeau, *La Peur en Occident* (Paris: Fayard, 1978), 75–87. Alain Croix, *La Bretagne aux 16e et 17e siècles. La vie, la mort, la foi* (Paris: Maloine, 1981), 1059. E. O. James, *Seasonal Feasts and Festivals* (London: Thames and Hudson, 1961), 226–27. Gouberville, *Journal*, 3:604.

15. BML, Fonds Coste 355, Registers of the Confrérie de la Trinité de Lyon, 9v, 15v–17v,

31r–32r. A. N. Galpern, *The Religion of the People in Sixteenth Century Champagne* (Cambridge, Mass.: Harvard University Press, 1976), 63–64.

16. Gouberville, *Journal,* 1:23–24, 81–82, 87, 147, 229, 240, 248, 304; 2:49, 52, 71, 153, 171, 204; 3:542, 585. "Livre de Raison de Gilles Satin, Sr de la Teillaye," in Paul Parfouru, "Anciens livres de raison de familles bretonnes conservés aux Archives d'Ille-et-Vilaine," *Bulletin archéologique de l'Association bretonne* (Rennes, 1897), 453 n. 2. "Papier ou Registre de Jehan de Gennes," 139r–v, 144v (BN, MSS., Nouv. acq. fr. 1723). AN, JJ238, 63v. [Nicolas Barnaud], *Le Miroir des Francois, Compris en Trois Livres* (n.p. [Geneva], n.p. [Guillaume de Laimarie?], 1582), 662, 665: "banquets des femmes accouchees," "une gessine de commere." Vaultier, *Folklore,* 1–2, 5.

17. Christiane Klapisch-Zuber, "Le complexe de Griselda. Dot et dons de mariage au Quattrocento," *Mélanges d'l'École française de Rome* 94 (1982): 7–43; Jane Fair Bestor, "Marriage Transactions in Renaissance Italy and Mauss's *Essay on the Gift*," *Past and Present* 164 (August 1999): 6–46. Bestor's interesting essay, appearing as this book goes to press, has implications for gift theory beyond the case of the groom's gifts to the bride.

18. AN, JJ257B, 16r, letter of remission for Guillaume Guillon, *laboureur* of Marcil-sur Mauldre in the Île-de-France, January 1545/1546.

19. Gaspard de Saillans, *Le Premier Livre composé Par Gaspar de Saillans, gentilhomme Citoyen en Valance en Dauphiné* (Lyon: Jean d'Ogerolles, 1573), 38–42, 46–49, 55, 60, 68–72. Marriage contract between Gaspard de Saillans and Louise de Bourges, 7 July 1564 (ADR, BP3660, 238r–240v).

20. AEG, Reg. Consist., 25, 37r–v, 25 March 1568. Charles Gouyon, *Mémoires de Charles Gouyon, Baron de la Moussaye (1553–1587),* ed. G. Vallée and P. Parfouru (Paris: Perrin, 1901), 98–99. A medical student at Montpellier, Felix Platter sent his fiancée in Basel sachets and two strands of coral and brought her on his return a printed German Bible with her initials on the cover (*Beloved Son Felix,* 110, 139).

21. Gouberville, *Journal,* 2:217. AN, JJ249B, 1r–v. Rabelais, *Le Quart Livre,* chap. 14, in *Oeuvres complètes,* ed. Mireille Huchon (Paris: Gallimard, 1994), 571–73.

22. Fleuriot, "Advis Moraux," 329.

23. Jean-Baptiste Molin and Protais Mutembé, *Le Rituel du mariage en France du 12e au 16e siècle* (Paris: Beauchesne, 1974), chap. 5. David Houard, *Dictionnaire analytique, historique, étymologique, critique et interprétatif de la Coutume de Normandie* (Rouen: n.p., 1780), 1:611–30. ADM, 5E14532, marriage contract of 6 January 1553 with a "don mobile" of one hundred livres tournois, given by Nicolas Le Faulconnier and his wife of the town of Valognes to Jean Mangin of the nearby parish of Brix, future husband of their daughter Peralle.

24. ADR, 3E1013, 31 May 1575. Other examples of sons receiving patrimonial gifts at the time of their marriage: ADR, BP3655, 37r–38v (29 December 1543); BP3897, 253v–256v (24 March 1554/1555); BP3899, 22v–25r (27 November 1558); BP3900, 244r–246v (12 October 1558), 252r–253v (30 October 1557); BP3906, 287r (9 December 1553); BP3907, 198r–200v (20 May 1560). L'Estoile, *Mémoires-Journaux,* 3:61–62 (wedding of the Duc d'Épernon and the Comtesse de Candales, 30 August 1587). Henri III also paid for much of the wedding and bridal garments for the marriage of Charles Gouyon, Baron de La Moussaye at the chateau of Gaillon (Gouyon, *Mémoires,* 114–15). ADPA, B16, 24r. Also, Henri de Navarre makes a "don" of 580 livres tournois in 1574 to one of the gentlemen of his chamber for the purchase of wedding dress for his bride (Paul Raymond, "Notes extraites des comptes

de Jeanne d'Albret et de ses enfants, 1556–1608," *Revue d'Aquitaine et des Pyrénées* 10 [1866]: 246). Gouberville, *Journal,* 2:229 (game for the wedding of the daughter of Captain du Teil); 2:56 (pays for minstrels); 1:193–94 (sends "présent des nopces" to Jean Le Febvre at Neuville for marriage of his daughter Tassine to the Sieur de Coucy). Coyecque, 1:20–21, no. 3690, agreement between the groom Nicolas de La Salle, laboureur of Vanves and four "compaignons à marier," February 1540/1541. Other examples include: a platter of meat given by a bridegroom of Therouanne in Picardy to the men in his craft "par bonne coustume," September 1541 (AN, JJ255B, 93r); and, in Mareil-sur-Mauldre, a basket of wheat promised by the bridegroom to his fellow laboureur for the wedding, January 1545/1546 (AN JJ257B, 16r).

25. Gouberville, *Journal,* 1:41, 184, 271; 2:33, 118–19, 211, 293, 371; 3:445, 588. Gilles Satin, "Livre de raison," 453. Claude de la Landelle, canon of Vannes, gives the choirboy Nicolas twenty-five sous on Saint Nicolas's day so that the lad can "pay for his feast" ("paier sa feste"), La Landelle, *Comptes,* 111.

26. Vaultier, *Folklore,* 178–79. Gouberville, *Journal,* 2:201. La Landelle, *Comptes,* 18, 99–100, 158.

27. Jeanne du Laurens, "La Généalogie de messieurs du Laurens," in Charles de Ribbe, ed., *Une Famille au XVIe siècle d'après des documents originaux,* 3d ed. (Tours: Alfred Mame, 1879), 57. *Le Premier [-Second] volume de la bible en francoys* (Lyon: Pierre Bailly, 17 December 1521), back flyleaf of copy at Houghton Library, Harvard University, Typ 515.21.210F): "Les noms de ceulx qui ont baille du pain benist en la maison des hoirs Me Claude Fyot a Villefranche." The Bible had been given by a priest to Benoiste Saladin, Fyot's widow.

28. Gouberville, *Journal,* 2:176 (handout outside his uncle's manorhouse at the death of Gouberville's cousin), 234 (oak wood given to two Franciscans for their services at funeral of local count). La Trémoille, *Les La Trémoille,* 3:49–52, 55–56, January 1541/1542: alms, payments to preacher, mourning garb for servants, etc., at death of François de La Trémoille. Shroud for priest in the village of Montaigut-le-Blanc in Auvergne (AN, JJ238, 165r). Will of Nicolas Vannchy, merchant, native of Foiano, residing in Lyon (ADR, 3E3908, 183v–192v).

29. Guillaume Terrien, *Commentaires du Droict Civil tant public que privé, observé au pays et Duché de Normandie,* 2d ed. (Paris: Jacques Du Puys, 1578), 196, and book 6: "De Succession et partages d'heritage." Jean Yver, *Égalité entre héritiers et exclusion des enfants dotés: Essai de géographie coutumière* (Paris: Sirey, 1966); Emmanuel Le Roy Ladurie, "Structures familiales et coutumes d'héritage en France au 16e siècle," *Annales.ESC* 27 (1972): 825–46. ADM, 5E14537 provides a good example of Normandy practice. The register of notary Augerat, going from 1561 to 1563, contains many marriage contracts and very few wills. The will of Thomas Laguelle, Sire de Quineville (in the same part of Normandy as the Sire de Gouberville) of 19 May 1562 seems to illustrate the Normandy custom: he gives half his "goods, movables, clothes and jewels" to his wife "in consideration of the good affection and good treatment that she gave him during his illness and before," and after bequests to his relatives and the poor, assigns the rest of his goods for the payment of his debts. The couple had no children, and he had already revoked a donation of a *rente* to his nephews.

30. Claude de Rubys, *Sommaire explication des articles de la Coustume du Païs et Duché de Bourgongne* (Lyon: Antoine Gryphius, 80), 42–49.

31. Examples of male bequests: ADR, 3E3908, 209v (canvas maker gives black wool cape to his brother); 4G6bis, 24v (priest gives his feather bed on which he's sick to male who took care of him); 3E346, 208r (spice merchant gives all his wool cloaks, bonnets, and hose to his servants and apprentices; 3E6442, 423r (armorer gives his lute and zither to wife of male friend, clothes to a male friend); 3E344, 204r (goldsmith gives all tools and lead

tools to his cousin, also goldsmith); 3E7185, 8 March 1562/1563 (boatman gives his clothes to another boatman). Examples of female bequests: ADPC, 9B24 (Boulogne widow gives all her clothes to her daughter, 1572); ADA, 5E5335, 122r (peasant woman in hamlet near Mas d'Azil leaves dress to her daughter and a linen sheet to each niece); ADR, 3E336, 132r; 3E348, 126v; 3E3766, 237v; 3E3908, 54v (saddler's wife leaves her red dress to her chambermaid, her rosary with a cross and silver ornaments to her daughter); 136r; 155r (dressmaker's widow leaves lined black wool dress to daughter, dress and four shirts to chambermaid); 199r (rope maker's wife leaves gray dress to be made into cloak for husband, gray skirt and new shirt to her husband's daughter by earlier marriage, dress to sister); 201v; 211r (pewterer's wife leaves coral silver rosary to sister and black dress with violet underskirt to niece); 219v (butcher-woman leaves her little wool skirt to her chambermaid, a little "round" dress to a barber's widow, her best dress and underskirt and all her rings to her daughter by her first marriage, and a good dress to her sister-in-law); 248r (dyer's wife leaves a dress and black skirt to her mother and a violet dress with violet skirt to her husband's niece); 254r (merchant spinner's widow leaves her serge dress to a man for a cloak, her furred dress with skirt to a woman, her best dress and skirt to the wife of a cabinetmaker, six shirts and headscarves to the daughter of a blind woman); 265v (wife of urban gardener leaves her good black dress with violet skirt to her niece and a black skirt to her god-daughter); 3E4494, 7v; 3E4981, 85v; E221, 25 May 1582 (Françoise Turquet, wife of an ennobled financial officer, leaves a costly chain and one of her best dresses and underskirt to a woman, a pearl necklace to her niece, her intimate lingerie to her cousin, a golden chain to her cousin's wife, an agate ring to the wife of another cousin, and a dress and rosary to Barbe Mathieu, "her cousin and good friend"); BP3837, 121v.

32. ADR, 3E1012 (1558).

33. Jean Papon, *Premier Tome des trois Notaires* (Lyon: Jean de Tournes, 1568), 325–78: Donations. Jean-Marie Ricard, *Traité des Donations entre-vifs et testamentaires*, 2 vols. (Paris: Jean Guignard and Arnoul Seneuze, 1692). Ralph Giesey, "Rules of Inheritance and Strategies of Mobility in Pre-Revolutionary France," *American Historical Review* 82 (1977): 271–89.

34. Benoît du Troncy, *Formulaire fort recreatif de tous Contractz, Donations, Testamens, Codicilles et aultres actes qui sont faicts et passez par devant Notaires et tesmoings. Faict par Bredin le Cocu, Notaire Royal et Contreroolleur des basses marches au Royaume d'Utopie* (Lyon: n.p., 1593), 193–99.

35. ADR, BP3655, 20r–21v (24 December 1540). AN, Y86, 219v–221v; Y95, 308v–309v (13 May 1550). ADR, BP3987, 148r–149v (13 April 1556/1557). ADR, 3E2810, 128v–129v (3 July 1572).

36. ADR, BP3908, 38r–41r.

37. See Papon, *Notaires*, 327–35 for discussion of the *donation entre vifs* as having contractual aspects but not properly being a contract, and the circumstances under which it could lead to a legal action. Charles Du Moulin, *Summaire du livre analytique des contractz, usures, rentes constituées, interestz et monnoyes* (Paris: Mathurin Du Puys, 1547), 1r–2r. Defense of Claude Bourbon, a financial officer for the king in the Beaujolais region, prosecuted in 1565 for non-fullfilment of a 1555 donation entre vifs to Geneviève Roussel (ADR, E221, 4 October 1565). Bourbon sought royal letters cancelling the donation on the grounds he was then a minor and that it had not been voluntary.

38. Words of acceptance of Claude Gerland of a donation of one-fourth of the goods and property of his father, peasant in the parish of Liergues in Lyonnais: "cette donation

[j]'ay accepte et accepte . . . et cette donation est agreable par tous ses points . . . et cy apres vous merciant humblement le bien qu'il vous a pleu me faire" (ADR, BP3655, 53v, 31 January 1540/1541).

CHAPTER 3. GIFT PRACTICES AND SOCIAL MEANINGS

1. Gilles de Gouberville, *Le Journal du Sire de Gouberville,* 4 vols. (Bricqueboscq: Les Éditions des Champs, 1993–94), 3:536: gives "trois miches pour fère le pain bénist." Accounts of René Lecoq, treasurer of the fabrique of Notre Dame de Vitré (BN, MSS., Nouv. acq. fr. 1723, 120r–133v). Guillaume Bouchet, *Premier Livre des Serees de Guillaume Bouchet, Sieur de Brocourt. Reveu et augmenté* (Paris: Jérémie Perier, 1608), a 5r.

2. See Gouberville, *Journal,* for a small sample of gifts exchanged between noble households from September 1553 to May 1554, 2:35 (partridge), 37 (hunting dogs), 47 (dog), 54 (woodcock), 60 (partridges), 62 (boar), 70 (goat), 97 (artichokes, wine, venison pâté); and 3:566 (artichokes, 21 May 1560). Studies of Gouberville: A. Tollemer, *Un Sire de Gouberville, gentilhomme campagnard au Cotentin de 1553 à 1562* (Paris and the Hague: Mouton, 1972 [reprint of edition of 1873]); Madeleine Foisil, *Le Sire de Gouberville, un gentilhomme normand au 16e siècle* (Paris: Aubier Montaigne, 1981). AN, 1AP251, no. 67, no. 98; Louis La Trémoille, *Les La Trémoille pendant cinq siècles,* 5 vols. (Nantes: Émile Grimaud, 1893–94) 2:87–88. ADHG, E916, Jean de Coras to Jaquette de Bussi, 13 August 1567, describing the gloves and letter of greeting sent to his wife by her sister, reprinted in Charles Pradel, ed., *Lettres de Coras, celles de sa femme, de son fils et de ses amis* (Albi: Imprimerie G.-M. Nouguiès, 1880), 18–19.

3. Gouberville's *Journal* is filled with mentions of visits back and forth between himself and his noble neighbors, especially his nearby kin. Charles Gouyon, *Mémoires de Charles Gouyon Baron de La Moussaye (1553–1587)* (Paris: Perrin, 1902), 128–29. See S. Amanda Eurich, *The Economics of Power: The Private Finances of the House of Foix-Navarre-Albret during the Religious Wars,* Sixteenth Century Essays and Studies, 24 (Ann Arbor: Edwards Brothers, 1994), 124–27, on the importance of hospitality in the Albret household as a demonstration of their liberality. For the changing situation in England, see Felicity Heal, "The Idea of Hospitality in Early Modern England," *Past and Present* 102 (February 1984): 66–93.

4. AN, JJ256C, 48r–v (April 1543/1544). *Livre de Comptes de Claude de La Landelle, 1553–1556,* ed. René de Laigne (Rennes: Société des Bibliophiles Bretons, 1906), 40–41, 44–45, 67–68, 79. Bouchet, *Serees,* a 4v. Bonaventure Desperiers, *Nouvelles Récréations et Joyeux Devis,* ed. Louis Lacour, 2 vols. (Paris: Librairie des Bibliophiles, 1874) nouvelle 3, pp. 18–23; nouvelle 14, pp. 74–49.

5. Edict of Charles IX, 1563, reproduced in Guillaume Terrien, *Commentaires du Droict Civil . . . observé au pays et Duché de Normandie* (Paris: Jacques Du Puys, 1578), 151–52.

6. Erasmus, "The Godly Feast," in *The Colloquies of Erasmus,* trans. C. R. Thompson (Chicago: University of Chicago Press, 1965), 75–76. Erasmus *The Correspondence of Erasmus,* trans. R. A. B. Mynors and D. F. S. Thomson, ed. James K. McConica, in *Collected Works of Erasmus* (Toronto: University of Toronto Press, 1974), vol. 3, no. 312, pp. 43–44.

7. Erasmus, *Correspondence,* vol. 4, nos. 451–53, pp. 37–40; no. 455, p. 43; no. 463, pp. 69–73; no. 486, pp. 123–24; no. 508, pp. 177–78. Among natural philosophers, specimens and rarities of various kinds were exchanged rather than books, as Paula Findlen has shown for Italy ("The Economy of Scientific Exchange in Early Modern Italy," in Bruce Moran, ed., *Patronage and Institutions* [Woodbridge, Boydell, 1991], 5–24).

8. Charles de Bouelles, *Proverbium Vulgarium Libri tres* (Paris: Galliot Du Pré, 1531), aa 1v–aa 2r, dedication to Joachim Michon, dated 16 February 1527/1528. *L'Aritmetique de Iaques Peletier du Mans, departie en Quatre Livres, A Theodore Debesze* (Poitiers: Jean and Enguilbert de Marnef, 1549; 2d ed., Poitiers: Jean de Marnef, 1552). I have discussed these editions and the subsequent withdrawal of Bèze's name in the edition published at Lyon in 1554 in Natalie Zemon Davis, "Peletier and Beza Part Company," *Studies in the Renaissance* 11 (1964): 188–222.

9. Erasmus, *Correspondence*, vol. 4, no. 457, pp. 54–57; no. 489, pp. 128–29: Luigi di Canossa, Bishop of Bayeux to Erasmus, 13 November 1516; no. 522, pp. 203–522: Guillaume Budé to Erasmus, 5 February 1517.

10. René Martin to François de La Trémoille, 1529, in La Trémoille, *Les La Trémoille*, 3:68. Amaury Gouron to the Duc d'Étampes, 11 May 1557 in Gouyon, *Mémoires*, 166. Sharon Kettering, "Gift-Giving and Patronage in Early Modern France," *French History* 2 (1988): 131–51.

11. J. Russell Major, " 'Bastard Feudalism' and the Kiss: Changing Social Mores in Late Medieval and Early Modern France," *Journal of Interdisciplinary History* 17 (1987): 509–35. *Archives historiques du départment de la Gironde* (Paris and Bordeaux, 1868), 10:174–75, quoting ADGironde, G304, Archevêché, Hommages, 1300–1726). ADPC, 9B24, donation of land to be held by the recipient "en plain fief, foy et homaige" from François de Luxembourg 29 July 1564. Luxembourg and the recipient agree "par les foy et serment de leur corps et mains," 29 July 1564.

12. Claude du Chastel to the Duc d'Étampes, 26 November 1555, in Gouyon, *Mémoires*, 165. Kristen B. Neuschel, *Word of Honor: Interpreting Noble Culture in Sixteenth-Century France* (Ithaca: Cornell University Press, 1989), chaps. 3–4. Paul Raymond, "Notes extraites des Comptes de Jeanne d'Albret et de ses Enfants," *Revue d'Aquitaine* 10 (1866): 47, 128–29, 185, 244, 388, 446, 545.

13. Gouberville, *Journal,* 2:64 (7 January 1553/1554), 100 (8 June 1554), 118 (19 August 1554), 310 (7 November 1556), 324 (16 January 1556/1557), 326–27 (21 January 1556/1557); and 3:457 (30 October 1558), 465 (30 October 1558), 467–70 (28 December 1558, 31 December 1558, 4 January 1558/1559, 6 January 1558/1559), 540–41 (23–24, 26 December 1559), 545–46 (21 January 1559/1560, 25 January 1559/1560), 550 (11 February 1559/1560), 562 (9 May 1560), 565 (18 May 1560), 577 (7 July 1560), 585 (11 August 1560), 621 (23 December 1560).

14. Gouberville, *Journal,* 2:91 (23 April 1554), 93 (30 April 1554), 99 (5 June 1554), 101 (11 June 1554), 120 (7 September 1554), 120–26 (8, 10, 14, 25, 26, 29 September 1554), 129 (10 October 1554), 131–34 (17, 19, 23, 28, 29 [the supper at his manor for fellow officers], 30 October 1554 [Hurtebye sends him four pigs]), 165 (12 March 1554/1555), 167–68 (19 March 1554/1555), 170 (28 March 1554/1555), 174 (9 April 1555), 214–15 (18, 21 September 1555).

15. Gouberville, *Journal,* 2:216–17 (31 September, 4–5 October 1555), 218 (8 October 1555), 224 (29 October 1555), 228 (13 November 1555), 233–36 (3, 7, 10, 11, 12, 14 December 1555, Gouberville's fight with the Viconte de Valognes, the failure of Hurtebye to reconcile them, his passage through Valognes "où je n'arresté guères pour que le viconte y étoit" — [the last six words were in Greek characters, indicating Gouberville's anxiety and anger about the whole matter]).

16. Gouberville, *Journal,* 2:302 (6–8 October 1556), 289 (17 August 1556), 325–26 (18–19 January 1556/1557), 355–56 (10–11 June 1557). Throughout all this period, Gouberville, who had previously had a gift relation with the Viconte de Valognes, avoids him, has some litigation with him, and makes fun of his family (e.g., 2:317 [10 December 1556]).

17. Gouberville, *Journal,* 2:397 (1 January 1557/1558), 407–9 (12, 20 February 1557/1558); and 3:452 (3 October 1558), 466–67 (18 December 1558, the hare and kid to Hurtebye at same time as payment of receipt on collecting from royal domain), 487 (13 April 1558/1559), 493 (21 May 1559), 513 (16 August 1559), 517 (14 September 1559), 609 (22 November 1560), 632 (8 January 1560/1561).

18. Gouberville, *Journal,* 3:589–669 (periodic stays at Russy). See, for example, 3:599 (15 October 1560), 602 (24 October 1560), 609 (22 November 1560), 613–16, (1, 2, 6–7, 10, 13 December 1560), 620 (22 December 1560).

19. Gouberville, *Journal,* 2:247–50.

20. Gouberville, *Journal,* 1:69 (16 January 1549/1550, cider and honey for the sick wife of a household servant), 234 (23 March 1551/1552, goat's milk for a sick villager), 241 (15 April 1551/1552, two bottles of cider for a sick villager); and 2:48–49 (2 November 1553, nutmeg and honey for the newly delivered wife of a villager), 71 (1 February 1553/1554, honey, cider, and white bread sent to a villager's wife, in danger of dying in childbirth), 161 (22 February 1554/1555, cider for the sick son of a villager), 177–78 (19–20 April 1555, beer for several sick villagers including a shepherd). For a good review of Gouberville's services to his peasants, see Elizabeth Teall, "The Myth of Royal Centralization and the Reality of the Neighborhood: The Journals of the Sire de Gouberville, 1549–62," in Miriam Usher Chrisman and Otto Gründler, eds., *Social Groups and Religious Ideas in the Sixteenth Century* (Kalamazoo: Western Michigan University Medieval Institute, 1978), 1–11, 139–51.

21. Gouberville, *Journal,* 1:89 (17 April 1550), 94 (11 May 1550), 96 (18 May 1550), 216 (5 January 1551/1552), 297 (6 January 1552/1553); and 2:64 (4 January 1553/1554), 152 (17 January 1554/1555), 155 (3 February 1554/1555), 162 (28 February 1554/1555), 168 (21 March 1554/1555), 186 (23 May 1555).

22. Gouberville, *Journal,* 1:241, 243–44 (15 April 1551/1552 and 6, 10 May 1552, chickens, apples, and rabbits during Gouberville's illness); 1:59 (1 December 1549, wife of tenant brings twelve blackbirds), 209 (4 December 1551, male villagers bring herring); 3:542 (31 December 1559, son of village woman brings two chickens); 1:298 (8 January 1552/1553, male villager, Joret Gaillard, brings butter); 2:189 (2 June 1555, male villager brings goslings); 3:524 (16 October 1559, Jacques Burnel pays seventy-five sous as his Michaelmas rent, for which Gouberville gives him a receipt, and also leaves two woodcocks); 1:95 (15 May 1550, Joret Gaillard brings pigeons the day before he must go to Valognes for a case at the church court involving Messire Guillaume Le Flamenc. Gouberville goes with him the next day and speaks to the curé presiding over the court).

23. Gouberville, *Journal,* 2:209 (for apprenticeship of Jacques Dauge); 1:73 (3 February 1549/1550, four sous to Combault, one sou to Le Landays, prisoners in Valognes, the latter for having stolen four pigs from Gouberville), 75 (13 February 1549/1550, Le Landays's wife sells Gouberville a cow for a price from which Gouberville has subtracted the cost of the four pigs), 199 (30 October 1551, buys a dozen laces [*aiguillettes*] and two hundred pins from a mercer and gives the laces—for tying up pants and sleeves—to Guillaume and Philippe dits Mesnage and one hundred pins each to Jeanne Birette and la Mangonne). Similarly, Gouberville buys one thousand pins from peddlers on 25 June 1549, half of which he gives to his cousin and the other half to three peasant wives and a male servant (1:20).

24. Gouberville, *Journal,* 1:210 (10 December 1551, Gouberville and Nicolas Quentin finally resolve their dispute with help of an arbitrator), 211 (13 December 1551, Nicolas Quentin one of those coming to Sunday dinner). The relationship continued to have ups and downs. The following month Gouberville seized Quentin's arquebouse because he had

been "shooting in violation of the ordinances" (1:222 [14 January 1551/1552]). In May 1557, Gouberville drew up an account of the back rent Quentin still owed him since December 1551, and Quentin and his wife paid what they could, after which Gouberville gave their little daughter a small coin (2:347–48 [1 May 1557]).

25. Gouberville's well-off tenant Thomas Drouet was for a time in trouble for allegedly hunting big game in the king's forest of Bricquebec. He denied it, and another non-noble was identified as the culprit (*Journal*, 3:572 [13 June 1560]).

26. Gouberville, *Journal*, 2:203 (28 July 1555), 214 (18 September 1555).

CHAPTER 4. GIFTS AND SALES

1. Noël du Fail, *Les Propos Rustiques. Texte original de 1547*, ed. Arthur de La Borderie (Paris, 1878; reprint Geneva: Slatkine, 1970), 18.

2. Du Fail, *Propos*, 20.

3. Marie de France, *Les Lais de Marie de France*, ed. J. Rychner (Paris: H. Champion, 1973), prologue.

4. G. Post, K. Giocarinis, and R. Kay, "The Medieval Heritage of a Humanist Ideal: 'Scientia Donum Dei est, Unde Vendi non Potest,'" *Traditio* 11 (1955): 195–234. Jacques Le Goff, *Les Intellectuels au Moyen Âge* (Paris: Éditions du Seuil, 1962), 104–8. J. W. Baldwin, *Masters, Princes, and Merchants: The Social Views of Peter the Chanter and his Circle* (Princeton: Princeton University Press, 1970), 1:121–30; 2:83–86. J. Destrez, *La 'Pecia' dans les manuscripts universitaires du 13e et du 14e siècle* (Paris: Éditions Jacques Vautrain, 1935). These pages on publishing are an expansion from material originally presented in Natalie Zemon Davis, " 'Beyond the Market': Books as Gifts in Sixteenth-Century France," *Transactions of the Royal Historical Society*, 5th ser., 33 (1983): 69–88.

5. Étienne Du Tronchet, *Lettres Missives et Familieres d'Estienne Du Tronchet, Secretaire de la Royne mere du Roy* (Paris: Nicolas Du Chemin and Lucas Breyer, 1583), 331r–v: Étienne Du Tronchet to Lucas Breyer, marchand libraire at Paris.

6. *Plaidoyé Second. Sur ce que M. Simon Marion, Pour Iacques du Puis, et Gilles Beys Libraires en l'Université, demandeurs, a dict* (n.p., n.d. [copy in the Newberry Library]).

7. *Plaidoyé*. The works of Seneca, with annotations by Marc Antoine Muret, had been published in Rome in 1585 by Bartolomeo Grassi and Francesco Zannetti. In 1587, Seneca's *Opera Omnia*, edited by Muret, were published in Paris by Gilles Beys and Jacques Du Puys, the two complainants in the 1586 case, as well as by Nicolas Nivelle. Nivelle was presumably the publisher who wanted a monopoly over the edition.

8. *Dialogo dell' Imprese Militari et Amorose di Monsignor Giovio Vescovo di Nocera; Con un Ragionamento de Messer Lodovico Domenichi nel medesimo soggetto* (Lyon: Guillaume Rouillé, 1559), a 2v. *Dialogue des devises d'armes et d'amours du S. Paulo Iovio Avec un Discours de M. Loys Dominique sur le mesme subiet . . .*, trans. Vasquin Philieul (Lyon: Guillaume Rouillé, 1561), 3–4.

9. *La Chronique lyonnaise de Jean Guéraud, 1536–1562*, ed. Jean Tricou (Lyon: Imprimerie Audienienne, 1929), 150. Pierre de L'Estoile, *Journal pour la règne d'Henri III (1574–1589)*, ed. Louis-Raymond Lefèbvre (Paris: Gallimard, 1943), 56–57.

10. Gabriel Naudé, *Advis pour dresser une bibliothèque* (Paris: F. Targa, 1627), 98–115, 151–61. Krzysztof Pomian, *Collectionneurs, amateurs et curieux. Paris, Venise, 16e-18e siècle* (Paris: Gallimard, 1987), chap. 1; English translation, *Collectors and Curiosities: Paris and Venice, 1500–1800*, trans. Elizabeth-Wiles-Portier (Cambridge: Polity Press, 1990), chap. 1. A

similar point has been made by Paula Findlen about the gift exchange of specimens and objects of importance to the natural philosopher (Paula Findlen, *Possessing Nature: Museums, Collecting and Scientific Culture in Early Modern Italy* [Berkeley and Los Angeles: University of California Press, 1994]). The same networks of exchange could be traced in sixteenth- and seventeenth-century France, and the scientific cabinet of curiosities also contributed to the collector's reputation and symbolic power. In addition, many of the specimens came from overseas trade or were connected with mining ventures; that is, here too there is a connection with the world of sale as well as the world of power. Publisher Guillaume Rouillé and the physician-botanist Jacques Dalechamps sought plant specimens from "Africans, Spaniards, and Italians" sailing in remote corners of the world (Jacques Dalechamps, *Historia Generalis Plantarum in Libros XVIII* [Lyon: Guillaume Rouillé, 1587], 3r–4v: Guillaume Rouillé to the reader).

11. James Farge, *Orthodoxy and Reform in Early Reformation France. The Faculty of Theology of Paris, 1500–1543* (Leiden: E. J. Brill, 1985), 53.

12. Farge, *Orthodoxy and Reform,* 16–41, 47–54.

13. Louis Dulieu, *La Médecine à Montpellier,* 2 vols. (Avignon: Presses Universelles, 1975–79), 2:45–70. E. Wickersheimer, *La Médecine et les médecins en France à l'époque de la Renaissance* (Paris: A. Maloine, 1906), 61–70. Felix Platter, *Beloved Son Felix: The Journal of Felix Platter, a Medical Student in Montpellier in the Sixteenth Century,* trans. Sean Jeannett (London: F. Muller, 1961). Platter's memoir offers a description of the banquet, "with an abundant supply of sugared almonds," given by Guillaume Héroard after receiving his doctorate of medicine (p. 94). According to Étienne Pasquier, gifts from students to teachers were customary at earlier stages of education as well: "nous voyons maintenant les Regens des Colleges prendre tous les ans des dons et presens de leurs disciples sous le nom de Lendiz" (Étienne Pasquier, *Les Recherches de la France,* book 4, chap. 9 in *Les Oeuvres* [Amsterdam: La compagnie des Libraires Associez, 1723], 387).

14. Wickersheimer, *Médecine,* 66. Farge, *Orthodoxy and Reform,* 25, 29–30, 51, 56.

15. Farge, *Orthodoxy and Reform,* 26, 48, 51–52. Dulieu, *Médecine,* 68–69.

16. *Anciens et Nouveaux Statuts de la Ville et Cité de Bourdeaus* (Bordeaux: Simon Millanges, 1612), 230–31. Gianna Pomata, *Contracting a Cure: Patients, Healers, and the Law in Early Modern Bologna,* trans. Gianna Pomata, Rosemarie Foy, and Anna Tarboletti-Segre (Baltimore and London: Johns Hopkins University Press, 1998), especially chap. 2, "Promising a Cure."

17. Gilles de Gouberville, *Le Journal du Sire de Gouberville,* 4 vols. (Bricquebosq: Éditions des Champs, 1993–94), 2:234–35 (7 December 1555). Another example may be the surgeon Jean Antoine de Bonnys who, claiming to have made "several beautiful cures" in the Reims area, promised to cure a local gentleman of leprosy by the following Christmas Day. Before that time, his "salaire" was to cover only the cost of necessary drugs, and here the gentleman, not cured, accused Bonnys of much overcharging (AN, X2A87, 8 July 1536).

18. The physicians attached to the household of Jeanne d'Albret had an annual salary, which may have been paid to them in four installments (Paul Raymond, "Notes extraites des Comptes de Jeanne de Navarre et de ses enfants," *Revue d'Aquitaine* 11 (1867): 122. Annual payments to physicians by the Hôtel-Dieu of Lyon (AHDL, E2, 15 November 1551); Roland Antonioli, *Rabelais et la médecine,* Études rabelaisiennes, 12 (Geneva: Librairie Droz, 1976), 87 n. 108. For an example of payment to an important physician after cure, see ADR, 3E561, 290v–291v (20 November 1558): Master Jean Chappelain owes doctor of medicine Pierre Tolet 120 livres tournois for a loan of 20 écus d'or and for having visited him, advised

him, had him bled, and consulted with other physicians about him for four months until he was cured. Here Chappelain had not paid Tolet along the way. Jeanne du Laurens, "La Généalogie de Messieurs du Laurens," in Charles de Ribbe, ed., *Une Famille au 16e siècle d'après des documents originaux* (Tours: Alfred Mame, 1879), 44. Pomata, *Contracting a Cure,* 48; *Statuts . . . de Bourdeaus,* 230.

19. François Rabelais, *Le Tiers Livre,* chap. 34, in *Oeuvres complètes,* ed. Mireille Huchon (Paris: Gallimard, 1994), 461.

20. Bonaventure Desperiers, *Les Nouvelles Récréations et Joyeux Devis* (1558), ed. Louis Lacour (Paris: Librairie des Bibliophiles, 1874), nouvelle 59, 236–42.

21. Gouberville, *Journal,* 1:242, 244, 246, 249, 258; 2:180–82, 187, 222, 407; 3:437, 488, 490, 515, 517, 600. In an episode similar to Gouberville's fee payment to physicians he hardly knew, Raoul Dager was summoned for a special visit to Gouberville's sister at another manor and her husband paid Dager a fee of two écus directly, which the physician accepted (3:555). The physician Antoine Du Lac, who was not on the salaried household staff of Antoine du Bourbon and Jeanne d'Albret (see n. 16), was given sixty livres as a "gift" ("don") in 1557 for visiting Antoine "during his illness at Nérac. ("Comptes de Jeanne de Navarre," 11:45).

22. Jean de Coras to Jacquette de Bussi, 2 April 1567, 10 April 1567 in *Lettres de Coras, celles de sa femme, de son fils et de ses amis,* ed. Charles Pradel (Albi: Imprimerie G.-M. Nougiès, 1880), 10–11, 13.

23. Pierre Franco, *Traité des hernies* (Lyon: Thibaud Payen, 1561), *5r–*7r.

24. Louise Bourgeois, *Observations diverses sur la sterilité, perte de fruict, foecondité, accouchements et maladies des Femmes . . . par L. Bourgeois dite Boursier, sage femme de Royne,* 2d ed. (Rouen: Widow Thomas Daré, 1626), book 2, 181–82, 192–93, 234, 245, 247.

25. *La Grande chirurgie de M. Guy de Chauliac . . . Restituée par M. Laurens Ioubert* (Lyon: Etienne Michel, 1579), e 3r–e 7r: dedication of Joubert to Catherine Genas, dated 15 August 1578. Joubert was one of Jacquette de Bussi's physicians in Montpellier back in 1567 and thus a recipient of gifts from her and Jean de Coras.

26. BN, Nouv. acq. fr. 1441, 1r (4 April 1580): "Pensions, gaiges, Estatz et Entretenementz," "Dons, pris et bienffaictz." BN, MS. fr. 25728, no. 786: "pour ses gaiges et entretenement" during 1542; no. 787: "ses gaiges ordinaires et autres dons et beneffaictz," 1543. Baron de La Garde to Charles IX, 16 December 1569, requesting a pension for the Sieur de Bealieu, currently serving in the navy off Normandy (BN, Fonds français 15550, 276, cited in *Archives historiques du Département de la Gironde,* 10 [1868]: 352, no. 157).

27. *Catalogue des Actes de François Ier* (Paris: Imprimerie Nationale, 1890), 260, no. 12215. BN, Fonds français, MS. fr. 25723, no. 785 (April 1543); MS. fr. 26149, 1725r. AN, KK133, 2532v. BN, MSS., Nouv. acq. fr. 1441, 9r.

28. See for instance, Paul Raymond, "Notes extraites des comptes de Jeanne d'Albret et se ses enfants," *Revue d'Aquitaine* 11 (1867): 116–50 and S. Amanda Eurich, *The Economics of Power: The Private Finances of the House of Foix-Navarre-Albret during the Religious Wars,* Sixteenth Century Essays and Studies, 24 (Ann Arbor: Edwards Brothers, 1994), 107–23. Mack P. Holt, "Patterns of *Clientèle* and Economic Opportunity at Court during the Wars of Religion: The Household of François, Duke of Anjou," *French Historical Studies* 13 (1984): 305–22, on the mixture of wages and pensions.

29. BN, MSS., Nouv. acq. fr. 1723, 91r, 95r. Other deniers à dieu on 90r, 90v.

30. ADR, 3E368, 28 May 1549; 3E3228, 288v; 3E566, 29 April 1562; 3E4542, January 1569, apprenticeship of Claude Grégoire.

31. BN, MSS., Nouv. acq. fr. 1723, 90r–v, 92r–v.

32. Gouberville, *Journal*, 1:78, 134, 148; 2:31, 35, 43, 44, 146; 3:481, 503, 541, 616–17, 625, among many examples. *Livre de Comptes de Claude de La Landelle, 1553–1556*, ed. René de Laigne (Rennes: Société des Bibliophiles Bretons, 1906), 16, 18, 54, 73, 80, 95, 137, 139. Another example from the phrase of the naturalist Pierre Belon: "when we give money to a chambermaid, we say it's 'pour ses épingles' " (*Les Observations de plusieurs choses memorables, trouvées en Grece . . . Arabie et autres pays estranges* [Paris, 1555], 199v).

33. La Landelle, *Comptes*, 15, 24, 31, 39, 46.

34. Gouberville, *Journal*, 1:26 (13 July 1549); 2:199 (12 July 1555); La Landelle, *Comptes*, 30; Paul Parfouru, "Anciens livres de raison de familles bretonnes conservés aux Archives d'Ille-et-Vilaine," *Bulletin archéologique de l'Association bretonne* (Rennes, 1897), 412–13; Paul Paris-Jallobert, "Registres de comptes de la paroisse d'Izé des 15e et 16e siècles," *Bulletin et Mémoires de la Société archéologique d'Ille-et-Vilaine* 13 (1879): 203.

35. *Remonstrances, et Memoires, pour les Compagnons Imprimeurs, de Paris et Lyon: Opposans. Contre les Libraires, maistres Imprimeurs desdits lieux: Et adiointz* (n.p., n.d. [Lyon, 1572]). AN, X1a, 77v–81r. On these claims and representations, see Natalie Zemon Davis, "A Trade Union in Sixteenth-Century France," *Economic History Review* 19 (1966): 48–69.

36. Gouberville, *Journal*, 2:152 (17 January 1554/1555). La Landelle, *Comptes*, 160. La Landelle also gave two sous in arrhes in striking the deal for the horse. In ordering a new cloak and stockings and the repair of his gown, La Landelle gave one sou of wine to the dressmaker "as stipulation that he wanted [these garments] made and repaired" (37–38).

37. Charles Du Moulin, *Summaire du livre analytique des contractz, usures, rentes constituées, interestz et monnoyes* (Paris: Mathurin Du Puys, 1547), 2v–7r, 17r–32r. Du Moulin read of the burger of Siena in the writings of the late medieval canonist Petrus Ancharanus (Pietro d'Ancarano), 1330–1416, to whom the bishop had submitted the case for judgment, 31r–v. The canonist took a more moderate position in his general reflection on cases of usury (*Consilia sive Iuris Responsa Petri Ancharani Iuresconsulti* [Venice, 1585], 96v). On Du Moulin's views, see Jean-Louis Thireau, *Charles Du Moulin (1500–1566). Étude sur les sources, la méthode, les idées politiques et économiques d'un juriste de la Renaissance* (Geneva: Librairie Droz, 1980), chap. 6.

38. BN, MSS., Nouv. acq. fr. 1723, 2r–5r, 21r, 37v–38r, 40r, 52r, 136v–137r. Émile Clouard, "Deux Bourgeois de Vitré. Journal inédit (1490–1583)," *Revue de Bretagne* (1914): 85–88, 206–9, 212–24. ADR, 3E345, 65v–69r; 3E372, 3 August 1555; 3E561, 290v–291v; 3E539, Easter 1559/1560; 3E3908, 219v–223r, 233r–240r, 245r–247v, 286v–290r; 3E4961, 24 December 1562, 29 December 1562, 31 March 1562/1563, 18 April 1562/1563; 3E5298, February 1550/1551; 3E7184, 444r–447r; 3E7598, 7 December 1541; 3E8029, 134r–136r. La Landelle, *Comptes*, 25–27, 37, 39, 56, 62, 75, 78, 153, 160.

39. BN, MSS., Nouv. acq. fr. 1723, 36v–37r. ADR, 3E3908, 245r–247v; 3E7184, 444r–447r. La Landelle, *Comptes*, 25, 61–62. Gouberville, *Journal*, 2:140 (1 December 1554); 3:524 (16 October 1559).

40. *Les Quatre premiers livres des Eneydes du Treselegant poete Virgile, Traduictz de Latin en prose Francoyse par ma dame Helisenne* (Paris: Denys Janot, 1542?): Crenne, wearing a coif, kneels before François Ier, who sits on his throne and wears a hat. Jacques du Fouilloux, *La Venerie de Iacques du Fouilloux, Gentil-homme, seigneur dudit lieu, pays de Gastine, en Poitou* (Poitiers: J. and E. de Marnef and J. and G. Bouchet, 1562): Fouilloux, his hat on the ground beside him, kneels before a standing and hatted François II, who was still alive when this woodcut was designed in 1561. *Quadrins historiques de la Bible* (Lyon: Jean de Tournes,

1553), B8r: Melchizedec presenting bread and wine to Abraham, picture designed by Bernard Salomon. *Figures de la Bible, illustrees de huictains francoys* (Lyon: Guillaume Rouillé, 1564), N3r: Abigail on her knees presenting many gifts, loaded on donkeys, to David, picture designed by Pierre Eskrich. BN., Cabinet des Estampes, Ea. 17 Rés. T. II: separate woodcut of the author Christofle de Savigny striding forward hatless, holding out his book *Tableaux accomplis de tous les arts liberaux* (Paris: I. and F. de Gourmont, 1587) to Ludovic de Gonzague, Duc de Nivernais, seated, with his hat on; also Georgette de Montenay, *Emblemes, ou devises chrestiennes* (Lyon: Jean Marcorelle, 1571), 90: disabled beggar on the ground receives alms in his bowl, picture engraved by Pierre Woeiriot.

41. *Livret des Emblemes de maistre Andre Alciat* (Paris: Chrestien Wechel, 1536), Q3v–Q4r: exchange of gifts between Ajax and Hector, woodcut designed by Jean Jollat.

42. *Ces presentes heures . . . a l'usage de Paris* (Paris: Widow Thielman Kerver, 1522), illustration for August. *Cy commencent les heures nostre dame a lusaige de Poitiers . . . avec plusieurs belles hystoires* (Printed in Paris for Jehan Varice, bookseller at Angers, 1525), B 1r: illustration for August. *Figures du Nouveau Testament, illustrees de huictains francoys* (Lyon: Guillaume Rouillé, 1570), Bb 6v, picture attributed to Pierre Eskrich or Jean Moni, illustrating Matthew 20:8–14, payment of the laborers in the vineyard, the farmer with a hat, the workers holding their hats.

43. *Figures de la Bible,* E 4v, picture designed by Pierre Eskrich illustrating Genesis 37: 27–28, Judah selling Joseph to the Ishmaelites. For market pictures in the Netherlands (a much more frequently treated subject there than in sixteenth-century France), see Keith P. F. Moxey, "The 'Humanist' Market Scenes of Joachim Beuckelaer: Moralizing Exempla or 'Slice of Life'?" *Koninklijk Museum voor Schone Kunsten-Antwerpen,* (1976), 109–87, and the important new book by Elizabeth Honig, *Painting and the Market in Early Modern Antwerp* (New Haven: Yale University Press, 1998), especially fig. 1, Sebastian Vrancx, *Harbor with the Children of Mercury* (wine-merchant and male purchaser; print-seller and female purchaser); fig. 18, Pieter Aertsen, *Market with Scenes from the Passion;* plate 14, Lucas van Valckenborch, *Vegetable, Fruit and Poultry Market;* and plate 19, Jacob Gerritsz. Cuyp, *Fish Market. Quadrins historiques de la Bible,* D 2r, Esau sells his birthright to Isaac, picture designed by Bernard Salomon.

44. *Figures du Nouveau Testament,* Bb 6v: payment of the workers in the vineyard, picture designed by Pierre Eskrich or Jean Moni.

45. Jean Bouchet, *Les Triumphes de la Noble et amoureuse Dame* (Paris: Guillaume de Bossonzel, 1536), 32r (referring to Seneca as well). The importance of the time interval in gift exchange has received valuable treatment by Pierre Bourdieu, *Esquisse d'une théorie de la pratique* (Geneva: Librairie Droz, 1972), 221–27.

46. Du Moulin, *Contractz,* 35r. BN, MSS., Nouv. acq. fr. 1723, 94v; La Landelle, *Comptes,* 23.

47. Jean Gilles de Noyers, "Proverbia," in *Thresor de la langue francoyse tant ancienne que moderne* (Paris: David Douceur, 1606), 10.

CHAPTER 5. GIFTS GONE WRONG

1. Henri Zerner, *The School of Fontainebleau. Etchings and Engravings* (London: Thames and Hudson, 1969), AF22, JM40. The pictures and drawings at Fontainebleau were also the source of many prints. "Un barbier rase l'autre": Jean Gilles de Noyers, "Proverbia," in

Thresor de la langue francoyse tant ancienne que moderne (Paris: David Douceur, 1606), 15. "One hand rubs another": Erasmus, *Adages,* I i 32, trans. Margaret Mann Phillips in *Collected Works of Erasmus* (Toronto: University of Toronto Press, 1982), 31:82.

2. Gilles de Noyers, "Proverbia," in *Thresor de la langue francoyse,* 2.

3. Jérome des Gouttes, "Recit de La Maizon et origine des des Gouttes," AEG, manuscripts.

4. ADR, 3E3908, 259r–261v, 183v–192v, 213r–216r. Another example in ADR, 15G120, 27 November 1559, is the will of widow Françoise Coyard, who says that by all right and reason she could cut her son off completely because "he had always been disobedient and had given her much trouble, torment, and sadness, having brought a suit against her and raised alarms against her." Still not wishing to use "all rigor" against him she leaves him five hundred livres, or else an annual pension of thirty livres. A legal discussion of what was required to disinherit a child who would customarily "be called to inherit" is given in Pardoux du Prat, *Theorique de l'art des Notaires, Pour cognoistre la nature de tous Contracts* (Lyon: Basile Bouquet, 1582), 200–203, chap. 5.

5. ADR, 3E3766, 237v–239v; 3E5294, 8 May 1547; 3E5295, 20 July 1557: wills of Clauda Carcande, widow of printer Claude Nourry, dit Le Prince, wife of printer Pierre de Sainte Lucie. Her daughter was Catherine Nourry, widow of printer Pierre de Vingle. On Vingle, see chap. 7 of this book.

6. AEG, Notaire Jean Jovenon, vol. 4, 125v–127r, will of François Bay, merchant of Lyon, inhabitant of Geneva, 24 December 1577. Claude de Rubys, *Sommaire explication des articles de la Coustume du Païs et Duché de Bourgongne* (Lyon: Antoine Gryphius, 1580), 42–46.

7. AN, 1AP281, no. 2, 21 January 1563/1564. AEG, Notaire Jean Du Verney, vol. 5, 45r–46r. ADR, 3E3908, 240v–243v. ADA, 5E5335, 123v; 5E6221, 8 May 1540; 5E6653, 54v. ADHG, 3E15280, 31 January 1547/1548; 3E15983, 322r–324v. See also the recommendations of René Fleuriot, gentleman of Bretagne, to his children to avoid "les grandes animosittés quy naissent aulx familles sur la division des biens que pères et mères delaissent à leurs enfants à leurs déscès et les grands procès qui s'engendrent entreulx" [The great animosity born within families over the division of the goods that fathers and mothers leave their children at their deaths and the big lawsuits bred among [the children]] (Jean Meyer, "Un témoignage exceptionnel sur la noblesse de province à l'orée du 17e siècle: les 'advis moraux' de René Fleuriot," *Annales de Bretagne* 79 [1972]: 324).

8. AN, 1AP251, no. 147: documents in the conflict between Anne de Laval, Dame de La Trémoille, and her son Louis de La Trémoille. The quarreling began already right after the death of Duke François, when Louis insisted that her goods be inventoried as well as those of his late father, which Anne said "was not customary for a woman of her estate" (1AP253, 218r–224r).

9. Jean Papon, *Premier Tome des Trois Notaires* (Lyon: Jean de Tournes, 1568), 341–55. Claude Le Brun de La Rochette, *Le proces civil et criminel* (Lyon: Pierre Rigaud, 1618), 172–73. Jean-Marie Ricard, *Traité des Donations entre-vifs et testamentaires,* 2 vols. (Paris: Jean Guignard and Arnoul Seneuze, 1692), vol. 1, part 3, chap. 6.

10. AN, Y95, 120r–121r, 158v–159v.

11. "Plaidoyé de Monsieur Brisson touchant le meurtre advenu au logis du Bailly de Colommiers, du vingt-deuxiesme Mars 1572," in *Recueil de Plaidoyez notables de plusieurs anciens et fameux Advocats de la Cour de Parlement* (Paris: Widow of Jean du Brayet and Nicolas Rousset, 1612), 246–64. Julien Brodeau, "La Vie de Maistre Charles Du Moulin," in Charles

Du Moulin, *Omnia quae extant Opera,* 5 vols. (Paris: Jean Cochart, 1681), 1:17–18, 57–59. Jean-Louis Thireau, *Charles Du Moulin (1500–1566): Étude sur les sources, la méthode, les idées politiques et économiques d'un juriste de la Renaissance* (Geneva: Librairie Droz, 1980), 26–27 and 27 n. 39.

12. ADR, BP3662, 63r–68r. Before approving the revocation, the local court at Condrieu had hearings on Jean Colombier's accusations, in which three other Condrieu priests supported Colombier's account.

13. ADR, 3E3908, 293r–295r, carter Lambert Michaud revokes inter vivos donations to his two oldest sons because they had been "ungrateful and disobedient," did not do what they were held to do by the contract of donation, and abandoned and left the family. Instead he divides his property at death equally among his four sons and one daughter. AN, Y87, 202r–v (9 August 1541) and Y93, 119v–122r (28 June 1547) Master Nicolas LeClerc, doctor regent in the Faculty of Theology at Paris revokes a donation of 1540 to one nephew, a judge in the king's chancellery court, because of "ingratitude" and refusing to live in peace with him and other relatives, and revokes a subsequent donation to two other nephews because they had tried to wrest away their sister's portion of the gift and to cheat him, their uncle, of an inheritance. See also E. Campardon and A. Tuetey, *Inventaire des registres des Insinuations du Châtelet de Paris. Règnes de François Ier et de Henri II* (Paris: Imprimerie Nationale, 1906), Y88, no. 890.

14. Shakespeare, *King Lear,* 1.1.50–52.

15. Ibid., 1.1.91–92, 96–98.

16. Ibid., 1.1.99–101.

17. Guillaume Budé to Erasmus, 1 May 1516 in *The Correspondence of Erasmus,* trans. R. A. B. Mynors and D. F. S. Thomson, annot. James K. McConica (Toronto and Buffalo: University of Toronto Press, 1976), 3:277–78, no. 403.

18. Louis La Trémoille, *Les La Trémoille pendant cinq siècles* (Nantes: Émile Grimaud, 1894), 3:85–86.

19. Antonio de Guevara, *Le Favori [sic] de court,* trans. Jacques de Rochemore (Antwerp: Christophe Plantin, 1557 [1st ed., Lyon: Guillaume Rouillé 1556]), 62v, 78r, 80v, 102v–103v.

20. Antonio de Guevara, *Du Mespris de la court et de la louange de la vie rustique,* trans. Antoine Alaigre (Lyon: Jean and François Frellon, 1543), F 5r, chap. 15: "Qu'entre Courtisans ne se garde amitié ny loyaulté." Philibert de Vienne, *Le Philosophe de court* (Lyon: Jean de Tournes, 1547), 95–106. On this whole genre see Pauline Smith, *The Anti-Courtier Trend in Sixteenth Century French Literature* (Geneva: Librairie Droz, 1966) and Rose Duroux, ed., *Les Traités de savoir-vivre en Espagne et au Portugal du Moyen Âge à nos jours* (Clermont-Ferrand: Association des Publications de la Faculté des Lettres et Sciences Humaines de Clermont-Ferrand, 1996).

21. Elizabeth Armstrong, *Ronsard and the Age of Gold* (Cambridge: Cambridge University Press, 1968), chaps. 1, 5; Daniel Ménager, *Ronsard: Le Roi, le Poète et les Hommes* (Geneva: Librairie Droz, 1979); Michel Simonin, *Pierre de Ronsard* (Paris: Fayard, 1990), part 3.

22. Michel de Montaigne, *Essais,* 3:9 in *Oeuvres complètes,* ed. Albert Thibaudet and Maurice Rat (Paris: Gallimard, 1962), 943 (translations mine). As always with Montaigne, his thought is full of paradoxes, and in other situations he can be critical of buying and selling as a threat to his honor (see Philippe Desan, *Les Commerces de Montaigne: Le discours économique des "Essais"* [Paris: Librairie A. -G. Nizet, 1992], chap. 3).

23. Montaigne, *Essais,* 3:9 in *Oeuvres,* 944–45.

24. Montaigne, *Essais,* 1:40 in *Oeuvres,* 247.

25. Michel de Montaigne, *Journal de voyage,* ed. François Rigolot (Paris: Presses Universitaires de France, 1992), 41–42, 68, 131, 171–74, 228–29. Montaigne, *Essais* in *Oeuvres,* 1: 26, p. 144, "De l'institution des enfans," to Madame Diane de Foix, Comtesse de Gurson; 2:8, p. 364, "De l'affection des peres aux enfans," dedicated to Madame d'Estissac. The sonnets of Étienne de La Boétie he dedicated to Madame de Grammont, Comtesse de Guissen, 1:29, p. 194. He also found a courteous language for a letter to Madame Paulmier, which accompanied a copy of his *Essais* (*Oeuvres,* 1396).

26. Montaigne, *Oeuvres,* xviii; *Journal de voyage,* 94.

27. Guevara, *Favori de court,* chap. 17. G. R. Owst, *Literature and Pulpit in Medieval England* (Oxford: Blackwell, 1966), 390–96; Natalie Zemon Davis and Arlette Farge, eds., *A History of Women in the West,* vol. 3: *Renaissance and Enlightenment Paradoxes* (Cambridge, Mass.: Harvard University Press, 1993), 59–63. Interestingly enough, Philibert de Vienne dedicated *Le Philosophe de court* to an unnamed woman, "l'amye de vertu," who had long reproached Vienne for being a manipulator and a liar (un prometteur, un menteur), p. 3. Marie de Gournay, "Peincture de Moeurs," (1626) in Mario Schiff, *La Fille d'alliance de Montaigne. Marie de Gournay* (Paris, 1910), 113. Montaigne, *Essais,* 3:2 in *Oeuvres,* 782.

28. Louise Labé, *Oeuvres complètes,* ed. Enzo Giudici (Geneva: Librairie Droz, 1981), 16–20, from the dedication to *Euvres de Louise Labe lionnoise* (Lyon: Jean de Tournes, 1555). Gournay's relation to Montaigne is characterized in her first publication, *Le Proumenoir de Monsieur de Montaigne, par sa fille d'alliance* (Paris: Abel L'Angelier, 1594) and in her preface to the 1595 edition of the *Essais* of Montaigne (Paris: Abel L'Angelier, 1595). I have discussed and given further bibliography on the relation between Gournay and Montaigne in Natalie Zemon Davis, "Neue Perspektiven für die Geschlechterforschung in der Frühen Neuzeit," in Heide Wunder and Gisela Engel, eds., *Geschlechter Perspektiven: Forschungen zur Frühen Neuzeit* (Frankfurt: Ulrkie Helmer Verlag, 1998), 20–28, and have considered more generally the strategies and language used by men and women to deal with autonomy in "Boundaries and the Sense of Self in Sixteenth-Century France," in Thomas C. Heller et al., *Reconstructing Individualism: Autonomy, Individuality, and the Self in Western Thought* (Stanford: Stanford University Press, 1986), 53–63, 332–35.

29. Sharon Kettering, "The Patronage Power of Early Modern French Noblewomen," *The Historical Journal* 32 (1989): 817–41. Louise Bourgeois, *Observations diverses sur la sterilité, perte de fruict, foecondité, accouchements et maladies des Femmes et Enfants nouveaux naix,* 2d ed., 2 vols. (Rouen: Widow of Thomas Daré 1626), 2:112–48. The first edition of this work (Paris: Abraham Saugrain, 1609) and the 1626 edition have dedicatory poems from Bourgeois to the aristocratic women (such as the Princesse de Conti, Madame de Montpencier, and Madame d'Elbeuf) whom she had served and who had helped her make her way (e.g., p. 117). André du Laurens received his post as royal physician to Henri IV in part by the intervention of a grateful patron of high birth, Madame de Crussol, Duchess d'Uzès (Jeanne du Laurens, "La généalogie de Messieurs du Laurens," in Charles de Ribbe, *Une Famille au 16e siècle d'après des documents originaux* [Tours: Alfred Mame, 1879], 72–75). Marcus Aurelius Antoninus, *Institution de la vie humaine* (Lyon: Widow of Gabriel Cotier [Antoinette Peronet], 1580), *3r–*5v, dedication of Antoinette Peronet to François de Mandelot, lieutenant-governor of the Lyonnais, 15 February 1570.

30. Du Laurens, "Généalogie," 49, 60–61, 65–66.

31. Gournay, preface to Montaigne, *Essais* (1595), a iii r–v. The whole question of women's dedications in their publications in sixteenth-century France and their strategies to get around the prescription of silence have been discussed recently by Susan Margaret

Broomhall, "Women and Publication in Sixteenth-Century France" (Ph.D. diss., University of Western Australia, 1999), chap. 6.

32. *Les Quatre premiers livres des Eneydes du Treselegant poete Virgile, Traduictz de Latin en prose Francoyse par ma dame Helisenne* (Paris: Denys Janot, 1542?), épître dédicatoire.

33. *Les Oeuvres de ma dame Helisenne de Crenne* (Paris: Estienne Groulleau, 1560): L'Espistre Dedicative de Dame Helisenne à toutes honnestes Dames, to *Les Angoisses douloureuses qui procedent d'amours* (first published with this dedication in Lyon: Denis de Harsy, 1538).

34. Christine de Pizan, *The Book of the City of Ladies,* rev. ed., trans. Earl Jeffrey Richards (New York: Persea Books, 1998), 2:50, pp. 170–76, 265–66.

35. Marguerite de Navarre, *Heptaméron,* ed. Simone de Reyff (Paris: Flammarion, 1982), story number twenty-one, 206–24, 508.

36. Montaigne, *Essais* (1962), 1:31 in *Oeuvres,* 204. For another approach to Montaigne's description of exchange among the Tupinamba, see the interesting study of Desan, *Commerces de Montaigne,* chap. 6.

37. "Declaration du voyage du Capitaine Gonneville et ses compagnons au Brésil (1503–1505)," ed. C. A. Julien in C. A. Julien, R. Herval, and T. Beauchesne, eds., *Les français en Amérique pendant la première moitié du 16e siècle* (Paris: Presses Universitaires de France, 1946), 29; "Voyage de Giovanni da Verrazano à la *Francesca*" (1524), trans. R. Herval, in *Les français en Amérique,* 58, 64–65, 69–70.

38. Jacques Cartier, *Premier Voyage* (1534) and *Deuxième Voyage* (1535–36), ed. Théodore Beauchesne, in *Les français en Amérique,* 100–2, 104–5, 131, 133, 144, 155. *The Voyages of Jacques Cartier,* trans. H. P. Biggar, introduction by Ramsay Cook (Toronto: University of Toronto Press, 1993), 21–22, 24–25, 49–51, 59–60, 67.

39. Jean de Léry, *History of a Voyage to the Land of Brazil,* trans. Janet Whatley (Berkeley and Los Angeles: University of California Press, 1990), 161, 164–69.

40. Cartier, *Voyages,* 33; Léry, *Voyage,* 180.

41. Cartier, *Deuxième Voyage,* 160; Cartier, *Voyages,* 70, 92.

42. Léry, *Voyage,* 65, 89, 99, 114, 170–71.

43. Erasmus, *Adages,* I i 100 ("Exchange between Diomede and Glaucus"), in *Collected Works,* 31:144–46.

44. Cartier, *Deuxième Voyage,* 179; Cartier, *Voyages,* 86. Jean Zeller, *La Diplomatie française vers le milieu du 16e siècle* (Paris: Librairie Hachette, 1881), 291.

45. Cartier, *Deuxième Voyage,* 131, 137, 171–72; Cartier, *Voyages,* 50, 54, 79–80.

46. Léry, *Voyage,* 62, 65, 99, 167, 169.

47. For the seventeenth and eighteenth centuries, see Cornelius J. Jaenen, "The Role of Presents in French-Amerindian Trade," in Duncan Cameron, ed., *Explorations in Canadian Economic History: Essays in Honour of Irene M. Spry* (Ottawa: University of Ottawa Press, 1985), 231–51.

48. Cartier, *Deuxième Voyage,* 135; Cartier, *Voyages,* 52–53. Léry, *Voyage,* 162–64, 170.

CHAPTER 6. GIFTS, BRIBES, AND KINGS

1. André Viala, *Le Parlement de Toulouse et l'Administration Royale Laïque, 1420–1525 environ* (Albi: Imprimerie-Relieure des Orphelins-Apprentis, 1953), 155–66. *Inventaire-Sommaire des Archives Communales antérieures à 1790. Ville de Lyon,* vol. 3, ed. M. C. Guigue et al. (Lyon: n.p., 1887), CC940, CC946, CC958. Eugène Vial, "Présents d'honneur et gour-

mandises," *Revue d'histoire de Lyon* 9(1910): 122–48, 277–300, 377–401. *Inventaire-Sommaire des Archives Municipales antérieures à 1790 de la Ville d'Orange*, ed. L. Duhamel (Orange: Imprimerie Martin-Peyre, 1917), BB13, 90, 131; BB14, 87; CC418, 22, 25; CC429, 30, 35; CC433, 8; CC445; CC448, 3, 51; CC457. Alain Derville, "Pots-de-vin, cadeaux, racket, patronage: essai sur les mécanismes de décision dans l'état bourguignon," *Revue du Nord* 56(1974): 341–64.

2. Hélène Michaud, *La Grand Chancellerie et les écritures royales au 16e siècle* (Paris: Imprimerie Nationale, 1967), 112–13. Gilles de Gouberville, *Le Journal du Sire de Gouberville*, 4 vols. (Bricquebosq: Les Editions des Champs, 1993–94), 3:27 (2 August 1553), 35 (10 September 1553), 58 (12 December 1553), 69 (25 January 1553/1554).

3. Bonaventure Desperiers, *Les Nouvelles Récréations et Joyeux Devis*, ed. Louis Lacour (Paris: Librairie des Bibliophiles, 1874), nouvelle 10, pp. 56–61: bringing gifts to attorney for better service. E. Campardon and A. Tuetey, *Inventaire des registres des Insinuations du Châtelet de Paris. Règnes de François Ier et de Henri II* (Paris: Imprimerie nationale, 1906), nos. 127, 157. Guillaume Bouchet, *Premier Livre des Serees de Guillaume Bouchet, Sieur de Brocourt. Reveu et augmenté* (Paris: Jérémie Perier, 1608), neuvième serée: description of the painting of the avaricious lawyer receiving gifts from both ends. Bouchet's *Serées* were first published in three volumes from 1585 to 1598. The picture by Pieter Brueghel the Younger exists in numerous signed oil paintings (1615–21) with various titles: *The Payment of the Tithe, The Peasants' Lawyer, The Tax-Collector, The Lawyer of Bad Cases, The Notary's Office* (Georges Marlier, *Pierre Brueghel Le Jeune*, ed. J. Folie [Brussels: Éditions Robert Finck, 1969], 435–40). The Art Gallery of South Australia, from which my illustration comes, initially used the title *A Lawyer's Office* and has now changed it to *The Tax-Collector's Office* (Letter of Angus Trumble, Curator of European Art, Art Gallery of South Australia, 20 August 1999). It may well be that the painting was interpreted in these different ways in the seventeenth century. There are two reasons for preferring *A Lawyer's Office* or *The Peasants' Lawyer*, with a lawyer at the main table and a notary or clerk working for him at the smaller table. First, the figure reading at the desk is wearing a characteristic lawyer's bonnet. Tax-collectors and tithe-collectors were not ordinarily men with law degrees; and indeed, the collection of tithes and taxes did not usually take place in such a setting. The papers and bags on the desk and wall are precisely like those used for decrees and requests in civil and criminal suits, whereas tithe and tax records were kept in large registers. The peasants lined up with eggs and chickens are bringing gifts to please the lawyer, a common occurrence, while tithe payments were made in grain. Second, as I have learned from the art historian Keith Moxey, there are at least two early seventeenth-century engravings of Brueghel's painting with Latin and German texts that criticize the avarice of lawyers, one by AE. Schal and one by Paulus Fürst. (Letter of Keith Moxey, 13 October 1983; phone conversation of 7 September 1999. See also Keith Moxey, "The Criticism of Avarice in Sixteenth-Century Netherlandish Painting," in Görel Cavalli-Björkman, ed., *Netherlandish Mannerism* [Stockholm: National Museum, 1985], 21–34). Thus, though gifts to men of the law may not have been the exclusive reference of Brueghel's painting for contemporary viewers, it was certainly a major reference. Jean Imbert, *Institutions Forenses, ou practique iudiciaire* (Poitiers: Enguilbert de Marnef, 1563), 494.

4. "De main vuyde, vuydes prieres." "Par dons et presens on vient à bout de ses affaires" from Jean Gilles de Noyers, "Proverbia," in *Thresor de la langue francoyse tant ancienne que moderne* (Paris: David Douceur), 4, 16.

5. *Inventaire-Sommaire des Archives Communales. Lyon*, vol. 3, CC940. *Edict du Roy prohibitif à tous Gouverneurs, leurs Lieutenans, Presidens, Tresoriers, Generaulx, et autres officiers*

Royaulx, de prendre n'exiger du peuple deniers n'autres presens, sans la permission expresse dudict seigneur Roy (Paris: Jean Dallier and Vincent Sertenas, 1560). Michaud, *Grande Chancellerie,* 113, 295 n. 8; Natalie Zemon Davis, *Fiction in the Archives: Pardon Tales and Their Tellers in Sixteenth-Century France* (Stanford: Stanford University Press, 1987), 10, 153 n. 14.

6. *Des États Généraux et autres assemblées nationales,* ed. Charles Joseph Mayer, 18 vols. (The Hague and Paris: Buisson, 1788–89), 11:195, *cahier* of the nobility. Bernard de La Roche-Flavin, *Treize Livres des Parlemens de France* (Geneva: Matthieu Berjon, 1621), book 8, chap. 17, pp. 608–13. *Recueil général des anciennes lois françaises depuis l'an 420 jusqu'à la Révolution de 1789,* ed. F. A. Isambert et al., 29 vols. (Paris, n.p. 1822–33), 14:76, Edict of Orléans, January, 1560/1561, art. 43; 14:409–10, Ordinance of Blois, May 1579, art. 114.

7. La Roche-Flavin, *Parlemens de France,* book 2, chap. 18, p. 240 (1494); book 3, chap. 4, pp. 343–44 (1550, 1566). ADHG, B22, 347v (18 August 1528). Jonathan Dewald, *The Formation of a Provincial Nobility: The Magistrates of the Parlement of Rouen, 1499–1610)* (Princeton: Princeton University Press, 1980), 146. A. Floquet, *Histoire du Parlement de Normandie,* 7 vols. (Rouen: E. Frère, 1840–42), 1:515–19; 2:1–16.

8. ADIV, 2Eb13, "Extraict du proces criminel Institué en la court de parlement au . . . poursuilte de maistre Francoys de Cahedeuc Lieutenant particulier du Rennes Contre maistre Gilles Becdelievre Juge magistrat criminel audict Rennes, 1559–1560." Becdelièvre did not get final payment for damages and lost salary until 1566.

9. ADIV, 2Eb13, 7v. Noël du Fail, *Les Contes et Discours d'Eutrapel* (Rennes, 1585) in *Oeuvres facétieuses de Noël du Fail,* ed. J. Assézat, 2 vols. (Paris: Daffis, 1874), 1:253–57. By the time Noël du Fail wrote this work, he had risen to the post of judge in the Parlement of Brittany.

10. La Roche-Flavin, *Parlemens de France,* book 8, chap. 17, p. 613. La Roche-Flavin claims he heard the story himself in 1583 in Limoges from the hotelkeeper.

11. The meanings of and quarrels about bribery over the centuries is the subject of a magisterial book by John T. Noonan, Jr., *Bribes* (New York: Macmillan Publishing Company, 1984). See especially chaps. 11–12 on the sixteenth and early seventeenth centuries.

12. *The Compact Edition of the Oxford English Dictionary* (Oxford: Oxford University Press, 1971), 273. Shakespeare, *Measure for Measure,* 2.2 and *Julius Caesar,* 4.3. Francis Bacon, *The Work of Francis Bacon,* ed. James Spedding, 7 vols. (London: Longmans, Green, Reader, and Dyer, 1874), 7:215, 226. On the emergence of the word *miet* in Basel and Strasbourg in the fifteenth century to indicate wrongful secret gifts given to government officers, see Valentin Groebner, "The Guard's Offer: Gifts, Corruption and the Visualization of the Invisible in Renaissance Basel," in Gadi Algazi, Bernhard Jussen, and Valentin Groebner, eds., *Negotiating the Gift* (Göttingen: Vandenhoeck and Ruprecht, 2000); see also Groebner's *Dangerous Liquids: Gift-Giving and Corruption in Renaissance Germany and Switzerland* (Philadelphia: University of Pennsylvania Press, forthcoming).

13. Gouberville, *Journal,* 2:154 (Supper at Saint Lô with the seneschal, a judge from the presidial court, and two members of Gouberville's household: "pour ung pot de vin, 3 sous"). On the vin de marché, see chap. 4 of this book. The critical biblical texts against judges accepting gifts (Exodus 23:8, Deuteronomy 16:19, 1 Samuel 8:3) use *munera* for gifts in the Latin Vulgate; the French Protestant Bible uses *le don* for Exodus 23:8, *présent* for Deuteronomy 16:19, and *des dons* for 1 Samuel 8:3 (*Biblia* [Paris: Robert Estienne, 1540], 25v, 64r, 92r; *La Bible* [Geneva: Pierre and Jacques Chouet, 1622], 37r, 94v, 136v). The "Geneva Bible" in English—that is the English translation printed in Geneva in 1560 by refugees from England—uses "gift" for Exodus 23:8 and "reward" for both Deuteronomy 16:19 and

1 Samuel 8:3, while the King James Version uses "gift" for the first two texts and "bribes" for 1 Samuel 8:3 (*The Geneva Bible. A Facsimile of the 1560 Edition* [Madison: University of Wisconsin Press, 1969], 10, 88, 124).

14. Spedding, *Francis Bacon*, 7:226, 238, 258. François Rabelais, *Le Tiers Livre*, chaps. 36, 39–43, in *Oeuvres complètes*, ed. Mireille Huchon (Paris: Gallimard, 1994), 466–67, 474–87. Charles Loyseau, *Cinq Livres du Droit des Offices* (Cologne: Isaac Demonthouz, 1613), 117–18.

15. For instance, Gouberville, *Journal*, 1:7, arbitration of a dispute between Messire Clément Rouxel, a priest, and Cossin, a local sergeant, because of an attack by Rouxel's brother on Cossin's stepson. Gouberville had them to dinner after mass, and it was agreed that Rouxel would pay Cossin two testons. The day before, Rouxel had given Gouberville a large fish (27–28 April 1549). *Journal*, 3:568, Gouberville had four tenants to midday dinner, and arbitrated a dispute among them about a promised payment of furniture (29 May, 1560). In both cases the arbitration solved disputes that were also before the courts. *Journal* 1:251 (4 June 1552), the curé de Cherbourg tells Gouberville stories from Rabelais's book 4, and promises to lend it to him. He may have read *Le Tiers Livre* as well.

16. Rabelais, *Le Tiers Livre*, prologue in *Oeuvres*, 352, and notes 7–11; *Cinquiesme Livre*, chaps. 11–15, in *Oeuvres*, 749–61. Noël du Fail, judge in the Parlement of Brittany and a reader of Rabelais, makes a similar contrast in his *Contes et Discours d'Eutrapel* between local magistrates, who receive foods from both parties in a case and solve things in a festive setting, and professional judges who compel their parties to give them money (*Contes d'Eutrapel*, 1: 312–13, 253–56).

17. Jean de Coras, *Petit Discours des parties et office d'un bon et entier iuge* (Lyon: Barthélemy Vincent, 1595), 54–66. The first edition of this book has never been found, but there is a reference in the text to Charles IX succeeding to the throne in December 1560 and to Antoine de Bourbon as co-regent during Charles's minority. Antoine de Bourbon, who died in 1562, is not referred to as "late," which suggests that the book was initially written and published between early 1561 and 1562.

18. Jean de Coras, *De Iuris Arte Libellus* (Lyon: Antoine Vincent, 1560). This work and the legal thought of Jean de Coras are treated by A. London Fell, Jr., *Origins of Legislative Sovereignty and the Legislative State*, vol. 1: *Corasius and the Renaissance Systematization of Roman Law* (Königstein and Cambridge, Mass.: Gunn and Hain, 1983). Jonathan Dewald stresses the king's concern to extricate his judges and other royal officials from service and ties to local aristocracies (*Formation of a Provincial Nobility*, pp. 146–47).

19. Quoted by La Roche-Flavin in *Parlemens de France*, book 8, chap. 17, p. 609, from one of Pibrac's harangues when he was Avocat général at the Parlement of Paris.

20. *Livret des Emblemes de maistre Andre Alciat, mis en rime francoyse* (Paris: Chrestien Wechel, 1536), H8v–J1r: "Ces gens sans mains qui sont assis / Sont ceulx dont iustice [*sic*] est pourveue: / Ilz soent ayans le sens rassis: / En don chose nest deulx receue." *Emblemes d'Alciat, de nouveau translatez en Francois* (Lyon: Guillaume Rouillé, 1549), 176–77: "Et les mains coupées pour ne prendre aulcuns dons, ne presentz, pour estre corrompuz."

21. Hans Holbein, *Les Simulachres et historiees faces de la mort* (Lyon: Melchior and Gaspard Trechsel for Jean and François Frellon, 1538), E 1r: "Du mylieu d'eulx vous osteray / Iuges corrumpus par presentz." For the many editions of this work, see Natalie Zemon Davis, "Holbein's *Pictures of Death* and the Reformation at Lyons," *Studies in the Renaissance* 3 (1956): 97–130. ADIV, 2Eb13, 3r.

22. Another gift network generating concern about bribery was diplomacy. Here the ambassador had to be bountiful in giving gifts and banquets on behalf of his prince, but restrained in spending on his own behalf. He also had to be wary of taking gifts from those to whom he was assigned. Jean Hotman, ambassador for Henri IV, gave the following advice in his manual on the Ambassador: "He will receive no gifts or presents, neither from the Prince to whom he has been sent, nor from any of his people for any reason whatsoever, unless it is just before he is to leave his post and ready to mount his horse . . . For gifts oblige, and blind the eyes of those who see clearly, as the law of Moses says. Those who receive them become slaves to those who give them. All the more if they accept a pension or other benefit [from the prince to whom they are sent], for they will either seem stained with avarice or suspect of treason." Jean Hotman, *De la Charge et Dignité de l'Ambassadeur* in *Opuscules françoises* (Paris: Widow of M. Gullemot, 1617), 499; Jean Hotman, *The Ambassador* (London: James Shawe, 1603), n.p.

23. Lawrence M. Bryant, *The King and the City in the Parisian Royal Entry Ceremony: Politics, Ritual, and Art in the Renaissance* (Geneva: Librairie Droz, 1986), 32. George A. Wanklyn, "Le présent offert à Henri II par la Ville de Paris en 1549," *Revue de l'Art* 46 (1979): 25–30. Georges Guigue, ed., *La magnificence de la superbe et triumphante entree de la noble et antique Cité de Lyon faicte au Treschrestien Roy de France Henry deuxiesme de ce Nom, Et à la Royne Catherine son Espouse le XXIII de Septembre MDXLVIII* (Lyon: Guillaume Rouillé, 1549; reprinted in Lyon: Société des Bibliophiles de Lyon, 1927), 67. Among other sources, see also Jean Boutier, Alain Dewerpe, and Daniel Nordman, *Un tour de France royal: Le voyage de Charles IX (1564–1566)* (Paris: Aubier, 1984), part 4; Victor E. Graham and W. McAllister Johnson, *The Royal Tour of France by Charles IX and Catherine de' Medici: Festivals and Entries, 1564–1566* (Toronto: University of Toronto Press, 1979); Victor E. Graham and W. McAllister Johnson, *The Parisian Entries of Charles IX and Elizabeth of Austria, 1571* (Toronto and Buffalo: University of Toronto Press, 1974); Margaret McGowan, ed., *L'Entrée de Henri II à Rouen 1550* (Amsterdam: Theatrum Orbis Terrarum, 1977), and Michael Wintroub, "Civilizing the Savage and Making a King: The Royal Entry Festival of Henri II (Rouen, 1550)," *Sixteenth Century Journal* 29 (1998): 465–94.

24. Bryant, *Parisian Royal Entry,* 24, 64, 208.

25. *Entree . . . de Lyon,* 3–79, 134–39, 141–42, 182–84. Bryant, *Parisian Royal Entry,* 42–45.

26. *Entree . . . de Lyon,* 67, 138–39.

27. Bryant, *Parisian Royal Entry,* 27–28. *Entree . . . de Lyon,* 79, 138–39, 184–85, 190–91. Roger Doucet, *Finances municipales et crédit public à Lyon au XVIe siècle* (Paris: Librairie des Sciences Politiques et Sociales, 1937), 40–42.

28. Bryant, *Parisian Royal Entry,* 36–40, 214. Roger Doucet, *Les Institutions de la France au XVIe siècle* (Paris: Éditions A. and J. Picard, 1948), 314–15, 556–77.

29. Jean Combes, *Traicté des Tailles, et autres charges et subsides, tant ordinaires, que extraordinaires, qui se levent en France* (Paris: F. Morel, 1584), 3v–4r, 13v. Alain Guéry, "Le roi dépenser. Le don, la contrainte, et l'origine du système financier de la monarchie française d'Ancien Régime," *Annales.ESC* 39 (1984): 1241–69. Charles Loyseau, *Traité des Seigneuries* (Paris: Abel L'Angelier, 1609), chap. 3, pars. 42–46, pp. 61–64. Antoine Loisel, *Institutes coutumieres* (Paris: Nicolas Gosselin, 1710), book 1, title 1, V: "Au Roi seul appartient de prendre tribut sur les personnes." Howell Lloyd, "The Political Thought of Charles Loyseau (1564–1627)," *European Studies Review* 11 (1981): 69–70.

30. Bryant, *Parisian Royal Entry*, 208–14. *Entrées royales et fêtes populaires à Lyon (XVe–XVIIIe siècles)*, exhibition catalog (exhibition at the Bibliothèque de la Ville de Lyon, 12 June–12 July 1970), 98–100.

31. Jean Savaron, *Traicté de l'Annuel et Venalité des Offices* (Paris: Pierre Chevalier, 1615), 4–16. Roland Mousnier, *La Vénalité des offices sous Henri IV et Louis XIII*, 2d ed. (Paris: Presses Universitaires de France, 1971), introduction. Christopher Stocker, "Public and Private Enterprise in the Administration of a Renaissance Monarchy: The First Sales of Office in the Parlement of Paris (1512–1524)," *Sixteenth Century Journal* 9 (1978): 4–29.

32. Guillaume Budé, *De L'Institution du prince* (Paris: Nicole Paris, 1547), chap. 3, pp. 20–22; chap. 39, p. 165. Budé had died in 1540, and the work remained in manuscript until 1547. On this text see David O. McNeil, *Guillaume Budé and Humanism in the Reign of Francis I* (Geneva: Librairie Droz, 1975), chap. 4.

33. Jean Bodin, *Les Six Livres de la République* (Paris: Jacques Du Puys, 1577), book 5, chap. 4, pp. 563–64, 576–77. In order to guarantee that recipients were worthy, Bodin was also totally opposed to payment for offices. Among many studies of Bodin's political thought, see Quentin Skinner, *The Foundations of Modern Political Thought*, 2 vols. (Cambridge: Cambridge University Press, 1978), 2:284–301.

34. Bodin, *Republique*, book 4, chap. 4, p. 457.

35. Claude de Rubys, *Les Privileges, franchises et immunitez octroyees par les roys treschrestiens, aux Consuls, Eschevins, manans et habitans de la ville de Lyon* (Lyon: Antoine Gryphius, 1574), 68–69. An excellent general study of the myth of "race" or stock and lineage and of quarrels about the social order is Arlette Jouanna, *Ordre social. Mythes et hiérarchies dans la France du 16e siècle* (Paris: Hachette, 1977). See also Davis Bitton, *The French Nobility in Crisis, 1560–1640* (Stanford: Stanford University Press, 1969), 79–82; Ellery Schalk, *From Valor to Pedigree: Ideas of Nobility in France in the Sixteenth and Seventeenth Centuries* (Princeton: Princeton University Press, 1986); Jonathan Dewald, *Aristocratic Experience and the Origins of Modern Culture: France, 1570–1715* (Berkeley and Los Angeles: University of California Press, 1993), chaps. 2–3; and the important new study of Jay M. Smith, *The Culture of Merit: Nobility, Royal Service, and the Making of Absolute Monarchy in France, 1600–1789* (Ann Arbor: University of Michigan Press, 1996), chaps. 1–2.

36. Bodin, *Republique*, book 4, chap. 4, p. 466; book 5, chap. 4, pp. 567–68, 578. Bodin especially praised François I for his gifts of office in his standoffish last years, "giving offices, honors, and benefits only to the deserving and men of honor." He contrasted this with the reign of Henri II, who was so sweet, gracious, and courteous he could deny no one, and then fell into financial need and sold great offices to those who could pay the most. The result was unworthy people in office (book 2, chap. 4, pp. 251–52).

37. Bodin, *Republique*, book 6, chap. 6, p. 755; also book 5, chap. 4, p. 578.

38. Jean Bodin, *The Six Bookes of a Commonweale*, trans. Richard Knolles (London: G. Bishop, 1606; facsimile ed. K. D. McRae [Cambridge, Mass.: Harvard University Press, 1962]), book 4, chap. 4, p. 486; book 3, chap. 8, p. 402. Jean Bodin, *De Republica Libri Sex* (Frankfurt: Widow Jonas Rose, 1641), book 4, chap. 4, p. 686; book 3, chap. 8, pp. 564–65. Bodin's translation of his book into Latin was first published in 1586.

39. Dewald, *Formation of a Provincial Nobility*, 22–29, 86–87, 136–41. Stocker, "First Sales of Office," 6, 10–11.

40. *Recueil général des anciennes lois*, 14:408, Ordinance of Blois, art. 109. ADR, BP3640, 80r–v, 16 November 1546; François Charlin was kin to the important Lyon poet

Louise Labé; 324r–328r, 27 December 1555–14 January 1555/1556. The *lettres de don de l'office* are found in BP3640 through BP3646, interspersed with other kinds of royal gifts.

41. Philibert de Vienne, *Le Philosophe de court* (Lyon: Jean de Tournes, 1547), 105, using the "misanthrope Timon" to compare ironically with courtiers who only act to please others. Pierre Boaistuau, *Le Théâtre du Monde (1558),* ed. Michel Simonin (Geneva: Librairie Droz, 1981), 67–69, 239–42. Geoffrey Bullough, *Narrative and Dramatic Sources of Shakespeare,* 8 vols. (London: Routledge and Kegan; New York: Columbia University Press, 1957–75), 6: 226–31. William Shakespeare, *Timon of Athens,* 1.2; 4.3.434–43.

42. Michel de Montaigne, *Essais,* 1:22 in *Oeuvres complètes,* ed. Albert Thibaudet and Maurice Rat (Paris: Gallimard, 1962), 105–6. Philippe Desan, "Montaigne et le 'moi gelé': 'Le profit de l'un est dommage de l'autre' (I,22)," *Romance Notes* 30, no. 2 (1990): 95–100.

CHAPTER 7. GIFTS AND THE GODS

1. James Lynch, *Simoniacal Entry into Religious Life from 1000 to 1260* (Columbus: Ohio State University Press, 1976), especially pp. 64–75. E. Amann, "Simon le magicien," *Dictionnaire de théologie catholique,* ed. A. Vacant and E. Mangenit, 15 vols. (Paris: Le Touzet and Ané, 1903–50), 14:2130–40. *Figures du Nouveau Testament, illustrees de huictains francoys* (Lyon: Guillaume Rouillé, 1570), Gg 4r (Acts 8:18–24). Jean Benedicti, *La Somme des Pechez et le Remede d'iceux* (Paris: Denis Binet, 1595), book 3, chap. 8, pp. 272–87; book 6, chap. 2, pp. 684–93.

2. ADR, 10G3626, journal and daily accounts of Antoine Richard, priest and co-vicar of the Church of Sainte Croix, Lyon, 1570–77. René Benoist, *Traicte Des dismes, auquel clairement est monstré que de tout droict et raison, tous Chrestiens sont tenuz de payer les Dismes, Premices et oblations aux Pasteurs de l'Eglise* (Paris: Nicolas Chesneau, 1564), 1r–5r, 52r–60r.

3. *Livre de Comptes de Claude de La Landelle,* ed. René de Laigne (Rennes: Société des Bibliophiles bretons, 1906), 32–33. Wax: ADR, 10G563, 11G195, 90r–91v. Masses founded by new canons: La Landelle, *Comptes,* 99–100; ADR, 13G77r–99r (1544–51).

4. ADR, 14G 10, 36v–37v; 14G 66. Moshe Sluhovsky, *Patroness of Paris: Rituals of Devotion in Early Modern France* (Leiden: Brill, 1998), chap. 3.

5. ADR, 27H30, document of 7 January 1614, describing the initial gift of relics in March 1517. ADR, 15G161; 15G22, 109r; 3E765, 151r–152v, the Confraternity of the Fifteen Joys of Mary and of Saint Anne, limited to the canons and priests of the church of Saint Nizier at Lyon, founded in 1466 and going strong for three hundred years. ADR, 3E7061, 1 February 1554, chapel of the twelve permanent priests (*pérpetuels*) of the Church of Lyon.

6. ADR, 11G56, 14 December 1528; 13G13, 405v–406r (provision by the chapter of Saint Paul for naming of Baronnat after the Memento); 14G35, 15 December 1571; 15G154, 25 July 1530; 16G18, 8 January 1549/1550; 15H25, 19 October 1577; 16H1, 23. ADR, 3E3908, 89v–92r, 109v–114r; 3E5295, 12 February 1554/1555; 3E37061, 151r–154r. Petty indebtedness among clerics: ADR, 3E345, 65v–69r; 3E3908, 120v–121v.

7. A. N. Galpern, *The Religion of the People in Sixteenth Century Champagne* (Cambridge, Mass.: Harvard University Press, 1976). L'Abbé Martin, *Répertoire des Anciennes Confréries et Charités du Diocèse de Rouen approuvées de 1434 à 1610* (Fécamp: L. Durand, 1936). Andrew Barnes, *The Social Dimension of Piety: Associative Life and Religious Change in the Penitent Confraternities of Marseille 1499–1792* (New York: Paulist Press, 1994). Marc Venard,

"La fraternité des banquets," in Jean-Claude Margolin and Robert Sauzet, eds., *Pratiques et discours alimentaires à la Renaissance* (Paris: Maisonneuve and Larose, 1982), 137–45. ADM, G, Cure de la Trinité à Cherbourg, A: Accounts of the Confraternity of Notre Dame des Accords, 1515–1571. BML, Fonds Coste 355, Register of the Confrérie de la Trinité, chapel at the church of Saint Nizier, Lyon, 1306–1608.

8. Joseph Lemarié, "Épiphanie," *Dictionnaire de Spiritualité ascétique et mystique: doctrine et histoire,* ed. Maravel Viller (Paris: Beauchesne, 1960), 4:869–72; Richard C. Trexler, "Träume der Heiligen Drei Könige," in Agostino Paravicini Bagliani and Giorgio Stabile, eds., *Träume im Mittelalter: Ikonologische Studien* (Stuttgart and Zurich: Belser Verlag, 1989), 55–71. H. Kehrer, *Die Heiligen Drei Könige in Literatur und Kunst,* 2 vols. (Hildesheim: G. Olm, 1976), 2:128–45, 186, on late medieval sculpture and manuscript illumination of the three kings presenting their gifts to the infant Jesus. On popular celebration of the Feast of Kings, see chap. 2 in this book.

9. Henri Hubert and Marcel Mauss, "Essai sur la nature et la fonction du sacrifice (1899)," in Marcel Mauss, *Oeuvres,* ed. Victor Karady, 2 vols. (Paris: Les Éditions de Minuit, 1968), 1:302–5. Émile Durkheim, *The Elementary Forms of Religious Life,* trans. J. W. Swain (New York: Free Press, 1965), 384–85. Inga Clendinnen, *Aztecs: An Interpretation* (Cambridge: Cambridge University Press, 1991), 74–75, 92, 183–84. Maurice Godelier, *L'énigme du don* (Paris: Fayard, 1996), part 3: "Le sacré."

10. Hubert and Mauss, "Sacrifice," 303–5. The literature on sacrifice is extensive. An interesting collection that includes reflection on the applicability of gift theory to ancient Greek and Roman sacrifice is Jean Rudhardt and Olivier Reverdin, eds., *Le Sacrifice dans l'Antiquité* (Vandoeuvres-Geneva: Fondation Hardt, 1981).

11. The references here are to Genesis 4:4–7, 14:18–20, 22:1–18.

12. *Cy commence une petite instruction et maniere de vivre pour une femme seculiere* (Paris: A. Lotrian, ca. 1520), B 5r.

13. *Missale ad sacrosanctae Romanae ecclesiae usum* (Lyon: Jean Moylin alias de Cambrai, 1520). A Catholic explication of the mass is found in [Émond Auger], *La maniere d'ouir la messe avec devotion et fruict spirituel* (Paris: Nicolas Chesneau, 1571); a Protestant explication, which reproduces the 1520 missal in Latin and French translation along with very critical commentary, is [Pierre Viret], *Les Cauteles, Canon et Ceremonies de la Messe* (Lyon: Claude Ravot, 1563).

14. Antonio Possevino *Trattato del Santiss. Sacrificio del l'Altare della Messa* (Lyon: Michel Jove, 1563); *A Treatise of the Holy Sacrifice of the Altar, Called the Masse,* trans. Thomas Butler (Louvain: Joannes Foulerus, 1570), chaps. 1, 4. Auger, *La maniere d'ouir la messe,* D 2v. René Benoist, *Traicté du sacrifice Evangelique: Où il est manifestement prouvé que la divine et saincte Messe est le sacrifice eternel de la nouvelle Loy* (Paris: Gabriel de La Noue, 1586), 2r. Catholic reflection on and defense of the mass in the sixteenth century has been treated by Francis Clark, *Eucharistic Sacrifice and the Reformation,* (Oxford: Basil Blackwell, 1967), and David N. Power, *The Sacrifice We Offer: The Tridentine Dogma and Its Reinterpretation* (Edinburgh: T. & T. Clark, 1987). My own account stays close to the sources in sixteenth-century France.

15. Bernhard Jussen, "Gift and Heart, Countergift and Deed: A Scholarly Pattern of Interpretation and the Language of Morality in the Middle Ages," paper given at the conference "Négocier le Don," Paris, 11–13 December 1998 and in Gadi Algazi, Bernhard Jussen, and Valentin Groebner, eds., *Negotiating the Gift* (Göttingen: Vandenhoeck and Ruprecht, 2000).

16. *Une petite instruction . . . pour une femme seculiere,* a 7r. Esprit Rotier, *Responce aux blasphemateurs de la sainte messe* (Paris: Jacques Kerver, 1564), 19r.

17. Possevino, *The Holy Sacrifice of . . . the Masse,* chaps. 28–30. Auger, *La maniere d'ouir la messe,* D 2r–v. Rotier, *Responce,* 26v. *Extraict des plusieurs sainctz docteurs propositions dictz et sentences contenant les graces fruictz proffitz utilitez et louenges du tressacre et digne sacrement de lautel* (Paris: Pierre Ricoart, 1568), B 3r–v. Benedicti, *Somme des Pechez,* book 3, p. 197; book 4, chap. 3, pp. 419–20. *Missale ad usum lugdunensem ecclesie* (Lyon: Jean Huguetan, 1510), 181–205. BML, Fonds général, MS. 1203 (with signatures from two sixteenth-century women owners): "Sensuyt lordonnance des messes que lon doyt faire dire quant une femme doyt enfenter" (2r); "Sensuyt les messes que une femme doyt faire dire quant elle est pres dacoucher enfant pour avoir bonne delivrance" (3r–4r).

18. Benedicti, *Somme des Pechez,* book 3, chap. 8, p. 272 (it is simony "to require money for administering spiritual things"; book 6, chap. 2, p. 692 (restitution not required in selling spiritual things like sacraments).

19. ADR, 15G29, 83v, 94v–95v.

20. Erasmus, "The Godly Feast," in *The Colloquies of Erasmus,* trans. Craig R. Thompson (Chicago: University of Chicago Press, 1965), 60–63. Desiderius Erasmus to Paul Volz, 14 August 1518, in *The Correspondence of Erasmus,* trans. R. A. B. Mynors and D. F. S. Thomson (Toronto: University of Toronto Press, 1982), 6:89. Juan Luis Vives, *On Assistance to the Poor,* trans. Alice Tobriner, in Alice Tobriner, *A Sixteenth-Century Urban Report* (Chicago: University of Chicago Social Service Monographs, 1971), 46. Natalie Zemon Davis, *Society and Culture in Early Modern France* (Stanford: Stanford University Press, 1975), chap. 2, "Poor Relief, Humanism, and Heresy."

21. Barbara Beckerman Davis, "Poverty and Poor Relief in Sixteenth-Century Toulouse," *Historical Reflections/Réflexions Historiques* 17 (1991): 267–96.

22. Michel de Montaigne, *Essais,* 1:28, in *Oeuvres complètes,* ed. Maurice Rat (Paris: Gallimard, 1962), 189. Among much writing on the friendship between Montaigne and La Boétie, see Jean Starobinski, *Montaigne in Motion,* trans. Arthur Goldhammer (Chicago: University of Chicago Press, 1985), 36–66, and François Rigolot, *Les métamorphoses de Montaigne* (Paris: Presses Universitaires de France, 1988), chap. 3.

23. Montaigne, *Essais,* 1:28, p. 189.

24. Montaigne, *Essais,* 2:27, p. 645. See also my essay on the friendship between Montaigne and Gournay, cited in chap. 5, note 28.

25. Eugénie Droz, *Chemins de l'hérésie,* 4 vols. (Geneva: Slatkine Reprints, 1970–76), 1:92–115; 2:35; 4:47. See also Henri Delarue, "Olivétan et Pierre de Vingle à Genève, 1532–1533," *Bibliothèque d'humanisme et renaissance* 8 (1946): 104–18.

26. *La Bible. Qui est toute la Saincte escripture. En laquelle sont contenu le Vieil Testament et le Nouveau translatez en Francoys. Le Vieil de Lebrieu et le Nouveau du Grec* (Neuchâtel: Pierre de Vingle, 1535), *2r–v. Olivétan's dedication is signed "Des Alpes ce XIIe de Febvrier, 1535." After the dedication, Olivétan writes a letter to Protestant evangelizers discussing technical issues in his translation. Copies in the Scheide Collection, Firestone Library, Princeton University, and in the Beinecke Library, Yale University.

27. *La Bible,* *2r–v.

28. *La Bible,* verso of the title page: "Joannes Calvinus, Cesaribus, Regibus, Principibus, gentisbusque omnibus Christi Imperio Subditis Salutem"; *6r–*7r: "V. F. C. a nostre allié et confederé le peuple de l'alliance de Sinai, Salut." Eugénie Droz has proved conclusively that "V. J. C." is "Vostre Frere Calvin," *Chemins,* 108–10.

29. [Antoine Marcourt], *Le Livre des marchans, fort utile a toutes gens* (Corinth [Neuchâtel]: n.p. [Pierre de Vingle], 1533). Among later editions in French: 1534, 1541, 1544, and 1548. I here quote from the first English translation: *The Boke of Marchauntes, Right Necessarye unto All Folkes* (London: Thomas Godfraye, 1534), A 3r–A 4v; A 6v–A 7v; B 1r–v; B 3r–v; B 6r–v; C 4v; B 8r. On Marcourt, see Gabrielle Berthoud, *Antoine Marcourt Réformateur et Pamphlétaire du "Livre des Marchans" aux Placards de 1534* (Geneva: Librairie Droz, 1973).

30. My pages on Calvin have been written before reading the splendid book of B. A. Gerrish, *Grace and Gratitude: The Eucharistic Theology of John Calvin* (Minneapolis: Fortress Press, 1993), which has come to my attention only in 1999 as I am completing my own. Our interpretations of Calvin's theology, language, and sensibility converge on the whole, though Professor Gerrish's study is focused on a deep understanding of Calvin's view of the Lord's Supper, while I am using the sacrament as a means of talking about the question of gift and obligation more generally.

31. Jean Calvin, *Institution de la Religion Chrestienne,* ed. Jean-Daniel Benoît, 5 vols. (Paris: Librairie Philosophique J. Vrin, 1957–63), book 2, chap. 3: "élection gratuite" (par. 10, p. 70); "don gratuit," "bénignité gratuite" (par. 11, p. 71). Adam's sin as "ingratitude" along with pride and ambition (book 2, chap. 1, par. 4, p. 11). *Sermons de M. Iean Calvin sur le V. Livre de Moyse nommé Deuteronome* (Geneva: Thomas Courteau, 1567), 150: "bonté gratuite."

32. *The Bible and Holy Scriptures conteyned in the Old and Newe Testament. Translated according to the Ebrue and Greke* (Geneva: Rowland Hall, 1560; facsimile edition, Madison: University of Wisconsin Press, 1969).

33. Calvin, *Institution,* book 3, chap. 18, par. 1, pp. 298–301. Calvin also uses the example of God's promise to Abraham, of seed as of the stars in the heavens, made before he has tested Abraham's obedience through the command to sacrifice Isaac. After Isaac has been saved, the Lord reminds Abraham of the prior promise, and makes it again, "And in thy sede shal all the nacions of the earth be blessed because thou hast obeied my voyce" (Genesis 15:5, 22:16–18). Calvin comments, "Here surely we see . . . without ambiguity that the Lord remunerates the works of the faithful by the same gifts that he has already given them, before [the faithful] had even thought of doing anything, and [remunerates them] at a time when he had no cause to do good to them except his own mercy (p. 300)." The Epilogue of Théodore de Bèze's tragicomedy, *Abraham Sacrifiant,* begins "Or voyez vous de foy la grand' puissance / Et le loyer de vraye obeissance." Bèze presumably hoped the words would be understood with Calvin's interpretation. Théodore de Bèze, *Abraham Sacrifiant,* ed. Keith Cameron, Kathleen M. Hall, and Francis Higman (Geneva: Librairie Droz, 1967), 112.

34. Calvin, *Institution,* book 3, chap. 18, par. 2, p. 299.

35. On this whole subject, see Kristin Elizabeth Gager, *Blood Ties and Fictive Ties: Adoption and Family Life in Early Modern France* (Princeton: Princeton University Press, 1996).

36. Émile Rivoire and U. van Berchem, *Les Sources du droit du Canton de Genève,* 4 vols. (Arau: H. R. Sauerländer, 1927–35), "Edictz passez en Conseil General, 29 janvier 1568," 3: 176ff., title 14: Mariage, Dots, Douaires; Title 27: Testaments.

37. Calvin, *Institution,* book 1, chap. 10, par. 2, p. 116; book 2, chap. 10, par. 8, p. 201; book 3, chap. 17, par. 5, p. 285; chap. 18, par. 7, p. 306; chap. 20, par. 45, p. 392. *Dictionaire [sic] Francoislatin, contenant les motz et manieres de parler Francois, tournez en Latin* (Paris: Robert Estienne, 1539), 23, 107, 347; Paul Imbs, ed., *Trésor de la langue française,* 16 vols. (Paris: Éditions du Centre National de la Recherche Scientifique, 1971–94), 2:564–65. Robert Letham,

"The *Foedus Operum:* Some Factors Accounting for Its Development," *Sixteenth Century Journal* 14 (1983): 457–67; John S. Coolidge, *The Pauline Renaissance in England: Puritanism and the Bible* (Oxford: Clarendon Press, 1970), chap. 5; Brian Armstrong, *Calvinism and the Amyraut Heresy: Protestant Scholasticism and Humanism in Seventeenth-Century France* (Madison: University of Wisconsin Press, 1969), 47–56, 140–57, 195–221. "Covenant" is the noun used in the 1560 Geneva Bible in places where Calvin's biblical citation uses "alliance": e.g., Deuteronomy 7:9, "The faithful God who kepeth covenant and mercie unto them that love him and kepe his commandements, even to a thousand generacions" (*The Geneva Bible,* p. 84); "Le Seigneur ton Dieu garde en mille générations son alliance et sa miséricorde à ceux qu'il ayment et gardent ses commandemens" (*Institution,* book 3, chap. 17, par. 5, p. 285). It would be interesting to explore the grid of meanings around "covenant" in English in comparison to those around the French "alliance."

38. Jean Calvin, *Commentaires de M. Iehan Calvin sur toutes les Epistres de l'Apostre Sainct Paul* (Lyon: Antoine Vincent, 1565), 53–54. Calvin, *Institution,* book 2, chap. 8, par. 53, p. 182.

39. Jean Calvin, *Commentaires sur l'Ancien Testament,* ed. André Malet, 5 vols. (Geneva: Labor et Fides, 1962), 1(*Livre de la Genèse*):95–102, 152–53. Similar comments on the altar built by Abraham in the plain of Moreh (Genesis 12:8), p. 200; and on the altar built by Jacob before the city of Schechem (Genesis 33:20), pp. 482–83.

40. Among notable attacks on the mass and transubstantiation are Antoine Marcourt, *Declaration de la Messe* (Neuchâtel: Pierre de Vingle, 1534; Geneva: Jean Michel, 1534), with several subsequent editions and an English translation: *A Declaration of the Masse* (Wittenberg [London]: Hans Luft [John Day], 1547); and Pierre Viret, *Les Cauteles, Canon et Ceremonies de la Messe,* of 1563 (see note 13). For a review of Continental and especially English Protestant criticism of the mass, see Clark, *Eucharistic Sacrifice.*

41. [Jean Calvin], *La Forme des Prieres et Chantz Ecclesiastiques, avec la maniere d'administrer les Sacremens* (n.p. [Geneva]: n.p. [Jean Gérard], 1542), a 3v; k 2v–k 3v; l 4v–l 8r. Calvin, *Institution,* book 4, chap. 17, par. 2, p. 376; par. 10, p. 384.

42. Calvin, *Institution,* book 4, chap. 18, par. 7, p. 455: "Autant qu'il y a à dire entre Prendre et Donner, autant il y a de différence entre le Sacrement de la Cène et Sacrifice." His Latin is "Quantum interest inter dare et accipere, tantum a sacramento coenae sacrificium differt" (Jean Calvin, *Institutio Christianae Religionis,* ed. A. Tholuck, 2 vols. [Edinburgh: T. and T. Clark, 1874], vol. 2, book 4, chap. 18, par. 7, p. 68.

43. Émile Benveniste, *Le Vocabulaire des institutions indo-européennes,* 2 vols. (Paris: Les Éditions de Minuit, 1969), vol. 1, chaps. 5–7. Benveniste (1902–76) was in touch with Mauss and his circle while doing his doctoral work and became Mauss's colleague at the Collège de France in 1937, when he acquired the chair of comparative grammar. Both men were forced to "retire" from the Collège in the late autumn of 1940 under Vichy's Statut des Juifs.

44. Calvin, *Institution,* book 4, chap. 18, par. 16, p. 463. Also Jean Calvin, *Sermons sur l'Harmonie des Trois Evangelistes. S. Matthieu, S. Luc et S. Marc* in *Ioannis Calvini Opera Quae Supersunt Omnia,* ed. G. Baum et al., 59 vols. (Braunschweig: C. A. Schwetschke, 1863–1900), 46:352 commenting on Matthew 2:9–11. Elsie McKee, *John Calvin on the Diaconate and Liturgical Almsgiving* (Geneva: Librairie Droz, 1984), 53–56. See also Antoine Marcourt, *Declaration of the Masse,* A 8r: If there is any sacrificing to be done, it is of ourselves to God and everyone should do this "wythout beyng shaven, shorne, ceremonyus, or dysguysed."

45. Charlotte d'Arbaleste, *Mémoires de Madame de Mornay,* ed. Henriette Witt, née Guizot (Paris: Société de l'histoire de France, 1858–59), 1:1–4.

46. Calvin, *Institution,* book 2, chap. 8, par. 55, p. 184; book 4, chap. 17, par. 44, p. 440.

47. Calvin, *Institution*, book 2, chap. 8, par. 55, p. 184.

48. Calvin, *Institution*, book 2, chap. 8, par. 55, p. 184; book 3, chap. 7, pars. 6–7, pp. 171–73.

49. Calvin, *Institution*, book 3, chap. 15, par. 3, p. 268.

50. Rivoire and Berchem, *Sources du droit*, 3:172, 388, 434, 608–9; 4:101–8, 353, 640.

51. Rivoire and Berchem, *Sources du droit*, 2:379; 3:322; 4:12–13, 51–52, 56, 95, 196, 208, 218–19, 243. AEG, Pièces historiques 1288, 1542 description of the "brigues" of 1538; AEG, Procès criminel 539, 1st series, testimony of 6 August 1555. E. William Monter, *Studies in Genevan Government (1536–1605)* (Geneva: Librairie Droz, 1964), 103–7. W. Deonna, "Les fresques de la Maison de Ville de Genève," *Revue suisse d'Art et d'Archéologie* 13, no. 3 (1952): 141–43. An interesting portrait of pre-Reformation political gifts in Basel is Valentin Groebner's "The Guard's Offer: Gifts, Corruption, and the Visualization of the Invisible in Renaissance Basel," paper given at the Conference "Négocier le Don," Paris, 11–13 December 1998, and in Godi Algazi, Bernhard Jussen, and Valentin Groebner, eds., *Negotiating the Gift*.

52. Robert M. Kingdon, "Social Welfare in Calvin's Geneva," *American Historical Review* 76 (1971): 50–69; Bernard Lescaze, ed., *Sauver l'âme, nourrir le corps. De l'Hôpital Général à l'Hospice Général de Genève* (Geneva: Hospice Général, 1985); McKee, *John Calvin on the Diaconate;* Jeannine E. Olson, *Calvin and Social Welfare: Deacons and the Bourse Française* (Selinsgrove, Pa.: Susquehanna University, 1989); Mark Valeri, "Religion, Discipline, and the Economy in Calvin's Geneva," *Sixteenth Century Journal* 28 (1997): 123–42, especially 135–39. For a similar Protestant institution of welfare reform, see Raymond A. Mentzer, Jr., "Organizational Endeavour and Charitable Impulse in Sixteenth-Century France: The Case of Protestant Nîmes," *French History* 5 (1991): 1–29. I have considered the shift in Genevan neighborhood life in Natalie Zemon Davis, "Charivari, Honor, and Community in Seventeenth-Century Lyon and Geneva," in John A. MacAloon, ed., *Rite, Drama, Festival, Spectacle: Rehearsals toward a Theory of Cultural Performance* (Philadelphia: Ishi Press, 1984), 42–57.

53. *Le Tiers Livre des faictz et dictz Heroïques du noble Pantagruel* was first published in Lyon and Paris in 1546. In the second edition, Paris and Lyon, 1552, the "noble Pantagruel" of the title becomes the "good Pantagruel," "bon Pantagruel." François Rabelais, *Oeuvres complètes*, ed. Mireille Huchon (Paris: Gallimard, 1994), 1221, 1343–44, 1356–57.

54. Rabelais, *Le Tiers Livre*, chaps. 1–5, in *Oeuvres*, 353–69.

55. Rabelais, *Le Tiers Livre*, chap. 5, in *Oeuvres*, 367–68.

56. Michael Screech, *Rabelais* (London: Duckworth, 1979), 225–31. Mireille Huchon in *Oeuvres*, 1351–53. In contrast, both V. L. Saulnier and Philippe Desan have seen the debate between Panurge and Pantagruel as having defensible arguments on both sides: V. L. Saulnier, *Rabelais: Rabelais dans son enquête* (Paris: Société d'Édition d'Enseignement Supérieur, 1983), 152–53; Philippe Desan, *L'Imaginaire Économique de la Renaissance* (Mont-de-Marsan: Editions InterUniversitaires, 1993), 70–76.

57. François Rigolot, *Les Langages de Rabelais,* Études rabelaisiennes, 10 (Geneva: Librairie Droz, 1972), 137–43.

58. Rabelais, *Le Tiers Livre*, chap. 9, in *Oeuvres*, 378.

CONCLUSION

1. Alexander Nagel, "Gifts for Michelangelo and Vittoria Colonna," *Art Bulletin* 79 (1997): 647–68; "Liberal Art and Reformist Critique: Competing Discourses of the Gift

in Italian Renaissance Art," paper given at the conference "Négocier le don," Paris, 11–13 December 1998, and in Gadi Algazi, Bernhard Jussen, and Valentin Groebner, eds., *Negotiating the Gift* (Göttingen: Vandenhoeck and Ruprecht, 2000). Paula Findlen, "The Economy of Scientific Exchange in Early Modern Italy," in Bruce Moran, ed., *Patronage and Institutions* (Woodbridge: Boydell, 1991), 5–24.

2. The entire corpus of women's publications in sixteenth-century France has been examined in the new thesis of Susan Broomhall, "Women and Publication in Sixteenth-Century France" (Ph.D. diss., University of Western Australia, 1999). Natalie Zemon Davis, *Women on the Margins: Three Seventeenth-Century Lives* (Cambridge, Mass.: Harvard University Press, 1995), chap. 2 on Marie de l'Incarnation.

3. Marguerite de Navarre, *Le Miroir de l'Ame Pecheresse*, ed. Renja Salminen (Helsinki: Suomalainen Tiedeakatemia, 1979), 209.

4. Elsie Anne McKee, *Katharina Schütz Zell*, vol. 1, *The Life and Thought of a Sixteenth-Century Reformer* (Leiden: Brill, 1999), 276–78, 287–88, 321–24. Georgette de Montenay, *Emblemes, ou devises chrestiennes* (Lyon: Jean Marvorelle, 1571), 46, 59, 71. Sara Matthews Grieco, "Georgette de Montenay: A Different Voice in Sixteenth-Century Emblematics," *Renaissance Quarterly* 47 (1994): 791–871.

5. Pierre Belon, *Les observations de plusieurs choses memorables trouvées en Grece, Asie, Iudée, Egypte, Arabie, et autres pays estranges* (Paris: Gilles Corrozet, 1555), 192v–193r. Guillaume Postel, *De la Republique des Turcs* (Poitiers: Enguilbert de Marnef, n.d. [ca. 1563]), 12, 56–65. Nicolas de Nicolay, *Les quatres premiers livres des Navigations et Peregrinations Orientales* (Lyon: Guillaume Rouillé, 1568), reprinted in Nicolas de Nicolay, *Dans l'empire de Soliman le Magnifique,* ed. Marie-Christine Gomez-Géraud and Stéphane Yérasimos (Paris: Presses du Centre National du Recherche Scientifique, 1989), 206. Lisa Jardine, *Worldly Goods: A New History of the Renaissance* (London: Macmillan, 1996), 334. The immensely valuable collection edited by Bartolomé Bennassar and Robert Sauzet, *Chrétiens et Musulmans à la Renaissance: Actes du 37e Colloque International du CESR, 1994* (Paris: Honoré Champion, 1998), has much on commerce but very little on gifts.

6. Leon Modena, *The History of the Rites, Customes, and Manner of Life, of the Present Jews, throughout the World,* trans. Edmund Chilmead (London: John Martin and John Ridley, 1650), 50–55: "Of Their Charity to the Poor." Shlomo Simonsohn, *History of the Jews in the Duchy of Mantua* (Jerusalem: Kiryath Sepher Ltd., 1977), 344–46, 519–21, 549–62. Natalie Zemon Davis, "Religion and Capitalism Once Again? Jewish Merchant Culture in the Seventeenth Century," *Representations* 59 (summer 1997): 64–67. Marc Venard, *L'Église d'Avignon au 16e siècle,* 4 vols. (Lille: Université de Lille, 1980), 1:204–10; 3:1317–34. Felix Platter, *Beloved Son Felix: The Journal of Felix Platter,* trans. Sean Jeannett (London: F. Muller, 1961), 107. Vivian B. Mann and Richard I. Cohen, *From Court Jews to the Rothschilds: Art, Patronage, and Power 1600–1800* (Munich and New York: Prestel, 1996), 54, 110–11. Avigdor Farine, "Charity and Study Societies in Europe of the Sixteenth–Eighteenth Centuries," *Jewish Quarterly Review* 64 (1973): 16–47, 164–75. Jacob R. Marcus, *Communal Sick-Care in the German Ghetto* (Cincinnati: Hebrew Union College Press, 1947).

7. Relevant studies here would be John Brewer and Susan Staves, eds., *Early Modern Conceptions of Property* (London and New York: Routledge, 1996); John Brewer and Roy Porter, eds., *Consumption and the World of Goods* (London and New York: Routledge, 1993); P. S. Atiyah, *The Rise and Fall of Freedom of Contract* (Oxford: Clarendon Press, 1979); Albert O. Hirschman, *The Passions and the Interests: Political Arguments for Capitalism before Its Triumph* (Princeton: Princeton University Press, 1977); Martha Woodmansee and

Peter Jaszi, eds., *The Construction of Authorship: Textual Appropriation in Law and Literature* (Durham: Duke University Press, 1994).

8. Amartya Sen, *On Ethics and Economics* (Oxford: Basil Blackwell, 1987).

9. George Dalton, introduction in Karl Polanyi, *Primitive, Archaic, and Modern Economies: Essays of Karl Polanyi,* ed. George Dalton (Boston: Beacon Press, 1968), xiii–xvi. Cynthia Earl Kerman, *Creative Tension: The Life and Thought of Kenneth Boulding* (Ann Arbor: University of Michigan Press, 1974), 9–13. Marshall Sahlins, *Stone Age Economics* (Chicago: Aldine Publishing Company, 1972), chap. 5: "On the Sociology of Primitive Exchange" (initially published in 1968).

10. Jacques Derrida, *Donner le temps* (Paris: Éditions Galilée, 1991), chaps. 1–2; English translation, *Given Time* (Chicago: University of Chicago Press, 1994). Among reactions to Derrida's approach, see Tim Jenkins, "Derrida's Reading of Mauss," in Wendy James and N. J. Allen, eds., *Marcel Mauss: A Centenary Tribute* (New York and Oxford: Berghahn Books, 1998), 83–94; Alain Caillé, *Don, intérêt et désintéressement* (Paris: Éditions La Découverte/Mauss, 1994), 251–61.

11. For a wide-ranging view of activities and attitudes in the non-profit, voluntary, or independent sector, as it is variously called, see Brian O'Connell, ed., *America's Voluntary Spirit* (New York: The Foundation Center, 1983).

12. For a similar approach to the mixed moral status of gifts and their potential danger, see Jonathan Parry, "On the Moral Perils of Exchange," in Jonathan Parry and Maurice Bloch, eds., *Money and the Morality of Exchange* (Cambridge: Cambridge University Press, 1989), 64–93.

13. Jean Starobinski, "Don fastueux et don pervers," *Annales.ESC* 41 (1986): 7–26.

14. Georges Bataille, *The Accursed Share,* vol. 1: *Consumption,* trans. Robert Hurley (New York: Zone Books, 1991), 169–90, 193 nn. 24–25. The first French edition was 1967; Bataille says he was working on the book for eighteen years. The notes to the section on the Marshall Plan refer to writings of 1948–49 and talk of President Harry Truman as still alive. On Bataille, see Michèle Richman, *Reading Georges Bataille: Beyond the Gift* (Baltimore: Johns Hopkins University Press, 1982). For another analysis of how international grants were complicated by political objectives, see Kathleen D. McCarthy, "From Cold War to Cultural Developments: The International Cultural Activities of the Ford Foundation, 1950–1980," *Daedalus,* special issue on "Philanthropy, Patronage, Politics" (winter 1987): 93–108.

15. Linda Levy Peck, *Court Patronage and Corruption in Early Stuart England* (London and Boston: Unwin Hyman, 1990). Sharon Kettering, *Patrons, Brokers, and Clients in Seventeenth-Century France* (New York and Oxford: Oxford University Press, 1986), 192–206; "Gift-Giving and Patronage in Early Modern France," *French History* 2 (1988): 147–51. Jean-Claude Waquet, *Corruption: Ethics and Power in Florence, 1600–1770,* trans. Linda McCall (University Park: Pennsylvania State University Press, 1984), especially the excellent introduction, pp. 1–18. John T. Noonan, Jr., *Bribes* (New York: Macmillan, 1984). Cf. Susan Rose-Ackerman, *Corruption: A Study in Political Economy* (New York: Academic Press, 1978); Arnold J. Heidenheimer, *Political Corruption: Readings in Comparative Analysis* (New York: Holt, Rinehart and Winston, 1970).

16. Richard Titmuss, *The Gift Relationship: From Human Blood to Social Policy* (London: George Allyn & Unwin, 1971); Kenneth J. Arrow, "Gifts and Exchanges" in Edmund S. Phelps, ed., *Altruism, Morality, and Economic Theory* (New York: Russell Sage Foundation, 1975), 13–28, quotation on p. 22. For a critical reaction to Arrow's essay, which first appeared in 1972, see Peter Singer, "Altruism and Commerce: A Defense of Titmuss against Arrow,"

Philosophy and Public Affairs 2 (1973): 312–20. Other relevant studies: Thomas Nagel, *The Possibility of Altruism* (Oxford: Clarendon Press, 1970); Gerald Dworkin, Gordon Bermant, and Peter B. Brown, eds., *Markets and Morals* (New York: John Wiley, 1977).

17. François Rabelais, *Le Tiers Livre,* in *Oeuvres complètes,* ed. Mireille Huchon (Paris: Gallimard, 1994), prologue, 351; Terence Cave, *The Cornucopian Text: Problems of Writing in the French Renaissance* (Oxford: Clarendon Press, 1979), 171, 183–204. Christine de Pizan, *The Book of the City of Ladies,* trans. Earl Jeffrey Richards, rev. ed. (New York: Persea Books, 1998), book 1, chaps. 35, 38, pp. 75–76, 79; book 2, chap. 11, pp. 115–16. Pizan has taken the traditional tale of "Roman charity," in which a woman breastfeeds her old father, and made it her mother instead, thus amplifying the gift return.

18. Bataille, *Accursed Share,* 23–24, 37–38. Lewis Hyde, *The Gift: Imagination and the Erotic Life of Property* (New York: Vintage Books, 1983), xiv. Eudora Welty and Ronald A. Sharp, eds., *The Norton Book of Friendship,* (New York and London: W. W. Norton, 1991), 35–40; Ronald A. Sharp, *Friendship and Literature: Spirit and Form* (Durham: Duke University Press, 1986), chap. 2: "Friendship as Gift Exchange."

Illustration Credits

Illustration Credits

Thielman Kerver, 1522). (Department of Rare Books and Special Collections, Princeton University Library)

11 Payment of the harvester, *Cy commencent les heures nostre dame a lusaige de Poitiers . . . avec plusieurs belles hystoires* (Printed in Paris for Jean Varice, bookseller at Angers, 1525). (Médiathèque François Mitterrand, Poitiers)

12 Sale of Joseph to the Ishmaelites, *Figures de la Bible, illustrees de huictains francoys* (Lyon: Guillaume Rouillé, 1564), designed by Pierre Eskrich. (Department of Printing and Graphic Arts, The Houghton Library, Harvard University)

13 Jacob Gerritsz. Cuyp, *Fish Market*, 1627 (Dordrechts Museum, Dordrecht)

14 Esau sells his heritage to Jacob, *Quadrins historiques de la Bible* (Lyon: Jean de Tournes, 1553), designed by Bernard Salomon. (Carnegie Mellon University Libraries Special Collections)

15 Pieter Brueghel the Younger (1546–1638), *The Tax-Collector's Office*, ca. 1615, Antwerp. Oil on wood panel, 74.5 × 106.5 cm. (Art Gallery of South Australia, Adelaide; bequest of Helen Austin Horn, 1934)

16 "Le Parlement du bon prince," *Livret des Emblemes de maistre Andre Alciat* (Paris: Chrestien Wechel, 1536), woodcuts by Jean Jollat. (Department of Printing and Graphic Arts, The Houghton Library, Harvard University)

17 Bribing the judge, Hans Holbein, *Les Simulachres et historiees faces de la mort* (Lyon: Melchior and Gaspard Trechsel for Jean and François Frellon, 1538). (Department of Printing and Graphic Arts, The Houghton Library, Harvard University)

18 Bribing the judge, Guillaume de La Perrière, *Le Theatre des Bons Engins, auquel sont contenuz cent Emblemes moraulx* (Paris: Denys Janot, 1539/1540), woodcut designed by unknown artist who worked for the Janot publishing house. (Department of Printing and Graphic Arts, The Houghton Library, Harvard University)

19 Simon and the Apostles, *Figures du Nouveau Testament, illustrees de huictains francoys* (Lyon: Guillaume Rouillé, 1570), design attributed to Pierre Eskrich or Jean Moni. (Department of Printing and Graphic Arts, The Houghton Library, Harvard University)

20 Thomas de Leu, *Sacrifice under the Law of Nature,* late sixteenth century. (Cliché Bibliothèque nationale de France, Paris [Cabinet des Estampes, Ed. 11. a. Rés. 203–1])

21 Thomas de Leu, *Sacrifice under the Law of Moses,* late sixteenth century. (Cliché Bibliothèque nationale de France, Paris [Cabinet des Estampes, Ed. 11. a. Rés. 204–2])

22 Thomas de Leu, *Sacrifice under the Law of the Gospel,* late sixteenth century. (Cliché Bibliothèque nationale de France, Paris [Cabinet des Estampes, Ed. 11. a. Rés. 205–3])

23 Charity figure, Georgette de Montenay, *Emblemes, ou devises chrestiennes* (Lyon: Jean Marcorelle, 1571), engraved by Pierre Woeiriot. (Department of Printing and Graphic Arts, The Houghton Library, Harvard University)

Acknowledgments

I first began to think about gifts in the early 1980s as a superb opportunity for connecting history and anthropology. It was also the dawn of the Reagan era in America, and gifts seemed, if not a panacea, then at least a critical option to the commercial and individualistic sensibility celebrated everywhere in the media. By the time I did a first presentation of my work—as the Curti Lectures at the University of Wisconsin–Madison in 1983—I realized gift relations were much more complicated and multivalent than I had thought. But I had the pleasure of offering my ideas to Merle Curti, a man of distinguished scholarship and generosity, who himself had contributed much to our understanding the history of American philanthropy.

But then *The Gift in Sixteenth-Century France* took many years to complete. Partly it was demoted by other books and other stories to tell. Partly *The Gift* seemed to resist closure by its demands for theory about broad historical change and about matters of gender. The fortunate side for me of this delay was the opportunity to present some of this material to different university communities and learn much from our discussion. Among these settings were Ben-Gurion University; Bryn Mawr College; the University of California, San Diego; Carnegie Mellon University; Christ's College Cambridge; the Collège de France; Columbia University; the Universität Konstanz; the University of Florida at Gainesville; the Folger Library; the University of Lancashire; La Trobe University; the University of Michigan; Montana State University; the Institute of World History of the Russian Academy of Sciences in Moscow; Pomona College; Princeton University; the Royal Historical Society; Stanford University; the Centre for Medieval Studies, University of Toronto; Wesleyan University; and Yale University. Subsequent correspondence with colleagues from these institutions brought many new ideas.

Two interdisciplinary conferences on the theme of gift exchange were also important intellectual events for me. "The Gift and Its Transformation" I co-organized with Rena Lederman of the Department of Anthropology at Princeton University and Ronald Sharp of the Department of English at Kenyon College, both of whom gave me fresh understanding of our subject. Funded by the National Endowment for the Humanities and the Wenner-Gren Foundation, this conference was held at the National Humanities Center in November 1990. In addition to many excellent papers, the comments of the late Annette Weiner were

Acknowledgments

memorable. The conference on "Negotiating the Gift" took place at the German Historical Institute in Paris in December 1998. Organizers Gadi Algazi, Valentin Groebner, and Bernhard Jussen brought together scholars in medieval and early modern studies. Their lively debates helped me clarify my own position in regard to "the gift register" as I approached the final stages of writing.

In the early stages of my research I received support from the National Endowment for the Humanities and the John Simon Guggenheim Memorial Foundation. Since these generous institutions have long and patient memories, I hope my return will not seem too delayed.

Then in 1998, I had the honor of presenting *The Gift in Sixteenth-Century France* as the Fifth Jerusalem Lectures in History in Memory of Menahem Stern, sponsored by the Historical Society of Israel. These lectures allowed me to pay tribute to the life of a distinguished historian and lover of peace, tragically snatched away before his time. Professor Stern was born in Poland and emigrated to Palestine in 1938. After studies at the Hebrew University of Jerusalem and Oxford University, he devoted more than thirty years to research and publication on Jewish history of the Hellenistic and Roman periods. His three volumes on *Greek and Latin Authors on Jews and Judaism* (Jerusalem, 1974–84) are widely recognized, throughout the scholarly world as a major contribution to Jewish studies. Meanwhile, he trained several generations of students at Hebrew University, all of whom remember his classes with appreciation.

My months in Israel also introduced me to exciting new scholarship on gifts. Discussions with Ilana Silber of the Sociology Department at Bar-Ilan University and Ilana Krausman Ben-Amos of the History Department at Ben-Gurion University were a precious aftermath of my lectures.

Since much of the research on and thinking about *The Gift in Sixteenth-Century France* was carried on during my years at Princeton University, I want to acknowledge the support of my colleagues, always ready to offer suggestions for books and new paths to follow. Especially I cite the generosity with which François Rigolot volunteered information about gift words and images in the French language. Further, in 1980 and 1993 I conducted graduate seminars on gift matters, which were outstanding because of the quality of the student participation. Also during those years Dean Dabrowski was providing me valuable secretarial and library help. In addition to that received at Princeton, I am appreciative of the kind service I received from librarians and archivists in numerous institutions in North America and France.

At the University of Wisconsin Press, Scott Lenz provided me with good counsel and expert editing. I enjoyed working with Hannah Nyala as she copyedited my text; our shared interest in history and anthropology was an added bonus. I also want to thank Carla Aspelmeier and Rich Felsing for their work designing this book.

Finally, my husband Chandler Davis has been a loyal listener, reader, and respondent throughout this project. Since our relation, like that of Michel de Montaigne and Étienne de La Boétie, is "beyond gifts, beyond benefits," I cannot truly say I am grateful to him. But in this book, dedicated to the future of our children and grandchildren, he has a rightful share.

Index

Index

Hospitality: feudal, 17. *See also* Banquets and feasts; Marriage, courtship, and engagement gifts

Hotman, Jean, 161*n22*

Houllier, Jean, 52

Households: as arena for gift troubles, 68–72; gifts to staff of, 51–53

Hubert, Henri, 104, 109

Hudson's Bay Company, 136*n8*

Human–divine links, 11–12

Hurtebye, Sire de, 38–39, 40, 41

Hyde, Lewis, 132

Île-de-France, 28, 29, 32–33

Indigent. *See* Charitable gifts; Poor, the

Inheritance. *See* Inter vivos donations; Wills/ inheritances/legacies

Insults, gross: and gifts gone wrong, 71

Interest charges, 54

Inter vivos donations *(donatio inter vivos)*, 31–33, 70, 71–72, 75, 86, 145*n37*, 155*n13*

Iroquoians, 80, 81–82

Isaac, 166*n33*

Italy: gift-giving in, 27–28, 125

Izé, 53

Jacob, 31; Esau and, 64, 65 (fig.)

Jeanne d'Albret, Queen of Navarre, 29, 38, 51, 150*n18*, 151*n21*

Jesuits, 83, 109–10

Jesus: gifts presented to infant, 21, 105; sacrifice of, 117

Jews, 116; Calvin's letter to, 113; gift bestowal between Christians and, 128; gift systems of, 126, 127; and neighborliness, 20; sacrifices of, 64, 65 (fig.), 105, 166*n33*

Jones, Gareth Stedman, 7

Joseph: selling of by Judah, 63 (fig.)

Joubert, Laurent, 50, 141*n4*, 151*n25*

Journeymen: payments and gifts to: 51–54

Judah: selling of Joseph by, 63 (fig.)

Judges: and gifts/bribes, 87–90, 92 (fig.), 93 (fig.), 159*n13*, 160*n16*

Judges of Thebes: portrayal of, 90, 91 (fig.)

Jussen, Bernhard, 105

Kettering, Sharon, 37

King's officers: wages and pensions for, 51

Kissing: and homage, 37

Knives: as gifts, 36, 80–81

Knowledge: teaching as example of gift–sale relationship 47–48

Kwakiutl potlatch, 4, 10, 136*n8*, 138*n17*

Labé, Louise, 76

La Boétie, Étienne de, 111, 114

Lac, Antoine du. *See* Du Lac, Antoine

Laguelle, Thomas, Sire de Quineville, 144*n29*

La Landelle, Claude de, 53, 54–55, 66

La Moussaye, Baron de. *See* Gouyon, Charles, Baron de La Moussaye

Language of gifts. *See* Postures of gift presenta- tion; Vocabulary of gifts and gift-giving

Languedoc, 69–70

La Noue, François de, 19

La Salle, Nicolas de, 144*n24*

La Trémoille, Duchess de. *See* Laval, Anne de, Duchess de La Trémoille

La Trémoille, François, Duke de, 37, 70, 73, 154*n8*

La Trémoille, Louis II de, 18, 70, 154*n8*

Laurens, André du. *See* Du Laurens, André

Laurens, Jeanne du. *See* Du Laurens, Jeanne

Laurens, Julien du. *See* Du Laurens, Julien

Laurens, Louis du. *See* Du Laurens, Louis

Laval, Anne de, Duchess de La Trémoille, 35, 70, 141*n3*, 154*n8*

Law, property. *See* Property, law

Lawyers: gifts to, 86–87; gifts of food for, 86 (fig.), 158*n3*

LeClerc, Master Nicolas, 155*n13*

Lecoq, René, 142*n9*

Legacies. *See* Wills/inheritances/legacies

Lent: at Paris, 25

Le Palle, Guyon, 52

Le Palle, Paulette, 52

Léry, Jean de, 81, 82, 83, 84

L'Estoile, Pierre de, 19

Leu, Thomas de, 105 (fig.), 107 (fig.), 108 (fig.)

Lévi-Strauss, Claude, 5

Liberal gift-giving, 17–19

Life cycle: days, 41; gifts related to family, 27–33

Limoges, 88

Little, Lester, 7

Loans: and debt (in Rabelais), 121–23; and usury (as examples of gift-sale relationship), 54–55

Lord's Supper, 125, 126; and Calvin, 117, 118–19

Louis XII, 93

Louis XIV, 95, 128

Loyseau, Charles, 95

Lucca, 75

Index

Index

Index

United States: blood system in, 131
University teaching: and compensation, 47–48, 50–51
Ursulines, 83
Usury, 54
Uzès, Duchess d'. *See* Crussol, Madame de, Duchess d'Uzès

Valence, 28
Valla, Lorenzo, 21–22
Valognes, 38, 39, 41, 49, 86
Valognes, Viconte de, 39, 40, 147*n16*
Vauzelles, Jean de, 110
Venette, Jeannette, 33
Verrazano, Giovanni da, 80
Vienne, Philibert de, 73–74, 154*n27*
Vingle, Pierre de (Pirot Picard), 38, 112, 114
Virgil, 77
Vitré, 52, 54, 142*n9*
Vives, Juan Luis, 110
Vocabulary of gifts and gift-giving, 14, 21, 37–38, 159*n12*, 159–60*n13*; Calvin and, 118; "friends," 18–20
Voluntary sector: contemporary, 129, 131
Von Reden, Sitta, 8
Vrancx, Sebastian, 64

Waldensians, 112
Weiner, Annette B., 5, 136*n6*

Welcome banquets. *See* Banquets and feasts
Welfare reform and institutions, 110, 120–21
Welty, Eudora, 132
Wills/inheritances/legacies: 14, 20, 30–32, 68–71, 144*n29*; animosity and, 154*n7*; Calvin's metaphor of, 115; of clerics, 103; and clothing, 31; and disinheritances, 30, 68–69, 154*n4*; female bequests (examples), 145*n31*; male bequests (examples), 144*n31*; and property, 31–32; quarrels over, 70–72; and religious choices, 69; revocation of, 70–72, 155*nn12, 13*; will-making and behavior, 68–69; of women, 140*n26*. *See also* Inter vivos donations
Wine: as a gift, 35, 53, 54
Women: book exchanges between, 101–2; friendship between, 20; and gifts gone wrong, 75–80; as givers and recipients, 125–26; as model for religious reciprocity, 125–26; responses of on pressure to obey, 78–80; seeking of public favor by, 76–77; vocation of, 76; voices of and gift-giving, 75–80; wills of, 140*n26*. *See also* Dowries; Marriage

Ypres, 110

Zannetti, Francesco, 149*n7*
Zell, Katharina Schütz, 125–26
Zwingli, Ulrich, 116